VENUS

Ronnie Gale Dreyer is a writer, teacher and consultant based in New York City. She studied Hindu Astrology at Sanskrit University in Benares and co-founded the first astrological computer service in Holland where she lived for ten years. She is the author of *Indian Astrology* and can be contacted at:
PO Box 8034, FDR Station, New York, New York 10150-8034.

Frontispiece: Aphrodite from Thrapsus, Africa, in terracotta; c.500-400 BC

VENUS

*The Evolution of the Goddess
and Her Planet*

RONNIE GALE DREYER

Aquarian
An Imprint of HarperCollins*Publishers*

Aquarian
An Imprint of HarperCollins*Publishers*
77–85 Fulham Palace Road,
Hammersmith, London W6 8JB
1160 Battery Street,
San Francisco, California 94111–1213

Published by Aquarian 1994
3 5 7 9 10 8 6 4 2

© Ronnie Gale Dreyer 1994

Ronnie Gale Dreyer asserts the moral right to
be identified as the author of this work

A catalogue record for this book
is available from the British Library

ISBN 1 85538 006 4

Typeset by Harper Phototypesetters Limited,
Northampton, England
Printed in Great Britain by
Redwood Books, Trowbridge, Wiltshire.

All rights reserved. No part of this publication may be
reproduced, stored in a retrieval system, or transmitted,
in any form or by any means, electronic, mechanical,
photocopying, recording or otherwise, without the prior
permission of the publishers.

This book is dedicated to my sisters
RANDI and KAREN
who are continual sources of love,
friendship and Venusian strength.

CONTENTS

Acknowledgements — 9
Introduction — 11

PART I *The Goddess*

1. *Early Mother Goddesses*
   Paleolithic Europe — 17
   Neolithic and Chalcolithic Era (8000 – 3000 BC) — 19
   Bronze Era (3500 – 1500 BC) — 24

2. *Mesopotamian Goddesses and Astrology*
   Inanna – Sumerian Goddess of Heaven and Earth — 28
   Ishtar – Babylonian Goddess of Love, Fertility and War — 40
   Babylonian Astrology: The Venus Tablet of Amisaduqa — 50

3. *Mediterranean Goddesses and Astrology*
   Semitic Fertility Goddesses — 61
   Aphrodite – Greek Goddess of Love and Beauty — 70
   Greek Astrology — 86
   Venus – From Goddess of Love to Divine
       Mother of Rome — 95

4. *The Renaissance Venus: Rediscovering the Goddess
   and Her Planet* — 108
   The Astronomy of Venus — 118

PART II *The Planet*

5. The Planet as Symbol	119
6. Taurus and Libra	127
7. Venus through the Signs	139
8. Venus through the Houses	173
9. Venus in Aspect	220
10. Venus in Prediction: Transits and Progressions	248
Appendix	263
References	265
Bibliography	270
Index	274

ACKNOWLEDGEMENTS

Because this book first took shape almost nine years ago, the list of people who influenced and aided me from its conception to its final publication is too vast to mention. I would like especially to thank all my students, clients, colleagues, friends and family members who, over the years, have become my greatest teachers; if I have not included your names, I hope you know the contribution you have made to this work. Special mention goes to Edith Katz, Rachel Pollack, Vera van Schaik, Dale Remley, Coen Cornellisen, Diana Blok, Ellen Perchonock and Eddie Woods, whose early dialogues shaped many of the ideas set forth in this book. Most of all, special thanks to my first mentor, Richard Lamm, whose insights helped formulate my approach to horoscope interpretation.

I'd like to thank Ken Stewart and P. J. Dempsey for their professional advice, Bea and Joe Siegel for allowing me the run of their home office, John Hartnett, Pasquale Crispo, Esq., and the law firm of Kera Graubard & Litzman for use of their equipment and, especially, Karen Dreyer and Dan Lieblein who bailed me out of computer problems by lending me their own.

The research and writing of this book took me to many places. Chrissie Richman, Dale Remley and especially Sue Budding were always hospitable on my visits abroad, as were the staff at Palenville Interarts Colony and the Ragdale Foundation, where some of the writing was completed. But, most of all, I could never have written this book without the hours spent in the Frederick Allen Memorial Room of the New York Public Library – a silent oasis in the chaotic, urban desert. Thanks also go to Ken Fields, who visited Aphrodisias and reported back about its magnificence, Diana Bloc and Nancy Spero for permission to use their photographs, Ken Negus for his poetry, Henry Weingarten and the New York Astrology Center for computer printouts, Demetra George and Rachel Pollack for their support and endorsements and Ken Irving for advice and encouragement. I would also like to thank Danelle McCafferty for her helpful suggestions and Annette Weir of Art Resources who helped research the photographs.

Everyone at Aquarian who worked with me on this project must be cited for their tenacity, especially Eileen Campbell, David Brawn, Barbara Vesey, Elizabeth Hutchins and my editor, Liz Puttick, whose suggestions, guidance and monumental patience through this book's many revisions are greatly appreciated. Georgia Hughes of HarperSanFrancisco was also extremely generous in her support of this project.

The emotional support and financial assistance of family and friends cannot go unmentioned, especially that of Fran and Herb Dreyer, Randi, Rene, Eric and Brett Jurgens, Karen Dreyer and Dan Lieblein, Bernice Napach, Marsha Berger, Carolyn Protz and Barry Napach. Ultimately, however, it was Fran Dreyer's unflagging belief in me and the worthiness of this project which overrode my frustrations and motivated me to keep going even when it looked as if there was no end in sight. If it were not for her superb editing and rewriting skills as well as the countless hours which she generously gave to this project, *Venus* might still be languishing at the bottom of the sea. For her tireless efforts, abiding faith and unconditional love, I am eternally grateful.

Ronnie Gale Dreyer
December, 1993

INTRODUCTION

One of the highlights of my vacation to Italy during the summer of 1984 was a visit to Florence's magnificent Uffizi Gallery where, among its countless treasures, two spectacular Renaissance paintings, Botticelli's 'Birth of Venus' and Titian's 'Venus of Urbino', commanded my undivided attention. Although I had been introduced to these masterpieces 10 years earlier by Dr Rodee, an inspirational Art History professor, it was not until I stood before them that I realised how perfectly these two distinct yet equally valid interpretations of the Love Goddess embody the planet Venus' dual assignment as ruler of Libra and Taurus. Whereas Botticelli's ethereal, delicate, svelte figure (modelled after Aphrodite/Venus, the Greco/Roman Goddess of Love and Beauty) epitomises the physical attributes of the air sign, Libra, Titian's luxurious, sensual, full-bodied figure typifies the earth sign, Taurus.

It suddenly dawned on me that no one had compiled a modern, comprehensive text assimilating the characteristics of both Taurus and Libra into descriptions of the astrological Venus. Although the planet was commonly interpreted from the Libran standpoint of love, beauty, creativity, tenderness and harmony – qualities evoked by Botticelli's image of the Goddess – it was rarely targeted as a Taurean symbol of fruitfulness, productivity, patience, wealth and sensual pleasure – traits manifested by Titian's portraiture. While most astrologers shared my belief that Venus had never been properly defined as the ruler of Taurus (my own Sun sign) some conceded that Libra was the 'unequivocal' recipient of Venus and that the rulership of Taurus would some day be allotted to a yet-to-be discovered planet named for Vulcan, the Roman God of Metallurgy, husband of the Goddess of Love.*

*Ironically, the Roman astrologer Manilius designated Vulcan as the ruler of Libra.

Upon returning home, I relentlessly questioned colleagues, clients, students and even friends as to which image was evoked when they envisioned the Goddess Venus. As I expected, most of their visualisations incorporated the Libran beauty, delicacy and serenity but failed to produce the Taurean earthiness, indulgence and luxuriousness. Determined to uncover the missing attributes which could link the Love Goddess – and, ultimately, the planetary symbol – to the fertile, persevering and stubborn sign of Taurus, I embarked on a journey which took me to international museums, art galleries, libraries and ancient sites in search of Venus.

To my amazement, I discovered countless representational artefacts, images and written documents which not only disclosed Aphrodite's origins as a Fertility Goddess (until she was transformed by literary characterisations into a *femme fatale*) but revealed a wealth of prototypical deities who preceded her. Ranging from Paleolithic 'Venuses' to Neolithic earth deities and from Mesopotamian Fertility Goddesses to Semitic patronesses of the sea, these agricultural Fertility Goddesses finally provided the key to the lost 'Taurean' attributes of the Love Goddess, and redefine Venus as a planetary symbol.

It was at this time that I stumbled upon the now classic book *Inanna: Queen of Heaven and Earth*, a beautiful retelling of the ancient Sumerian legend surrounding the Fertility Goddess Inanna and her consort, the Vegetable God Dumuzi, whose separation and passionate reunion invoked the death and regeneration of the growing season. Most intriguing, however, was the revelation that the sensual, regal, persevering, fruitful and powerful Inanna, from whom Aphrodite descended, was considered by the earliest Mesopotamian astrologers to be the actual manifestation of the planet Venus. Moreover, Inanna's attributes – epitomised by her legends, artefacts and rituals – stemmed from the planet's physical characteristics. Most significant was the fact that during the period preceding and following its heliacal risings and settings*
the planet cannot be seen with the naked eye. It was these

---

*The heliacal setting and rising of any planet is its last setting before and first rising after a period of invisibility due to conjunction with the overshadowing Sun.

'appearances and disappearances' of the Goddess/Planet that led to its association with the agricultural cycle. This proved rather conclusively that the 'Taurean' characteristics of the Goddess and the planet Venus were one and the same and that the sign of Taurus was, indeed, an appropriate domain for the planet Venus.

To my amazement I also discovered that an overwhelming profusion of North, Central and South American, African and Asian fertility Goddesses were not only regarded as personifications of the planet Venus but even shared the same myths. Although these diverse cultures – some of whom traded with one another – covered different parts of the globe, they all lived under the same sky, and though certain peoples shared similar folklore they all derived the same conclusions concerning the abundance wrought by Venus – the Goddess and the planet. (Due to the enormity of material, I have chosen to focus only on the direct prototypes of Aphrodite/Venus.)*

At present, libraries and bookstores are glutted with riveting material about Goddess worship as well as recent archaeological discoveries revealing the existence of peaceful matriarchal communities which thrived for centuries prior to the rise of male-dominated warring cultures. And while the idea for this book first took shape more than seven years ago, the shelves are still devoid of a text delineating the evolution of Venus, the Goddess and the Planet – a gap I hope, in part, to fill.

Accordingly, I have divided this book into two major sections which link the development of the prototypical Love and Fertility Goddess (Part I) with the interpretation of Venus as a planetary symbol (Part II). Although originally a predominantly astrological study, this book became for me a compelling and, at times, obsessive quest for the quintessential Goddess, the people who worshipped her and her manifestation as an archetypal symbol within the horoscope. By recounting the history of her transformation from a powerful fertility Goddess to a superficial Goddess of Love and Beauty, I hope the horoscopic Venus can once again represent not only love, beauty, sensuality, creativity and harmony but fertility, prosperity, abundance and personal power.

*For more information on the Mesoamerican Venus, I refer the reader to Bruce Scofield's article 'The Other Side of Venus', *American Astrology*, May 1993.

PART 1
The Goddess

1

EARLY MOTHER GODDESSES

> Some of the symbols . . . derive from what Dr Jung has called 'the collective unconscious' – that is, that part of the psyche which retains and transmits the common psychological inheritance of mankind. These symbols are so ancient and unfamiliar to modern man that he cannot understand or assimilate them.
>
> *Man and his Symbols*, C. G. Jung[1]

Paleolithic Europe

As far back as the late Paleolithic Era (25,000–10,000 BC), when the Earth was covered with sheets of ice and plagued by frigid weather conditions, the feminine image was embodied in miniature sculptures, stone engravings and magnificent pictograms which dotted the cavernous, mountainous regions of Europe – from Spain and southern France to the northernmost region of Siberia. Collectively called Paleolithic or cave art, these finely carved images and wall drawings form our only link to a time when the population lived in mountain grottoes and survival was tested each and every day. Illustrated scenes of daily life attest to the existence of a prehistoric society where men hunted for food and clothing while women prepared meals, protected the hearth and brought forth new life.

The 'great mother', an archetypal term coined by Jungian analyst Dr Erich Neumann in his book of the same name, appropriately describes the multitude of clay, bone and ivory likenesses unearthed from mountain caves and surrounding burial grounds. Labelled 'Venuses' by nineteenth-century archaeologists, these reverential sculptures portrayed pregnant-looking women with accentuated breasts, abdomens and buttocks. Originally dismissed as erotic replications, these effigies were ultimately re-evaluated by numerous scholars who recognised that these 'expectant mother' figurines and pictographic childbirth sequences represented wonderment with the female anatomy and its reproductive miracles. Because they were discovered carefully positioned in cave hearths, sanctuaries and graves, these statuettes, 'mother guardians of the daily life, death and rebirth of the people'[2] presumably served as both idols and sacrificial objects during fertility rites and ritualistic burial services. When meticulously placed alongside corpses laid to rest in the foetal position, these figurines signified the child who, in death, was returning to the source of life – the mother. At some grave sites, the bones were covered with red ochre, a mineral dye, symbolising the flow of blood which constitutes menstruation, death and, ultimately, life.

The oldest 'Venus' figurine dates back to 30,000–25,000 BC and was discovered in a cave near the Austrian Alpine village of Willendorf. Appropriately called 'Venus of Willendorf', the now famous limestone statuette has come to represent the quintessential Paleolithic Fertility Goddess. Although her swollen breasts, protruding abdomen and massive thighs all seem to indicate a woman in the throes of pregnancy, her hand does not rest on the abdominal region as in other expectant 'Venuses' of the same period. For this reason, Dr Marija Gimbutas, author of *The Civilization of the Goddess*, refers to this particular statuette as a personification of abundance rather than actual pregnancy.[3] Whether or not 'Venus of Willendorf' depicts maternity is of little consequence; what *is* significant is that the statue was an object of adoration which symbolised fruitfulness and honoured the strength of women.

Fascination with the pregnant anatomy and the squatting position of childbirth was continually evident throughout statuettes and cave drawings of both the Paleolithic and subsequent Neolithic Eras. Most notable was Venus of Lespugue, an exaggerated and reconstructed ivory figurine (23,000 BC) made up of a series of juxtaposed eggs forming her breasts, abdomen and buttocks. The triangle, carved around the midriff area, was symbolic of the vulva – the outer genital area associated with reproduction and female sexuality. Limestone carvings of triangular vulvas and sandstone quartz engravings of the vulva's enlarged outer lips (indicating gestational changes) were discovered throughout the Dordognes in southwest France (25,000 BC) and throughout Germany/Yugoslavia (6000 BC).

The most extensive series of cave wall engravings, uncovered in the Dordogne village of Laussel, consists of rituals 'that associated pregnancy in women with rutting, migration, and calving in animals'.[4] Most recognisable is the 'Venus of Laussel' (also known as 'Venus with the Horn'), portrayed with accentuated breasts, heavy thighs, one hand placed on her protruding abdomen and an uncharacteristic face lacking individuality. Her uplifted right hand grasps a crescent-shaped notched horn of either a bull, ox or buffalo which 'may represent the crescent moon symbolising new life [while] the thirteen lines incised on the horn may mark the months of the lunar calendar'.[5] There appears to have been an early awareness that women's menstrual cycle and the completed Moon cycle (full Moon to full Moon) each lasted approximately 28 days and that conception only occurred during a certain phase, most likely, the crescent stage.

Because there was no apparent understanding of the causal relationship between sexual intercourse and childbirth, it may have been thought that reproduction stemmed from autoeroticism or emanated from the sky or wind. Due to a multitude of engravings depicting females positioned in close proximity to animals or holding the animals' bodily parts, women may have been thought to become impregnated by animal spirits, notably the bison or bull. An early symbol of male fertility, the bull was frequently sacrificed in hopes that its spirit would reemerge as new life inside the womb – a ritual that continued throughout the subsequent Neolithic, Bronze and Iron Eras.

Neolithic and Chalcolithic Era (8000–3000 BC)

The Neolithic Era was marked by the Earth's meteorological transformation from Arctic weather conditions to a moister, warmer climate which fostered dense forests, lakes and streams.

Countless prehistoric beasts, now immortalised in stone, could not adapt to the new environment and, as a result, either disappeared from the European continent or became extinct. Once the sole providers of food and clothing, mammoths, wild bison, sabre-toothed tigers and musk oxen were replaced by rabbits, sheep and fish who could easily survive in moderate temperatures. Castrated wild bulls, known as oxen, were domesticated and utilised as beasts of burden for transportation and clearing the land which, due to improved environmental conditions, was ripe for growth and development.

As the alternating dormant and growing seasons revealed themselves, the pursuit of a systematised method of providing an abundant and dependable harvest generated the formation of self-sustaining farming communities throughout Europe, Anatolia (Turkey) and Mesopotamia (Syria and Iraq). Agrarian society created the need for community dynamics which included the apportionment of food and fair division of labour. While men continued to hunt, fish and tame wild animals, women's duties entailed planting seeds and grinding the harvested grains into bread. Not only were females an integral part of the labour force but they formed the nucleus of the community responsible for the unit's day-to-day operation.

Quite naturally, these early agricultural co-operatives became matriarchal – governed by women – and, as a result, matrilineal – where property is passed down through the female line (possibly due to paternal uncertainty). It is important to note, however, that matriarchal rule was not indicative of a system where women were dominant and men submissive. On the contrary, these farming villages were more likely egalitarian societies held together by a common goal – providing sustenance and shelter for every member of the community.

With the advent of this new agricultural epoch, the Paleolithic pregnant idol evolved into the Neolithic fertility deity glorifying woman's ability to bring forth sustenance from the earth *and* life from the womb. Due to her participation in planting and gathering of the annual harvest, the epithet 'Mother Earth' perfectly describes the reciprocity between women and the land – the two esteemed sources of life.

Owing to the profusion of countless relics excavated from the sites of Neolithic farming communities throughout Europe and Western Asia, an incredible wealth of information has been amassed concerning the Grain Goddess and her probable relationship to these agrarian societies. I have chosen briefly to discuss the matrifocal* cultures of Old Europe, Anatolia and Crete, whose fertility deities were the earliest forerunners of Aphrodite/Venus.

OLD EUROPE

Dr Marija Gimbutas uses the term 'Old Europe' to describe the excavated farming villages which extended 'from the Aegean and Adriatic, including the islands, as far north as Czechoslovakia, southern Poland and the western Ukraine'[6] during the Neolithic and Chalcolithic Eras (between 7000-3500 BC). Agricultural tools, ovens and kilns discovered adjacent to the remains of shrines, sanctuaries and temples confirm that the worship of a fertility Goddess was directly linked to the cultivation of grains and legumes which were then ground into bread. In addition, private residences and public shrines were inundated with sacrificial artefacts ranging from ritual vessels to vases, from weaving to pottery, from music boxes to 'miniature sculptures of clay, marble, bone, copper and gold'.[7] Placed atop altars and throughout burial grounds, these votive objects were ceremoniously presented to the Grain Goddess who, if pleased, would certainly reward the earth with an abundant harvest.** Another customary rite (which began during the Paleolithic Era) involved the ritualistic slaughter of the wild bull (a symbol of male potency) and the offering of its dismembered genitals, consecrated horns and miniature replicas of the authentic animal whose spirit was said to invoke fecundity in women and nature.

*The term 'matrifocal' has been coined to describe later egalitarian societies where women did not necessarily govern but did, in fact, share the responsibility of running the community with their male counterparts.
**An extremely common tradition throughout the ancient world, tombs laden with gifts were thought not only to please the deities but to inform the dead about life among the living.

The most common sculptures discovered at altars and entombed in coffins, however, were female effigies in varying shapes and sizes – carved primarily from stone. Bone and ivory cross-shaped figurines were rampant throughout Old Europe and, when pierced at the forehead, may have been worn as pendants or earrings to protect wearers from danger. Copper and gold gradually replaced bone and stone for sculpting figurines and, due to the pliability of these metals, the feminine form acquired actual facial features and a shapelier body. Although Goddess figurines still displayed overemphasised breasts, abdomens and buttocks, they were less corpulent than her Paleolithic counterparts.

According to Gimbutas, the plenitude of sculpted bird deities (with beak heads and women's bodies) as well as reptilian Goddesses (women entwined with serpents) attests to the fact that these animals were life-affirming symbols likened to women and the earth. Bird Goddesses were often depicted with protruding buttocks which correlated egg-hatching with human gestation, while later myths infer that a cosmic snake or bird dropped the egg from which the world emerged. Due to the snake's ability to moult and, thus, rejuvenate, the serpent became a universal emblem of regeneration while its elusiveness gave it the reputation for infinite wisdom, making the reptile interchangeable with the Goddess. The snake was also said to have emerged from water – an archetypal significator of purification and renewal; later fertility rituals held in Phoenicia and Greece often included anointing oneself with water or bathing in the sea. Other common Goddess symbols included the fish or Fish-Goddess and the labris, or double axe, whose resemblance to a butterfly symbolised the metamorphic transformation of the dormant earth into harvested grain.

ANATOLIA

Contemporaneous with the productive southeastern Europe, thriving agrarian societies emerged throughout Anatolia (present-day southern Turkey), most notably Catal Huyuk, a 30–35 acre community and major trading centre (7000–5500 BC), whose religion centred around the veneration of a Grain Goddess. Due to the inordinate number of female bodies discovered in burial sites, archaeologist James Mellaart contends that Catal Huyuk was governed primarily by women who may even have been responsible for developing farming methods which advanced agricultural productivity. Resembling the Paleolithic 'Venuses', Anatolian Earth Mother statuettes possess massive abdomens, breasts and buttocks attesting to the continuing worship of a pregnant Goddess – frequently sculpted in the squatting position of childbirth. The prevalence of grain storage bins and sophisticated farming implements near shrines and temples replete with female idols indicates that the worship of fertility deities was systematised, ritualistic and well integrated into daily life. Genuine bull horns, skulls and heads adjacent to images of the Goddess ('as if to assert and strengthen her powers')[8] dominated the walls of shrines and private dwellings – tantamount to the way pictograms of women, hunters and prehistoric animals dominated Paleolithic Europe. Due to the similarity of motifs (double axes, doves, trees and bulls) and rituals, it has been surmised that the Catal Huyuk population may have either migrated from Old Europe or descended from her inhabitants.

Another major nucleus of Neolithic farming settlements, Halaf was located in Eastern Anatolia near the source of the Tigris and Euphrates Rivers. Migrating from Russia (5000 BC), the Halafians also incorporated miniature horned bulls, doves and double axes into their religion. Goddess figurines now 'became more vigorous and less obese' and the emphasis on the bellies and buttocks suddenly shifted to a more marked accentuation of the upper torso with forearms folded and hands placed on or below the breasts.[9] One groundbreaking element which distinguished Halafian sculptures was the appearance of miniature Goddesses either fondling and nursing their children or embracing their male lovers. Because so many double axes were uncovered throughout southern Iraq, the Halafians probably settled the Mesopotamian Valley (4500 BC)[10] where their culture was eventually absorbed by the Sumerians, whose Fertility Goddess Inanna was a direct forerunner of Aphrodite/Venus.

Mediterranean Islands

Straying from the massive fertility idols of Old Europe and Anatolia, figurines with elongated necks, short extended arms and disproportionately accentuated hips were uncovered throughout Malta, Sicily, the Cyclades and Aegean Island chains and, most notably, Cyprus (3500–2500 BC) – where Aphrodite's worship originated. Used as amulets and good luck charms, these limestone, marble and terracotta (baked clay) idols resembling stick figures frequently contained v-shaped marks highlighting the breasts and the genitals, reminiscent of the triangular vulvas carved on stone dating from earlier eras.

There is no evidence of human slaughter throughout the entire Neolithic and Chalcolithic Eras (8000–3000 BC) – a testament to the success of peace-loving matriarchal and matrifocal communities which dominated the epoch. Unfortunately, harsh winters and lack of knowledge concerning irrigation techniques caused the soil to erode and these self-sustaining communities to disperse throughout Europe and Asia in search of natural resources and more favourable weather conditions. As the agrarian co-operatives disbanded, the first wave of Indo-European hunters, herders and shepherds from present-day Russia and Mongolia migrated to southeastern Europe, Western and Central Asia. These patriarchal tribes, whose mobile and aggressive lifestyle precluded long-term agricultural planning, ultimately replaced the peace-loving, matrifocal societies of the Neolithic and Chalcolithic Eras.

Bronze Era (3500–1500 BC)

CRETE

Although fierce Indo-European tribes had already infiltrated most of Europe and Asia, the tranquil Minoan civilisation*, who

*The earliest Cretan settlers were comprised of Anatolian hunters and fishermen, who may have migrated to the island as early as 7000 BC, and Libyan settlers who arrived around 3500 BC.

worshipped the earth in the form of a Mother Goddess, flourished on the Mediterranean island of Crete between 3500 and 1500 BC – a period which coincided with both the Bronze Era and the Age of Taurus (*ca.* 4000–2000 BC). According to ancient recorded descriptions, Crete's terrain was a veritable paradise varying between rugged mountains and fertile, wooded areas at sea level – not much different than it is today. Because weather patterns remained stable and water was constantly replenished, early farmers quickly learned that the moist, fertile soil not only yielded bountiful harvests but produced a surplus for commerce. Due to the island's strategic Mediterranean location, Minoan commerce thrived and Crete became a rich maritime empire trading extensively with Sumer, Cyprus, Anatolia and Egypt.

It was British archaeologist Sir Arthur Evans whose expeditions to Crete in the early 1900s first uncovered the remnants of the progressive civilisation which he named 'Minoan' after the island's legendary King Minos. The highlight of Evans' archaeological excavations was the unveiling of the now-restored sprawling palace at Knossos (nearby Crete's present capital Heraklion). Its labyrinthine rooms, halls and chapels were filled with a plethora of sacrificial altars, shrines and remarkable wall frescoes and murals whose scenes of ritualistic worship illustrated Priestesses or Queens seated on their thrones attended by male and female devotees bearing gifts and votive offerings.

> To judge by the frequency of shrines, horns of consecration and the symbol of the double-axe, the whole palace of Knossos must have resembled a sanctuary. Wherever you turn, pillars and symbols remind one of the presence of the Great Goddess . . . This situation is related to that found in Neolithic and Chalcolithic Europe: in houses there were sacred corners with ovens, altars (benches) and offering places, and there were separate shrines dedicated to certain goddesses.[11]

Although Minoan women held powerful positions, it has never been completely ascertained whether they were *sole* policy-makers – i.e. matriarchal – or if Crete was a matrifocal, egalitarian society. Linear A and B tablets (1500 BC), primitive forms of Greek writing, have revealed that matrilinear law had indeed been instituted.

The extent to which the Mother Goddess was revered on Crete may be ascertained from the countless sacrificial artefacts* crafted from bronze, the newly discovered alloy of copper and tin, from which the epoch derives its name. When cast in bronze, stronger and more malleable than copper (which replaced stone and clay), Goddess figurines acquired even finer facial and bodily features and, most important, human physical proportions were sleeker and more curvaceous. Frequently accompanied by Old European and Anatolian motifs of doves, lions, fish and double axes, the Minoan Goddess ornamented cult vases, dishes and altar tables. Most often, however, she is represented as a beaked lady with snake curls, snake arms or a snake crest on her head.[12] In fact, the abundance of miniature Snake Goddesses and decorative snakes, symbols of wisdom and regeneration, have led archaeologists to use the term 'Serpent Goddess' interchangeably with the 'Cretan Goddess'.[13]

It was, however, the veneration of the bull whose image decorated and shaped a multitude of artefacts and the consecration of its horns (often anointed with the animal's blood) which became practically synonymous with Cretan Goddess worship. In order to invoke his sacred power and capture the horns, games and sporting events were held in arenas and courtyards in which men and women pitted their reflexes and physical strength against those of the bulls. The finale of these games was the ceremonial sacrifice of the bull – the symbol of male fertility and identifying symbol of the Taurean Epoch.

Crete's unique terrain accommodated the formation of natural sanctuaries which precluded the necessity for man-made temples – none of which has ever been uncovered anywhere on the island. To this day, some of Crete's most spectacular landmarks include remains of these 'natural' sanctuaries located on mountain peaks, amidst groves or inside caves where the fertility Goddess was ritualistically honoured.

*For detailed descriptions of most of the cult objects uncovered at Knossos, the author refers the reader to *The Goddesses and Gods of Old Europe* by Dr Marija Gimbutas.

While most matriarchal and matrifocal agrarian societies had already dissolved, Crete's ability to remain independent must be attributed not only to its insular location but to its egalitarian government and Goddess-worshipping religion. While the rest of the civilised world was actively engaged in territorial disputes, Crete enjoyed two millennia of peace and prosperity with women's sexual freedom, independence and generally high status firmly implanted within Minoan society. Ultimately, the island was overrun by the Indo-European Achaeans (1500 BC), herders and shepherds from the Russian steppes, whose wind and thunder Gods formed the prototype for Zeus, the Greek thunderbolt God. Later named Mycenaeans for Mycenaea, the region in Central Greece where they had originally settled (2000 BC), the Indo-European Achaeans integrated the earlier Minoan-Cretan culture into their own to such an extent that the worship is often described as the 'Minoan-Mycenaean religion.'[14] The amalgamation of Mycenaean Sky Gods with Minoan Mother Goddesses was especially evidenced by the illustrated seals on signet rings which displayed Earth Goddesses on mountain tops and Sea Goddesses accompanied by aquatic mammals. Although Mycenaean Linear B tablet inscriptions discovered at Knossos and Pylos (the southern tip of Greece) describe early prototypes of the Olympian deities, there were no indications of a deity which paralleled Aphrodite – the Greek Goddess of Love and Beauty. And while she inherited qualities of fierceness and fruitfulness from the Cretan Mother Goddess, Aphrodite's earliest prototype was Inanna, the Sumerian Love and Fertility Goddess, worshipped throughout southern Mesopotamia as the Morning and Evening Star.

2

MESOPOTAMIAN GODDESSES AND ASTROLOGY

Lady of all the me's, resplendent light,
Righteous woman clothed in radiance, beloved of Heaven and Earth . . .
Omniscient sage, lady of all the lands,
Sustenance of the multitudes, I have verily recited your sacred song!
True goddess, fit for the me's, it is exalting to acclaim you.
Merciful one, brilliantly righteous woman . . .

Like a dragon you have deposited venom on the land
When you roar at the earth like thunder, no vegetation can stand up to you.
A flood descending from its mountain,
Oh foremost one, you are the Inanna of heaven and earth!
The Exaltation of Inanna, Enheduanna (2300 BC)[1]

Inanna – Sumerian Goddess of Heaven and Earth

Inanna, the embodiment of the planet Venus, was worshipped throughout Sumer, an empire situated in the arid southern Mesopotamian valley between the Tigris and Euphrates Rivers (present-day southern Iraq from Baghdad to the Persian Gulf). Thriving during the Bronze Era and the Age of Taurus, Sumer (4000–1750 BC), a contemporary of both Egypt* and Crete, epitomises the zodiacal sign of Taurus, and Inanna, the Love and

---

*Because Egypt was an agricultural civilisation centred in the Nile River Valley, the Egyptians' observations of the heavens resulted in an array of astral deities whose great mother Nut, the Goddess of the Heavens, created the universe. Due to the greatness of Egypt's empire, which spanned three millennia, it will not be covered in this book.

Fertility Goddess, characterises the quintessential Taurean Venus.*

Emigrating from south-central Asia (3500–3200 BC), the progressive Sumerians were a conglomeration of farmers, fishermen, herders and shepherds whose language and culture immediately dominated the region. Their self-sufficiency, resourcefulness, productivity and practicality – attributes of the sign of Taurus – established her as a powerful yet culturally and technologically advanced empire. Despite the fact that the desert was totally unsuitable for vegetation, the ingenious development of irrigation canals by which water was transported from the Euphrates River transformed unfarmable southern Mesopotamia into a fertile river valley which yielded an abundance of food for sustenance and commerce. The fertility Goddess took on an entirely new significance as she did in all Bronze Age cultures: not only was she responsible for watering the earth and sustaining the land, but she was also looked to for the bestowal of wealth in an age of competitive commerce.

Sumerian navigators travelled the globe and were even thought to have opened new routes as far as India which would, of course, explain the wealth of cultural similarities existent in a myriad of Near and Far Eastern societies. In addition to agricultural superiority and a first-rate merchant class, Sumer's cultural supremacy was enhanced by the introduction of exotic spices, gems, fabrics and other natural resources as well as through excellence in the Taurean endeavours of gem-cutting, architecture, music, sculpture and the invention of the first potter's wheel. Sumer's greatest contribution to Western culture, however, was the development of one of the earliest forms of letter writing. Cuneiform writing, which first appeared between 3500–2900 BC, entailed the preservation of recorded materials by utilising a reed stylus or pressing wedge-shaped leaves containing marks and symbols into wet clay tablets. While early cuneiform writing was comprised of pictographics resembling Egyptian

---

*Because the word 'Venus', derived from the Latin vernacular, conjures up too many preconceived images, it will be referred to throughout much of this book as the Morning and Evening Star.

hieroglyphics, later inscriptions contained letter-symbols which evolved into the sophisticated characters of the Babylonian, Phoenician and, ultimately, the Greek alphabet – the forerunner of the 26 letters we use today.

Although the Sumerian city-states were, from inception, centrally united under a succession of kings, each boasted a somewhat egalitarian society. In addition to being part of the agricultural workforce, women partook in policy-making, held government positions and owned land which, according to matrilinear law, was passed down to her children. By the end of the third millennium, however, family holdings fell under the auspices of the father and brother even though women were still allowed to hold property and engage in business. As Sumer evolved from an agricultural nation into both a militaristic and maritime empire with outside threats and increased trading outlets, women were no longer a vital part of the workforce and their status steadily declined. As long as an agricultural surplus remained Sumer's primary trading staple, however, the Fertility Goddess continued to be worshipped as the giver of life and regenerator of death.

As early as the fourth millennium, the Sumerians had cultivated two numerical systems – a decimal system (based on 10s and 100s) used for everyday counting and record-keeping, and a sexagesimal system (based on 10s and 60s) which was applied to more complex mathematics. It was the Sumerians' affinity with numerical concepts which enabled them to calculate the movements of the heavenly bodies evolving into the more advanced astronomical calculations of the later Babylonians.

This epoch also marked the introduction of the first Ziggurat, a towering pyramid-shaped dome with each terraced story smaller than the one below, which became the standard model for Mesopotamian temples.* These unique temple towers, which may have had seven platforms (identified with the seven planets), were later used by the Babylonian astronomer-priests as observatories from which they probed the heavens and recorded celestial omens.[2]

---

*The Ziggurat at Ur is thought by some scholars to have been the model for the biblical Tower of Babel.

To reflect their increased knowledge about the heavenly bodies as well as the meteorological conditions which affected the seasonal cycles and, in turn, agricultural growth, the Sumerians created a pantheon of anthropomorphic sky, wind, thunder and earth deities who protected particular regions and maintained rulership over different areas of daily life. These divinities, more complex than the Neolithic Earth Goddess, mirrored Sumer's hierarchical society and accommodated their vision of the universe.

The Sumerians believed that the universe was under the watchful charge of a pantheon, human in form but superhuman in nature and powers, who controlled the cosmos in accordance with well-laid plans and duly prescribed laws. Although there were countless divinities in charge of every aspect of daily life, the leading Sumerian deities were the four creating Gods controlling the four major components of the universe: the Sky God An; the Earth Goddess Ki or Ninhursag; the Air God Enlil, who gradually became the leader; and Enki, God of the Waters and Wisdom.[3] The other important deities were the Sun Goddess Nannar and Moon God Nanna, whose children were the Sun God Utu and his sister Inanna, Goddess of the Morning and Evening Star.

To comprehend fully the nature of the relationship between luminary and corresponding deity, it must be understood that their names signified both their heavenly *and* earthly manifestations. Utu, for example, was not merely the Sun God but the Sun itself; by the same token, when the Sumerians invoked Inanna, their Fertility Goddess, they were also adulating Inanna, the star, whose magnificent white light made it, next to the Sun and the Moon, the brightest object in the sky.

Judging by their mathematical notations and recorded myths, the Sumerians were quite sophisticated in their knowledge of astronomy. They knew, as we do today, that for part of the year the brilliant 'Inanna' could be seen rising, sometimes as early as three hours before the Sun; during the rest of the year, the star rose and set after the Sun and remained in the sky long after the Sun had set. Fostering the visual illusion of 'accompanying' both the rising and setting Sun in the eastern and western sky, respectively, this luminary, with its resplendent white hue, was referred to as the Morning and Evening Star by most ancient cultures.* It was even said that the Morning Star's appearance in the eastern sky roused the soldiers to war, while the Evening Star's arrival in the western sky induced passionate lovemaking followed by restful sleep. As a result, the aggressive Morning Star and the soothing Evening Star exemplified the two faces of Inanna – 1) the wrathful Goddess of War and 2) the tranquil Love and Fertility deity.

By the same token, the Sumerians knew that when the Morning Star was farthest from the Earth in what we now know as superior conjunction with the Sun** Inanna's view was obstructed by the Sun and was thought, therefore, to have 'disappeared'. After two months of 'darkness' Inanna once again emerged as the Evening Star and resumed her journey towards inferior conjunction with the Sun when she disappeared for approximately three days, after which time she reappeared as the Morning Star. Due to the fact that the 'appearances' and 'disappearances' of the magnificent 'Inanna' often coincided with the moist and dry seasons, respectively, it was easy to see why the Sumerians personified her as the beautiful fertility Goddess who watered the earth and symbolised the nation's profitable agrarian economy. Because she descended from the sky but received her powers from the earth, Inanna was worshipped as 'Queen of Heaven and Earth'.

Since the Grain Goddess was interchangeable with the Morning and Evening Star, Inanna's artefacts, rituals and recorded legends provide insight into how the star was viewed. Excavations throughout the sites of burial grounds, palaces and temples (4000–3000 BC) revealed votive bronze and ivory Goddess statuettes with reptilian heads, pubic triangles and either prominent breasts or arms folded across the breasts (the classic reverential position), emphasising the Sumerians' persistent faith

---

*Although these two phases were originally thought to represent two different luminaries, the Sumerians were aware that it was simply two faces of the same heavenly body.

**Superior conjunction with the Sun occurs when Venus is farthest from the Earth and the Sun lies directly between the Earth and Venus. Inferior conjunction occurs when Venus is closest to the Earth and lies directly between the Earth and the Sun.

in a regenerative Earth Goddess. Just as prevalent were sacrificial bulls and vulvas cut from bronze, gold and, most frequently, lapis lazuli, a blue semi-precious stone considered to be the Goddess' personal jewel and a Venusian, Taurean gem. Due to the skill of Sumerian sculptors and the malleability of bronze, gypsum and alabaster, likenesses of the Goddess were finely executed and had delicate, naturalistic facial and bodily features.

As the legendary Queen of Sumer, Inanna was depicted as a regal, beautiful but stern ruler seated on her throne, ornately attired, bedecked with jewels and flanked by lion pillars. Whereas jewels represented her duty to uphold Sumer's wealth, the lions personified her fierceness and power as both law-maker and Patroness of War. In other reliefs of the period, Inanna, *sans* regalia, is clasping sheaves of grain acknowledging both her role as Fertility Goddess and her affinity with Sumerian women who, as part of the labour force, boosted the agrarian economy. Relief sculptures which display the nude Goddess embracing her lover celebrate physical love and attest to the absence of inhibition among the Sumerians.

The largest percentage of temple relics uncovered consisted of thousands of engraved cylinder seals, finely crafted miniature 'tubes of stone' which were 'rolled in wet clay' – the same substance as the inscribed tablets. The most recurrent scenes were enactments of deities and royalty accepting offerings of live animals and inanimate objects. Each seal was usually illustrated with a display of astral symbols – Suns, crescent Moons and star-shaped designs – each associated with a particular deity. Because it was placed above Inanna's head, the eight-pointed star became the identifying symbol of both the Goddess and the planet.*

Because agricultural cycles dominated their lives, the Sumerians' most important celebrations took place during: 1) the autumn equinox (the Sumerian New Year's Day), to honour the rainy season and annual planting, and 2) the spring (vernal) equinox, or secondary New Year's Day, marking the months-long gathering and storing of the harvest in anticipation of the dry

---

*The eight points represent the eight years it takes for the Venus/Sun conjunction to return to its original zodiacal placement. This will be further discussed later in this chapter.

summer. As part of the festivities, Sumerian temples hosted ecstatic marathons and public celebrations infused with music, dancing, lovemaking and sacrifices to the Goddess culminating in the Sacred Marriage Rites – when the reigning monarch was symbolically wed to Inanna, Goddess of Procreation.

Inspired by the legendary love affair between Inanna and her husband, Dumuzi, the Vegetable Lord, whose consummated passion was said to ignite the growing season, this mock ceremony served to ensure the Sumerian King's powers of leadership, fertility and immortality.[4] By mythologising the King of Sumer as the omnipotent and immortal husband of the Fertility Goddess, the Sumerians were assured there would always be plenty to eat and a surplus to sell. Amidst crowds of enthralled onlookers, the reigning monarch (playing Dumuzi) and a temple priestess (playing Inanna), both attired in full regalia, would re-enact the royal couple's wedding night, beginning with the ceremony and ending with simulated passionate lovemaking.

THE CYCLE OF INANNA

Prior to the advent of the written word, bards and storytellers wove lyrical tales about the characteristics and attitudes of the nation and its people while mythologising its rulers as Gods and Goddesses. Much of our knowledge of Sumerian civilisation is derived from approximately 30,000 inscribed clay tablets and tablet fragments dating from 2000 to 1750 BC uncovered at the site of the Sumerian capital, Nippur, by the University of Pennsylvania's team led by the late Dr Samuel J. Kramer. Although the majority of tablets contained economic, legal and administrative documents, approximately 3,000 to 4,000 were inscribed with hundreds of myths, laments and other compositions honouring the entire pantheon of Sumerian Gods and Goddesses.[5] Orally transmitted from generation to generation until recorded for posterity, these epic tales probably surfaced as early as 3400–2950 BC when Sumer was ruled by an actual king named Dumuzi who probably participated in the very first Sacred Marriage Rites.

Diane Wolkstein, a folklorist and storyteller, collaborated with Dr Kramer by weaving four translated stories into one epic prose-poem entitled 'The Cycle of Inanna'.* Her inspiring version of Kramer's original translations elucidates the three stages of Inanna's development: 1) The young maiden's emergence as fertility deity and accession to the throne; 2) Her initiation into womanhood through her marriage to the Vegetable God, Dumuzi, with whom she reigns; and 3) Inanna's descent to the Land of the Dead and subsequent resurrection as ruler of Heaven, Earth and the Underworld. As told by Kramer and Wolkstein, this epic reveals the extent to which Goddess worship prevailed in Sumer despite the fact that attitudes and laws less favourable to women were being enacted at a frighteningly accelerated pace. Because Inanna is the earliest personification of the Morning and Evening Star and the forerunner of Aphrodite/Venus, I have elaborated on her *rite de passage*.

Inanna as a Young Girl

'The Cycle of Inanna' opens in Inanna's garden in Uruk around 3000 BC, shortly after the great flood of Eridu – the probable model for the biblical deluge. Using her regenerative powers, the young maiden revives a huluppu tree which had been felled by the wind and carried downstream by the overflowing Euphrates River. The huluppu tree, a forerunner of the Tree of Knowledge in the Garden of Eden, was a date palm tree whose fruit was nutritional and profitable while its leaves, fibre and timber provided other profitable by-products. (In period reliefs, Inanna, often called 'Lady of the Date Clusters', is frequently depicted alongside the huluppu tree – both symbols of Sumer's agricultural and economic strength.)

After miraculously nursing the fallen tree back to life, Inanna recognises her ability to heal and rejuvenate nature and becomes fully cognizant of her burgeoning sexuality and capacity for procreation. Anxious to marry and succeed her uncle, King Enki,

*Throughout this chapter, I have used Wolkstein's version as my point of reference. Although this epic is based on four separate tales translated by Kramer, Wolkstein divided it into Inanna's three phases.

as Sumer's reigning monarch, Inanna sets out to build a bed and throne from the wood of the huluppu tree. In order to protect their respective homes in the tree's roots and trunk, a serpent and the Goddess Lilith (pictured in period reliefs as a bird-woman) attempt to thwart Inanna's decision to cut it down. In retaliation, Gilgamesh kills the snake, chops down the tree and helps construct a marriage bed and throne. Ironically, Enki, King of Sumer and God of the Waters, has arranged for Gilgamesh to aid Inanna but must now relinquish his own crown as Inanna's powers now surpass his.

Although this tale predates the Book of Genesis, the story of Inanna and the huluppu tree was almost certainly the basis for the biblical tale of the Garden of Eden. Just as the serpent and Eve conspire to obtain the knowledge of Yahweh (God), the snake and Lilith vie with Inanna (the Goddess) for mastery over nature. And just as the serpent and Eve are banished from the Garden of Eden, the snake and Lilith lose their homes – and, in the case of the snake, his life.

Inanna as Queen

Revelling in her emerging sexuality and great procreative abilities, the mature, self-proclaimed Queen of Sumer is introduced to Dumuzi, a shepherd, who competes with a farmer for her hand in marriage. Although Inanna prefers the tranquil life offered by the farmer, she ultimately weds Dumuzi, crowns him immortal King of Sumer and vests in him the fruitful powers of Vegetable Lord. In addition to epitomising the prosperity of the nation, the royal union represents the waning of the Taurean Age (personified by the gentle farmer) and the advent of the Arian Age (symbolised by Dumuzi the shepherd).

Just as Neolithic Goddesses received their procreative powers from the earth, Inanna is empowered by the great love and unabashed passion she shares with Dumuzi ('the young bull') and the consummation of their union was said to regenerate the earth.

> Inanna sang:
> He has sprouted; he has burgeoned;
> He is lettuce planted by the water

> He is the one my womb loves best.
> My well-stocked garden of the plain
> My barley growing high in its furrow,
> My apple tree which bears fruit up to its crown,
> He is lettuce planted by the water.
>
> Dumuzi sang:
>
> O Lady, your breast is your field
> Inanna, your breast is your field
> Your broad field pours out plants
> Your broad field pours out grain
> Water flows from on high for your servant
> Bread flows from on high for your servant
> Pour it out for me, Inanna,
> I will drink all you offer.[6]

While sculpted reliefs of this period are rampant with visual images of the nude couple embracing or making love, sensual passages use the burgeoning earth to describe metaphorically Inanna and Dumuzi in the throes of passion. When the great Goddess is sexually fulfilled, she is omnipotent; the harvest abounds and Sumer flourishes. If she is deprived of sensual pleasures, the land becomes sterile and the nation suffers economically.

Unfortunately, the couple's happiness is short-lived. Inanna journeys to the Land of the Dead to visit her adversarial older sister, Ereshkigal, Queen of the Underworld.

Inanna's Descent

The Goddess' descent is a story constant throughout the folklore of diverse cultures (Sumer, Babylonia, Canaan, Egypt and Greece) and describes the Fertility Goddess' search for a loved one who has been abducted – usually to the Underworld. Although this tale, which I call 'the Mourning Myth', varies from place to place, it always elucidates: 1) the Goddess' rite of passage into the mysteries of the Universe (often her inner or higher self); and 2) the distinction between the rainy, growing season and the dry, dormant one.

'Inanna's Descent', a story of separation, loneliness, grief, death, and ultimately, rebirth, unfolds as Inanna prepares for her impending visit to the Underworld. Sensing the perils which await her, she dons a protective amulet of lapis lazuli and arrives in the Underworld with the excuse of attending her brother-in-law's funeral. Inanna secretly hopes, however, to confront the darker side of herself as represented by her sister Ereshkigal and, perhaps, reconcile their differences.

Instead, the Queen of Heaven and Earth must pass through the seven gates of hell, relinquishing a layer of clothing and jewels at each gate until she is naked and, very simply, Ereshkigal's sister. To retaliate for being doomed to rule the Underworld, a jealous and vengeful Ereshkigal condemns Inanna to death so that she, too, may experience the wretched void below the earth. When Inanna fails to return, Enki, God of the Waters, knows that without Inanna the nation will perish. Using his bargaining skills, Enki pleads for Inanna's freedom until Ereshkigal reluctantly consents with the stipulation that, upon her release, someone be sent in her stead. Returning to Sumer, Inanna discovers to her chagrin that Dumuzi has enjoyed sole rulership and has not even missed her. Emotionally wounded and infuriated, Inanna displays her dictatorial side and, in a moment of rage, banishes Dumuzi.

Separated from her lover, a grief-stricken Inanna is incapable of watering the earth. The agonising heat and lack of rain renders the land so parched that vegetation shrivels and eventually dies. Responding to her own loneliness and to the agony of her subjects, who desperately fear there will be no harvest, Inanna travels to the steppes where she encounters a battered Dumuzi beaten by the demons from hell. To save him from death and her kingdom from disaster, Inanna revives her lover and sends him to the Underworld for half the year, while his sister replaces him the other half.

Overjoyed at the reconciliation of their beloved rulers whose passionate lovemaking ends the arid summer and inaugurates the autumn planting, the Sumerians celebrate the Sacred Marriage Rites. According to legend, Dumuzi and Inanna will rule during the fertile, wet season, until the annual spring bounty is gathered and Dumuzi will once again join Ereshkigal in the Land of the

Dead. When the dormant, parched summer is over, he returns to Sumer to reunite with Inanna and renew the cycle.

This allegorical tale has important connotations on a variety of levels. Because several versions of this legend were recorded during Sumer's transition from an agricultural to militaristic nation, Inanna is portrayed as a multi-faceted figure whose attributes can readily be linked with the sign of Taurus and its ruler Venus. While the earlier rendition portrays her as a sad, peace-loving Goddess who mourns the loss of her lover, the later version depicts a wrathful, belligerent deity who banishes Dumuzi to the Underworld. By allowing Inanna to first react hurt and angrily to Dumuzi's indifference and, later, to reverse his sentence due to her own loneliness and capacity for forgiveness, she became a very human Goddess with whom many women could identify.

Psychologically viewed, this legend, like so many myths and fairy tales, may be interpreted as a morality tale which conveys the polarities of good and evil which exist in us all. These contrasting traits are frequently exemplified by an individual's split personality or through opposites – the hero and villain, the good witch and bad witch, the loving, natural parent and wicked step-parent and, in the case of the 'Cycle of Inanna', the good and evil sister. According to Wolkstein, Inanna, the pastoral Queen of Heaven and Earth, and Ereshkigal, Queen of the dark and dry Underworld, comprise two aspects of the female psyche. Whereas Inanna is the quintessential 'good' sister whose sexuality results in procreation, Ereshkigal's libido is 'bad' because it is compulsive and lustful. By sharing Dumuzi, who spends half the year with Inanna and the other half with Ereshkigal, the sisters are bonded – each able to recognise the part of herself reflected in the other.

Inanna and Dumuzi's experiences in the Underworld also reflect the Sumerian view of the hereafter which, like most ancient cultures, propounded that death was not a finality but a place of refuge where one awaited reincarnation. Inanna's revitalisation from the Netherworld completes her rite of passage; as fertility Goddess she rules the Earth, as the Morning and Evening Star she governs the Heavens and now, having survived the Land of the Dead, she has added the Underworld to her domain.

Inanna's descent and resurrection typifies the initiatory journey which Joseph Campbell describes in his classic work *Hero of 1,000 Faces*. Although the author attributed this journey to the archetypal *hero* as opposed to *heroine*, Inanna's journey to hell and back, 'the oldest recorded account of the rite of passage through the gates of metamorphosis',[7] decidedly conforms to Campbell's paradigm outlining the initiate's path.

According to Campbell, the hero's journey involves 'the physical deed, in which the hero performs a courageous act in battle or saves a life . . . [and] the spiritual deed, in which the hero learns to experience the supernormal range of human spiritual life and then comes back with a message'.[8] While the archetypal hero journeys into the unknown to overcome insurmountable adversity, the heroine's initiation has traditionally involved either a menstrual rite or sexual experience which marks her passage into womanhood. Inanna's journey is, therefore, twofold – her journey to the Underworld suits the *hero's* rite of passage while her marriage to Dumuzi suits the *heroine's* initiation. At the end of each journey, however, both the hero and heroine are rewarded with the miracle of self-discovery – 'missing in your consciousness in the world you formerly inhabited'.[9]

Finally, Sylvia Perrera, a Jungian analyst, has implied that Inanna's journey through the seven gates of hell represents 'the seven planetary positions with which the planet Venus would move into conjunction on her descent and return'.[10] Inanna's imprisonment in the Underworld corresponded to the periods when the Morning and Evening Star could not be seen with the naked eye; conversely, her return to Sumer parallels the star's 're-emergence' in the sky. It seems quite likely, therefore, that 'Inanna's Descent' was intended to be an allegory of: 1) the seasonal cycles; and 2) the passage of the Morning and Evening Star which influenced those very cycles.

Ishtar – Babylonian Goddess of Love, Fertility and War

Throughout the Age of Taurus and early Bronze Era, a period of relative harmony prevailed among the three major empires of the era – Crete, Egypt and Sumer – whose search for new trading outlets and exotic resources created a competitive arena in which commerce flourished. Often preoccupied with the perpetuation of their agrarian economies, these empires were unprepared for the widespread territorial invasions by fierce Indo-European and Semitic tribes whose quest for a place to settle permanently altered the demographics of the ancient Near and Middle East. (This changeover also represented the transition from the agricultural Age of Taurus to the militaristic Age of Aries.)

Hailing from the Caucasus Mountains and Russian Steppes, the fair-skinned Indo-Europeans, or Aryans (Sanskrit for 'nobles') settled the Indus River Valley (India), Persia, Greece, Palestine, Syria, Anatolia and northern Mesopotamia. In contrast, the dark-skinned Semites migrated from southern Arabia and Africa to form settlements throughout the Levant (Syria, Lebanon, Jordan and Israel) and Mesopotamia (modern-day Iraq and northeastern Syria).

Originally hunters, herders and fishermen, these toughened Indo-Europeans and Semites were superb fighters whose continual pursuit of wild herds into unknown regions frequently forged bloody border disputes resulting in the victor's occupation of the embattled territory.[11] Without an agricultural society to accommodate their labour, nomadic women, necessarily excluded from hunting and fishing, tended to domestic chores and were ultimately less valued within the community.

The Semitic Akkadians* migrated to Mesopotamia (modern-day Iraq and eastern Syria) as early as the third millennium. Desirous of fertile land, the Akkadians encroached upon the Sumerians until the entire southern Mesopotamian region was cohabited by both groups and the entire territory was officially renamed Sumer-Akkad. Because their nomadic lifestyle precluded any sustained level of cultural development, the Akkadians enthusiastically incorporated Sumer's high civilisation into their own, taking advantage of Sumer's spiritual and artistic legacy. While origins and lifestyles were markedly dissimilar, their

---

*The three basic Semitic languages – Aramaic, Hebrew and Akkadian – were each further broken down by dialect. Akkadian consisted of Babylonian and Assyrian, after which its peoples were named.

commitment to agricultural productivity and economic prosperity enabled the Sumerians and Semites initially to co-exist under Semitic rule. Due to a mutual dependence on seasonal cycles and reverence for the land, the Akkadians easily assimilated Inanna's complex rituals, hymns and legends into the worship of their own Fertility Goddess – Ishtar.

Despite the similarities which bonded the two Goddesses, the cultures' disparate languages, values and religious precepts distinguished the Semitic Ishtar from the Sumerian Inanna. Just as Inanna conferred the gift of immortality upon the King of Sumer, Ishtar was said to endow the king with boundless might through the Sacred Marriage Rites – the ruler's symbolic nuptials in which the role of the Fertility Goddess was enacted by one of her priestesses.

According to Akkadian lore, however, Ishtar's power never superseded the authority of the king – an attitude which reflected the lowlier position of women in Semitic society. Sargon I, Sumer-Akkad's first king, was mythologised as the abandoned son of a High Priestess forbidden by law to bear children. Discovering the baby in a basket afloat in the Euphrates River, Ishtar not only adopts him but primes him for his future role as King.* After Sargon is enthroned, the Goddess becomes his lover and a priestess in her own temple – mirroring the privileged position of the king's concubine who, as Ishtar's priestess, even advised him on matters of state.

In an attempt to dominate the region, the Akkadians rededicated many Sumerian temples to Ishtar but were unable to obliterate completely the worship of Inanna, who had evolved into a defiant war deity and strong symbol of Sumerian nationalism. Although the mere mention of Inanna's name could rouse Sumerian fervour, her worship was tolerated by Sargon to gain the trust of the Sumerian people and maintain the nation's unity. Even Enheduanna, King Sargon's daughter and high priestess of Nanna, the Sumerian Moon God, paid homage to Inanna's beauty, wisdom, compassion and victoriousness in battle

*The story of Sargon's birth is, obviously, a forerunner of the tale of the infant Moses, found in the bulrushes of the Nile River by the Egyptian princess who raised him as her own.

in a series of devotional poems (2300 BC) later entitled *The Exaltation of Inanna* (see p.28).

But Enheduanna, the earliest known poetess and rare female scribe, also portrayed Inanna as a venomous, all-devouring predator willing to stop at nothing to annihilate her enemies and protect her nation. Because terrifying images dominate Enheduanna's lamentations, Inanna's belligerence and fierceness became her hallmarks and overshadowed the magnanimity for which she had heretofore been revered. No longer the humane and bountiful fertility Goddess whose powers over life and death targeted nature's regeneration, Inanna's new dimension as creator and destroyer of humanity characterised later versions of Ishtar and was a harbinger of the Hindu Kali, the Canaanite Anat, the Greek Athena and certain regional versions of Aphrodite.

Despite Enheduanna's privileged status as both a princess and person of letters, she was atypical of most Semitic women who, for the most part, were not as highly valued as their Sumerian counterparts who always held respected positions within Sumer's structured society.

Emblematic of Sumer-Akkad under constant siege, Inanna and Ishtar, the subject of innumerable Sumerian and Akkadian cylinder seals often accompanied by bilingual inscriptions (2300–1750 BC), were primarily venerated as martial deities and symbols of unity for their respective peoples. Armed with lion-headed clubs and astral weaponry, these Goddesses were recurrently depicted battling adversaries – their fierce expressions and tense body language conveying an eagerness to fight.

THE ASSYRO-BABYLONIAN EMPIRE
(1792–539 BC)

Neighbouring invasions finally weakened Sumerian strongholds and the reinforced Akkadians seized power for the final time. In a symbolic gesture which signified the demise of the Sumerian dynasty, Uruk's devastated shrines (including Eanna, Inanna's renowned temple) were restored and rededicated to Ishtar, the Semitic Fertility Goddess.

The destruction of Sumer-Akkad by the Semitic Amorites gave rise to the Assyro-Babylonian Empire (1792-539 BC) known for its remarkable intellectual, technological and cultural achievements. With King Hammurabi (1792-1750 BC) at its helm, the newly formed Empire escalated into a commercial land and sea power; its capital, Babylon, a previously unimportant town on the Euphrates River, became one of the world's greatest scientific, cultural and religious centres. Although agriculture remained a vital industry throughout southern Mesopotamia, a mercantile economy and military expansionism further contributed to the declining status of Babylonian women who were no longer needed to uphold the economy.

Because the temple, once the centre of Mesopotamian life, no longer administered the revenues of an elaborate estate, Ishtar's priestesses were no longer politically influential. They still resided, however, in Ishtar's temples, participated in the Sacred Marriage Rites and continued to serve the community through ritual prostitution – promising fertility and providing sexual favours, as Inanna's priestesses had before them.

As agricultural dominance gave way to Babylonia's emerging military and naval strength, Ishtar's omnipotence and influence declined in accordance with women's diminished position in society. Although the trinity of Shamash, the Sun God, Sin, the Moon God, and Ishtar, the Morning and Evening Star,* were still highly venerated, Marduk, the Akkadian King of the Gods and manifestation of Jupiter, the largest visible 'star', became the supreme deity and patron God of Babylon. Marduk's heroic rise heralded a new theme which appeared in creation myths of many patriarchal cultures – the Warrior-King's usurpation of the Goddess and ascendancy to the throne either by marrying her, making her his concubine and/or, in extreme cases, even murdering her. Ishtar, now secondary to Marduk, was often depicted as the King's mistress or as a priestess in her own temple which mirrored the actual king of Babylonia's relationship with

---

*These deities replaced the practically interchangeable Sumerian triad of Nanna, the Moon God, Utu, the Sun God, and Inanna, the Morning and Evening Star. Most of the other Sumerian deities, however, either vanished or merged into the far less complex Babylonian pantheon.

his priestess/concubine. According to the *Enuma Elish*, the Babylonian creation myth, Marduk attained kingship by slaying Tiamat, Goddess of Watery Chaos. After proclaiming himself king, Marduk created heaven and earth, assigned each deity a domain, created humankind and founded the great city of Babylon. In later versions of the myth, Marduk 'defined the year and its zodiac of twelve signs, the days of the year, the various stellar and planetary orders, and the manner of the moon: its waxing to the middle of the month in opposition to the sun, after which, its waning and disappearance, in approach to the stating of the sun.'*[12]

Because the Fertility Goddess no longer vested the king's powers, Hammurabi proclaimed Marduk patron deity of Babylon and declared himself – as did each successive king – Marduk's earthly manifestation. To reflect the new hierarchy of divinities, the Babylonian New Year, the primary holiday, was celebrated on Marduk's Saints Day (during the month of Nisan), which coincided with the burgeoning harvest and the occurrence of the spring equinox. The autumn Akitu Festival, which took place during the autumn equinox, was designated a secondary New Year's Day. Both holidays embraced the Sacred Marriage Rites in which the king participated to ensure the fertility of the land.

As Indo-European invasions became an omnipresent threat, however, Ishtar, revered as the Morning and Evening Star, was most valued as a Love and War Goddess and her priestesses were called upon to support the cause. In times of war, the 'Ishtaritu' provided not only physical satisfaction but, as incarnations of the holy spirit, empowered their patrons by boosting their morale and spurring them on to victory. These customs became so commonplace that the city of Uruk, once the centre of Inanna's worship and now enshrined to Ishtar, was coined the city of 'courtesans and prostitutes' by Herodotus, the Greek philosopher, who chronicled his fifth-century visit to Babylonia in his *Histories*.

Throughout the duration of the Assyro-Babylonian Empire,

---

*Although the *Enuma Elish* was originally recorded during the Old Babylonian period, it was revised during later centuries. Because this version mentions the 12 signs of the zodiac, it was probably recorded during the later Neo-Babylonian era.

Ishtar is almost exclusively portrayed on cylinder seals and reliefs as a martial deity – attired with protective helmet, combat uniform and either arrows or double-headed lion clubs slung over her shoulder. In other reliefs and seals, she holds an authoritative sceptre and is fully equipped with lethal weaponry ranging from taut bows and arrows to the most deadly weapon of all – the sharp-edged scimitar. Her most characteristic pose, however, depicts her upright with one foot triumphantly atop a lion – signifying a reciprocity of power and the ability to tame the fiercest of beasts. In later Assyrian-dominated times, the Goddess frequently commandeered a horse or lion-drawn chariot – an archetypal symbol of fortitude. The divine vehicle appeared throughout world mythologies alternately driven by the Hindu God Shiva, the Biblical Elijah and the Greek Phaethon.

> Images of Ishtar were known throughout Semitic lands: armed with bow and arrow; wearing the tiara crown upon Her head; holding the double serpent scepter; holding Her hands beneath Her breasts; standing upon the lion beneath Her feet; mushrusshu dragons by Her sides; riding in Her chariot drawn by seven lions; holding a bull by the horns; seated upon Her lion throne; riding upon the back of a large bird; holding the sacred branches in Her hands; brandishing sword or scimitar; priestesses sitting on the ground before Her – knowing Her as the most sacred eight-pointed star, the guiding light of the planet Masat Venus.[13]

Babylonian attitudes towards the Fertility Goddess and women in general are best epitomised by Ishtar's characterisation in two legends – 'Ishtar's Descent into the Netherworld' and 'Epic of Gilgamesh'.*

'Ishtar's Descent to the Netherworld', the Akkadian tale of Ishtar and her consort, Dumuzi, is an abridged version of 'Inanna's Descent' and focuses on Ishtar's sojourn to the Land of the Dead. Replacing Sumerian with Akkadian names, the story opens with Ishtar's journey to the Netherworld where she demands access to

---

*Based on earlier Sumerian legends, the most extensive versions of these myths were excavated from the Assyrian royal library (seventh century BC). These renditions, based upon Stephanie Dalley's translations in *Myths from Mesopotamia*, are composites of Sumerian, Babylonian and Assyrian fragments.

Ereshkigal, her sister and Queen of the Underworld. Adhering to Ereshkigal's orders, the gatekeeper admits Ishtar and treats her like any mortal entering the gates of Hell. Passing through each of the seven gates, Ishtar must relinquish an article of clothing or jewellery until she stands completely naked before her sister, who strikes her dead. With Ishtar's demise, the earth becomes parched, plants and animals cannot procreate and the Akkadians are terrified that there will be no harvest. King Ea (the equivalent of the Sumerian King Enki and God of the Waters) rescues Ishtar by tricking Ereshkigal into first reviving and ultimately releasing Ishtar with the stipulation that Dumuzi be sent to the Underworld in her place.

In the Akkadian version of the story, however, Ishtar is unable to resurrect Dumuzi in time for the spring harvest and, instead of grieving, acquires a new lover whom she names Dumuzi and with whom she participates in Sacred Marriage Rites to inaugurate the harvest and celebrate the fruitfulness of the earth. When the annual crop is finally gathered and the hot, dry summer approaches, the young lord is sent to his death. And so the cycle continues – each autumn a new paramour is chosen and each spring he is condemned to death.* Although 'Ishtar's Descent' still allegorised the seasonal cycles, Babylonia's waning agrarian economy and rising imperialism dictated that the Fertility Goddess become a less compassionate deity who put her lovers to death. While Ishtar was primarily extolled for her combativeness and carnality, a new literary hero emerged in the character of Gilgamesh.

The Epic of Gilgamesh

Although the 'Epic of Gilgamesh',** the most important and

---

*In certain Semitic dialects (including biblical writings), Dumuzi is also called Tammuz. The Babylonian/Hebrew month of Tammuz, which begins in mid-June, was named after the young god whose death occurred during the summer heat.

**The *Epic of Gilgamesh*, whose Hittite and Hurrian translations were discovered throughout the Near East, was based on Sumerian fragments about the heroic Gilgamesh, an actual king of Uruk who reigned during the third millennium. The figure of Gilgamesh, who appeared in the legend of Inanna and the Huluppu Tree, was based on this Sumerian king.

lengthiest Akkadian legend, concerns the mythical Sumerian king's heroic quest for immortality, our interest in the tale concerns the hero's interaction with Ishtar – a brief but significant episode which elucidates the Goddess' fall from grace in Babylonian society.

After slaying the monstrous guardian of the cedar forest, Gilgamesh returns home to Uruk where he encounters Ishtar at her temple Eanna, renowned for its ritual prostitution. Aroused by the temptingly handsome and heroic Gilgamesh, Ishtar proposes marriage by enticing him with promises of unlimited wealth and power in the form of magnificent jewels, chariots and all the treasures of the earth. After enumerating the long list of Ishtar's deceased lovers, the Sumerian cum Babylonian hero rejects her offer for fear that he, too, will come to a tragic end.

Incensed by his rejection and motivated by overwhelming revenge, Ishtar persuades her father to release the powerful Bull of Heaven from the Underworld, whose snorting causes the earth to open up and entraps and kills many of Uruk's young men. Escaping from the chasm in which they too were ensnared, Gilgamesh and his mortal companion, Enkidu, kill the Bull of Heaven – further angering Ishtar. As retribution for her misuse of the Bull of Heaven, Ishtar is stripped of her powers to bestow kingship – which, from this point on, must be inherited, earned or won by the might of the sword.*

Whereas earlier peace-loving, agricultural societies emulated the Fertility Goddess as their heroine, 'Epic of Gilgamesh' marked Ishtar's decline and the emergence of the archetypal mortal warrior-hero whose initiation entailed journeying into the unknown, battling obstacles and emerging unscathed. (Gilgamesh was the precursor of later epic protagonists – the Hindu Krishna, the Greek Odysseus, the Roman Aeneas, St George the Dragonslayer and the Knights of the Round Table in search of the Holy Grail.)

---

*The primary theme of the *Epic of Gilgamesh* involves the hero's search for the secrets of eternal life. Gilgamesh fails the only test of strength that would have qualified him for immortality. Gilgamesh does not live for ever, but by continuing to perform heroic deeds he learns to savour life and take pride in his achievements.

ASSYRIAN AND NEO-BABYLONIAN PERIOD (1000 BC-539 BC)

One of the most powerful and terrifying empires the ancient world had ever known, the Semitic Assyrians emerged as northern Mesopotamia's dominant power (1400 BC). The Assyrian Empire heralded the new Iron Age characterised by the production of heavier and more 'efficient' tools, weapons and military equipment – particularly the war chariot, whose incomparable speed and power transformed the way wars were fought.[14] Because Northern Mesopotamia was a land of consistent rainfall with little need for man-made irrigation canals, the Assyrians, a Semitic and Indo-European hybrid culture, had no need for a fertility Goddess whose sexual powers regenerated the earth. Whereas the Indo-European Hittites, who first settled the region, honoured an erotic 'dominant deity, depicted with wings, golden accoutrements, a lion and two attendants',[15] Ishtar, whose worship had spread throughout the Near and Middle East, was revered by the Semitic Assyrians in her capacity as War Goddess.

Because of their shared religious and cultural heritage, the Assyrian pantheon of deities was practically identical to that of Babylonia. Ishtar, sometimes referred to as Ashtart, was primarily an erotic warrior deity second only to Ashur, the Assyrian King of the Gods and equivalent of Marduk. Although most Ishtar temples which dotted major Assyrian cities were veritable brothels, the magnificent sanctuary in Nineveh served as an international cultural and religious centre. Due to its proximity to the Neolithic site of Halaf (see Chapter 1), artefacts arrayed with serpents, doves, double axes and lions dating as far back as 5000 BC distinguish Ishtar of Nineveh from other regional manifestations of the Goddess.

Like Babylonian images, Assyrian likenesses of Ishtar depict her almost exclusively as a martial deity attired in protective armour and helmet, weapons in hand and surrounded by an array of militant symbols. Her trademark stance, by which she is most recognisable, displays her atop lions or commandeering both horse and lion-drawn chariots. In accordance with their firm belief in celestial omens, the Goddess also appears in Assyrian seals and sculptures as an astral deity 'surrounded by a nimbus of stars'. The rosette, or eight-pointed star, continues to be pictured above the heads of deities to indicate their affinity with the luminaries, and it became Ishtar's personal symbol – as it had been Inanna's.

Although their assumption of supreme authority defied the power of the Gods, Assyrian kings humbly implored the divine guidance of both astronomer-priests (*Baru* priests) and certain temple priestesses who possessed remarkable skills of prognostication. In providing strategic counsel, these particular priestesses (often well-versed in astronomy) recited oracles which were said to have been directly transmitted by Ishtar in her capacity as warrior deity.

> You shall not fear, O Esarhaddon. It is I, the Lord, who speak with you. I watch over your innermost heart, like your mother who gave you being. Sixty great gods are stationed with me to guard you. The god Sin [is at your right hand, the god Shamash] at your left. Sixty great gods are stationed round you, grit with the hurricane. Put not your trust in man; cast your eyes on me, gaze on me. I am Ishtar of Erbil. Ashur has granted you well-being. When you were small I carried you. Have no fear; revere me.[16]

After dominating Western Asia for three centuries, the Assyrian Empire succumbed to the Babylonians, who unified Mesopotamia, inaugurating the Neo-Babylonian Era (612–539 BC) – a century of unprecedented imperialism and barbarism headed by Nebuchadnezzar, whose armies conquered Palestine and Syria (Judah). Alongside this reign of terror, however, was the reaffirmation of Babylon as a leading commercial port and prominent intellectual, educational and cultural centre which attracted international scientists and scholars – most notably the Greek philosopher Herodotus and the Greek mathematician Pythagoras – and opened the door to the Greek acceptance of astrology.

Babylonian Astrology: The Venus Tablet of Amisaduqa

The oldest forms of divination, practised first by Sumerian and later by Babylonian priests and priestesses, ranged from observing sounds and movements of birds in flight to scrutinising human facial and bodily aberrations. The most 'reliable' and commonly practised method of prognostication, however, was *extispicy*,* an early horary technique which entailed posing a question to a particular deity at the moment an animal (usually a goat or sheep) was sacrificed and obtaining a 'heavenly answer' in the form of configurations, sizes, colours, spots and/or other abnormalities.[17]

The demand for a more sophisticated and reliable method of predicting mundane occurrences and growing patterns led the Babylonian Baru ('observer') priests to log meteorological phenomena (floods, windstorms, thunder, lightning) – believed to be divine manifestations – alongside their accompanying events onto thousands of cuneiform tablets. The desire to know beforehand when to expect these climactic conditions as well as astronomical phenomena (equinoxes, solstices, Moon phases) created the need for an accurate calendar which chronicled the harvest cycle as well as pagan and religious celebrations. The pursuit of accurate scientific data to support the formation of a calendar led the Baru priests, whose schooling incorporated astronomical and mathematical techniques formulated by the Sumerians, to devise the world's earliest recorded astrological system.

Continuing the Sumerian legacy, the Baru priests spent countless hours in their towering temple observatories (Ziggurats) studying the configurations and movements of the Sun, Moon and the five 'stars'* whom they worshipped as celestial deities. In the eyes of the clergy, the desert skies of Mesopotamia must have indeed resembled a great arena where, night after night, the skirmishes and romances of their stellar Gods and Goddesses were dramatised before their eyes. Just as the Sun, Moon and the Morning/Evening Star were personified by Shamash, Sin and Ishtar respectively, Jupiter, Saturn, Mercury and Mars were assigned complementary divine rulers.

*When this process specifically involved the liver, it was called *hepatoscopy*.
**The five stars refer to the five planets – Mercury, Venus, Mars, Jupiter and Saturn – which were visible to the naked eye. Uranus, Neptune and Pluto were not discovered until the eighteenth, nineteenth and twentieth centuries, respectively.

To Marduk, the foremost, was assigned Jupiter, whose golden light burns most steadily in the sky, Venus fell to Ishtar, Saturn to Ninib, Mercury to Nebo, Mars, by reason of its blood-red color, to Nergal, patron of war. As for the fixed stars, singly or grouped in constellations, they were correlated with the less important lords, heroes, or genii. This was no impediment to regarding Ishtar, for instance, always as the goddess of the fertility of the earth, and worshipping her as such.[18]

By studying and methodically logging celestial patterns onto cuneiform tablets, the priests quickly concluded that the luminaries were superior forecasting tools which could time natural phenomena and accompanying events. Unlimited access to libraries and advanced instruments enabled the priests to correlate growing patterns, meteorological occurrences and ensuing periods of war and peace with recurrent configurations: moon phases, planetary conjunctions, sunspots, eclipses, comets and, most important, the heliacal risings and settings of the planets.

ENUMA ANU ENLIL

While the Sumerians were quite knowledgeable about the correlation between celestial movements and mundane events, it was the Babylonians who, as far as we know, *recorded* the first standard astrological text that charted the positions of the luminaries accompanied by their coinciding events. Although these listings were independently recorded over several centuries, they were first catalogued in one volume entitled *Enuma Anu Enlil* during the Middle Babylonian Period (1000 BC) and, as a result, lined the walls of countless Mesopotamian temple and palace libraries.

The volume's popularity as a standard astrological reference peaked during the Assyrian Empire when it was utilised by military commanders, royal personages and scholars alike. With the constant threat of invasion, Assyrian kings rarely made a strategic decision without consulting either oracular priestesses or Baru priests who made their predictions based on examples recorded in the *Enuma Anu Enlil*. Astrologers were also consulted by merchants, sailors and farmers.

The most complete version (housed in the British Museum and dating between the ninth and seventh centuries BC), was reconstructed from thousands of cuneiform tablets and tablet fragments containing celestial omens excavated in 1852 by British archaeologist Sir Henry Layard from the site of the palace of the Assyrian King Ashurbanipal (668-663 BC) in Nineveh – the city enshrined to Ishtar. Named for the first three words of the series, the *Enuma Anu Enlil*, literally meaning 'When the Gods Anu and Enlil',* was comprised of 70 tablets listing the positions of the Sun, Moon, five planets and their accompanying mundane events. The collection was numbered according to the importance of the luminaries (Moon, Sun, Jupiter, Venus, Saturn, Mercury, Mars): Tablets 1-22 concerned the Moon; Tablets 23-41 related to the Sun; Tablets 41-50 recorded meteorological phenomena such as eclipses and sunspots; and Tablets 51-70 described the five planets and the fixed star constellations.[19] Although the Moon was the most valued heavenly body with its waxing phase promoting plant growth, the *earliest* inscribed tablet lists the brilliant Morning and Evening Star's periods of invisibility and visibility, which correlated to both the growing season and the human gestation cycle.

THE VENUS TABLET OF AMISADUQA

Because the individual tablets of the *Enuma Anu Enlil* were not categorised chronologically, the Venus Tablet of Amisaduqa, originally written in the Babylonian dialect during the reign of King Amisaduqa (1646-1626 BC), was numbered Tablet 63. Translated from the Assyrian by Dr David Pingree of Brown University and Dr Erica Reiner of the University of Chicago, the tablet lists a series of 59 Omens** attributing mundane events to the Morning and Evening Star's periods of visibility and

---

*Anu and Enlil were the Sumero-Babylonian deities of Heaven and Earth.

**In addition to futuristic omens, the inscriptions also logged events that had already taken place and upon which the prognostications were based.

invisibility spurred by its heliacal risings and settings – that is, the first rising after and last setting before a period of invisibility due to conjunction with the blinding Sun.

The Venus Tablet of Amisaduqa divides its 59 omens into four sections: Section I – Omens 1-21, Section II – Omens 22-33, Section III – Omens 34-37 and Section IV – Omens 38-59. The following examples are from Section I:

Omen 1

In month XI, 15th day, Venus in the west disappeared, three days in the sky it stayed away, and in month XI, 18th day, Venus in the east became visible: springs will open, Adad his rain, Ea his floods will bring, king to king messages of reconciliation will send.

Omen 2

In month VIII, 11th day, Venus in the east disappeared; two months n days in the sky it stayed away, and in month X, nth day, Venus in the west became visible: the harvest of the land will prosper.[20]

Each Omen in Sections I, III and IV cites the duration of the star's period of invisibility, that is, the elapsed time between its last appearance before conjunction with the Sun (heliacal setting) and its re-emergence in the sky of the opposite direction after conjunction with the Sun (heliacal rising). The Omens in Section II, on the other hand, cover the duration of the star's period of visibility in the sky of same direction – that is, the elapsed time between its heliacal rising and setting (see Figure 2.1, page 56). Completing the astrological equation is the simultaneous terrestrial occurrence and/or deities precipitating that phenomenon. These resulting events either related to the fertility of the earth (such as drought, floods, wind) or to the king's ability to wage war, as in the following examples:

- Harvest of land will prosper
- Harvest of irrigated land will prosper, land will be happy

- Scarcity of barley and straw
- Hard times will befall the land
- Land will assemble in fortresses
- Downfall of large army
- Hostilities
- Hostilities – harvest will prosper
- King will send messages of wrath
- Mourning
- Rains
- Rains from the sky
- Floods
- Harvest[21]

Some of the so-called Omens simply mention the precise month and day when the star disappeared from view. An example is Omen 10, which reads: 'Venus disappeared in east on 25th of month 12.'[22]

The Evening Star remained invisible for three days – when inferior conjunction with the Sun occurred during the winter – and for two weeks – when the conjunction took place in the summer – until its heliacal rising, or, emergence as the Morning Star in the East. On the other hand, the Morning Star disappeared from the eastern sky for two months due to the blinding superior conjunction with the Sun until its heliacal rising or, emergence as the Evening Star in the West (see Fig. 2.1, page 56). These two months whereby the Star disappeared from view correlated, in certain years, to the approximately two-month long intolerable Mesopotamian summer and destruction of the crop. Since Inanna/Ishtar personified the Morning/Evening Star, the legendary sojourn in the Underworld of first the Goddess and then her lover allegorized the star's respective three-day and two-month long disappearance into the depths of the sky. Like the return from the Underworld, the re-emergence of the Evening Star at the end of summer heralded auspicious climactic conditions when, according to Omen Two, above, 'the harvest of the land will prosper'.

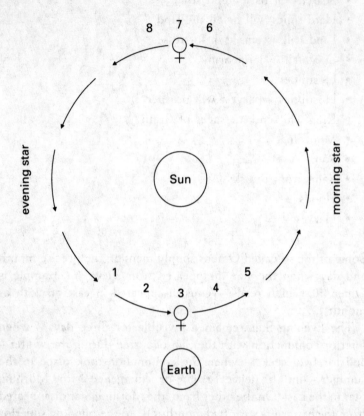

Fig. 2.1 The cycle of Venus as seen from the Earth.

The different positions of Venus as seen from the Earth are noted by the numbers in the above diagram:

1 Venus retrograde
2 Heliacal setting of Evening Star in the western sky
3 Inferior conjunction with the Sun
4 Heliacal rising of Morning Star in the eastern sky
5 Venus direct
6 Heliacal setting of Morning Star in the eastern sky
7 Superior conjunction with the Sun
8 Heliacal rising of Evening Star in the western sky

It is quite likely that the star's personification as Fertility Goddess in most cultures came about in response to the recognition of the Morning and Evening Star as an indicator of agricultural productivity. Additionally, its two periods of visibility as Morning and Evening Star, which each last approximately 263 days, roughly correlate with the length of human gestation.

Although it takes Venus approximately 225 days to orbit the Sun, it takes approximately 584 days (one synodic period), more than double that time, for the planet to return to superior conjunction with the Sun. After five synodic periods, or eight years (584 × 5 = 2920 days/8 years) have elapsed, Venus will be situated at approximately the same zodiacal degree as it was during the superior conjunction of eight years earlier. (This also applies to synodic returns of inferior conjunctions, see p.118.) Astronomically speaking, this means that every eight years the zodiacal positions for the Sun and Venus will be repeated, reiterating the horoscopic relationship between these two planets. (The eight-year Venus/Sun cycle is discussed in Chapter 10.)

Because the plotting of these five synodic returns through the zodiac resembled a large five-pointed star across the sky, the pentagram, the cuneiform symbol for the Morning and Evening Star became synonymous with Ishtar. By the same token, the rosette – the eight-pointed star which accompanied engravings of the fertility Goddess as early as the fourth millennium – was also inspired by these five synodic periods which equalled a duration of eight years.

Throughout the reign of King Nebuchadnezzar (604–561 BC), astrology and astronomy continued to flourish and, as a result of Babylon's growing reputation as an educational centre, the astronomer-priests devoted themselves to serious scientific research. Their innovative achievements included the invention of the first astrolabe (an instrument used to measure altitudes), the discovery of equinoctial and solstitial points, the perfection of lunar measurements and early usage of the constellations of the zodiac. Although astrology was primarily concerned with agricultural forecasting and formulating military strategies, the groundwork was laid for the construction and interpretation of the first horoscopes calculated for the precise moment of an individual's birth.

The first horoscopes were drawn up for royal personages, most notably the king, whose destiny represented that of the nation. Individual birth charts may have actually been recorded as early as the sixth century BC but, due to the delicacy of papyrus, which replaced cuneiform tablets, they were destroyed during the Persian and Greek invasions of Babylon. For this reason very few horoscopes exist that predate the first century AD.[23]

> The earliest horoscope we know of, written in Babylonia in cuneiform script, is presently exhibited at the Ashmolean Museum in Oxford and dates from about 410 BC. It lists only the position of the Sun, Moon and planets at the time of the child's birth, but other examples also give predictions of character and fortunes.[24]

During Persian rule (539–330 BC), a new breed of researchers emerged who were interested in mathematical astronomy and who were not necessarily members of the clergy. As a result, the planets' religious overtones became less significant and more emphasis was placed on credible scientific breakthroughs such as perfecting the measurements of the constellations and furthering the construction of individual horoscopes. Although the Indo-European Elamites (Persians) venerated Anahita as their Fertility Goddess and the embodiment of the Morning and Evening Star, their primary deity was her consort, Mithras, the warrior Sun-God, whose worship incorporated astrological symbolism. Also known as the bull slayer, Mithras, like Gilgamesh, may have represented the demise of the Age of Taurus (the era of fertility deities) and the arrival of the Age of Aries (the epoch of warrior deities).

Due to the lack of extant Babylonian horoscopes, it is difficult to ascertain the precise interpretation afforded to the planets in early individual horoscopes. It was during Greece's takeover of Persian-ruled Babylonia (Seleucid Era, 312–364 BC) that the planets were assigned many of the qualities by which they are known today. The Morning and Evening Star was viewed as the

Lesser Benefic (second only to Jupiter – the Greater Benefic), which bestowed good fortune when well placed in the chart. The following is a typical horoscope inscription from that period:

> 'The place of Venus means: Wherever he may go, it will be favourable; he will have sons and daughters' and 'If a child is born when Venus comes forth and Jupiter has set, his wife will be stronger than he.'[25]

Because the Greeks viewed the luminaries strictly from a scientific viewpoint, it was only after Babylonian cum Persian astrology was introduced into Greek culture that the planets adopted the qualities of the Gods and Goddesses on Mount Olympus – by which they are known today. Due to her resemblance to Inanna/Ishtar, Aphrodite, the Greek Goddess of Love and Beauty, was assigned the domain of the Morning and Evening Star.

3

MEDITERRANEAN GODDESSES AND ASTROLOGY

A Prayer to Aphrodite

On your dappled throne, Aphrodite,
sly eternal daughter of Zeus,
I beg you: do not crush me with grief,

but come to me – now as once
you heard my far cry, and yielded,
slipping from your father's house

to yoke the birds to your gold
chariot, and came. Handsome swallows
brought you swiftly to the dark earth,

their wings whipping the middle sky.
Happy, with deathless lips, you smiled:
'What is wrong, why have you called me?

What does your mad heart desire?
Whom shall I make love you, Sappho,
who is turning her back on you?

Let her run away, soon she'll chase you;
refuse your gifts, soon she'll give them.
She will love you, though unwillingly.'

Then come to me now and free me
from fearful agony. Labour
for my mad heart, and be my ally.

                                    Sappho
Translated by Willis Barnstone[1]

Semitic Fertility Goddesses

To trace the roots of Aphrodite, the Greek Goddess of Love and Beauty, it is appropriate to begin with Astarte, the Phoenician fertility Goddess – one of several Semitic Goddesses whose legends and symbols continued the legacy left by the Mesopotamian fertility deities and embodiments of the Morning and Evening Star – Inanna and Ishtar.

CANAAN

Canaan, the ancient name for the Levantine fertile plain extending from the Mediterranean Sea to the Syrian desert (modern-day Syria, Lebanon, Jordan and Israel), was inhabited by Semitic agriculturalists and herders from southern Arabia as early as the third millennium. Although these Nomadic tribes spoke diverse dialects, they were bonded by their worship of Baal, the Vegetable Lord, and his consort the Fertility Goddess, alternately called Anath, Asherah, Ashteroth, Attar and Atargatis. Most commonly, however, she was called Astarte.

Artefacts uncovered from the Levant's early Bronze period (3500–1500 BC) included miniature fertility deities with arms crossed over their breasts and cuneiform tablets (1500–1300 BC) discovered at the ancient site of Ugarit along the Northern Syrian coast. Like the bulk of agrarian lore, these Ugaritic* inscriptions unveiled legends which revolve around the perpetuation of the land by an array of deities: El,** the Thunder Lord/King of the Gods, Ashtoroth, a Fertility and Water Goddess, whose name literally means 'She that marches upon the sea',[2] and their children – Anath, the Warrior Goddess; Baal, the Vegetable God; and Mot, Lord of Death. Whereas El, Baal and Mot each have a counterpart in Mesopotamian folklore, Anath and Ashteroth are both aspects of Ishtar.

*Ugaritic, the language in which the Bible was written, was the Semitic language of the Canaanites and Hebrews.

**El was an early version of the Greek Zeus, who was also Thunder Lord/King of the Gods.

Canaan's most popular deity was Baal, the Vegetable God of Heaven and Earth, whose death (during the parched season) and reunion with his sister/lover, Anath (during the rainy, nurturing season) inspired ritualistic worship not unlike the ecstatic sexual rites commemorating Inanna/Ishtar and Dumuzi. Their story however, veers from Mesopotamian myth in that Baal is not banished to the Netherworld; instead, he is killed battling his nemesis – Mot, God of the Underworld. After burying her lover, a vengeful Anath kills Mot, thereby resurrecting Baal and heralding fertility among animals, plant life, human beings and the Gods.

Because Canaan was characterised by two or three moist years followed by two or three years of drought and locusts, the Goddess was not directly affiliated with the Morning and Evening Star, whose cycle did not coincide with the Middle Eastern seasons as it had with Mesopotamian cycles. Anath, portrayed as both a nature deity and a blood-thirsty Warrior Goddess, heralded the rain and the dew by devouring her enemies. Because 'ancient Near Easterners cut off heads and hands to boast of their victims slain in battle', Anath who 'slew men and exulted as their cut-off heads and hands flew through the air'[3] was honoured as a Victory and War Goddess.

PALESTINE

The Old Testament relates that Abraham, the Chaldean* biblical patriarch, migrated from the Sumerian city-state of Ur to Canaan (later renamed Palestine) where he founded the Hebrew religion. This new creed revolved around the worship of Yahweh, or Adonai (Hebrew for 'Lord'), the sole anthropomorphic God who, unlike the deities of other faiths, was devoid of human emotions and mortal vulnerabilities.

Although the Old Testament included many stories which were rooted in Near and Middle Eastern lore, the development of a monotheistic God may have been a backlash against Canaanite

---

*The Chaldeans were purported to have produced the first astronomer-priests; for this reason, some texts claim that Abraham himself practised the art of astrology.

monotheistic God may have been a backlash against Canaanite worship of fertility deities. Witnessing the ecstatic sexuality invoked by Sacred Marriage Rites, the Hebrews denounced the Goddess, whom they called Asherah, as an 'abomination' (1 Kgs 18.19) and forbade idolatry of all nature deities and the patronage of temple priestesses.

Because the Canaanites had long indulged in Goddess worship, it was virtually impossible for the agricultural Hebrews to prevent the adoration of fertility deities among farmers, women longing for a child, or lustful men who continued to patronise temple priestesses. Although the Old Testament rejects glorification of the Goddess, it lauds valiant heroines Ruth, Esther, Deborah and Judith who fought for the preservation of their homeland – a primary theme of Hebrew life.

The Old Testament tale about the expulsion of Adam and Eve from the Garden of Eden allegorises the repudiation of nature deities and supremacy of patriarchal law. Provoked by a desire to attain divine knowledge, Eve follows the wily serpent's advice by eating from the tree of knowledge and offering its fruit to Adam. This act resulted in her exile from Paradise and the eternal suffering of humanity which included woman's distress during childbirth.

This allegory reverses the symbolism contained in the Sumerian legend of Inanna, whose regenerative powers are received from the huluppu (date palm) tree. While Inanna's sexuality promised fecundity of the earth, Eve's 'fruitful' offer resulted in expulsion from Eden and the stripping of her powers. Whereas earlier societies embraced women's sexual, fertile powers, the Hebrews feared feminine strength and, as a result, forbade the worship of Asherah, the Fertility Goddess whose name literally means 'date palm tree'. (Hebrew patriarchal attitudes were also conveyed by the portrayal of Lilith, omitted from Genesis but known throughout Babylonian and Hebrew lore as Adam's first wife, who was banished from Eden for refusing to make love in the missionary position.)*

---

*As a dark Goddess, Lilith's name stems from the same root as 'laila' – Hebrew for 'night'. Derived from the Babylonian-Assyrian word 'Lilitu', meaning female demon or wind spirit, Lilith is described in Sumerian lore as the villainous Bird-Goddess killed by Gilgamesh, and in Isaiah (34.13) as 'dwelling among the desolate ruins'.

PHOENICIA

Contemporaneous with the Hebrew occupation of Palestine, Phoenicia, noted for its purple dye and fine metalwork, emerged as the most powerful maritime empire of its era (1300 BC). Excavations scattered throughout Lebanon and Syria have revealed countless Phoenician shrines and artefacts attesting to the widespread worship of the Fertility Goddess Astarte and her consort, Baal, whose rituals and legends were practically indistinguishable from those associated with Canaanite nature deities. Engravings which depicted Astarte either in mermaid form or surrounded by doves displayed motifs that most likely were passed down by the Neolithic settlers from Old Europe and Anatolia who worshipped Bird and Fish Goddesses.

By far the Levant's most prevalent icons were oval-shaped plaques, appropriately named 'Astarte Plaques', which bore sculpted impressions of the Goddess, often in the form of grasping serpents – a symbol of wisdom and affirmation of life.[4] Often depicted as a triangular vulva, Astarte's figure was also 'engraved on small gold pendants probably worn as protective amulets' as well as on 'mass-produced moulds used as household objects'.[5]

As Baal's adoring cults dominated the Middle East, Astarte's function as fertility deity was enacted through her influential priestesses who, in addition to granting sexual favours, practised the art of soothsaying. At ancient Phoenician sites, temples hosted rituals (akin to Mesopotamian Sacred Marriage Rites) wherein eunuchs and priestesses enacted the love affair between Astarte and Baal. Initiatory fertility rituals were also perpetuated at the lavish temple at Heliopolis (Syria) in which virginal maidens were compelled to make love with a stranger in preparation for marriage and motherhood. While men expressed their loyalty and humility by presenting Astarte with their shaven facial hair, women offered locks of their tresses – symbolic of the loss of virginity.[6] In return, a male was rewarded with sexual favours and promises of fertility for his land and family, while a female was assured she would conceive a child.

One of Astarte's most magnificent shrines was located at

Byblos* near Mt Carmel on the Syrian Coast, where the Goddess 'descended' as the fiery Morning and Evening Star alighting in the lake at Aphaca.[7] This shrine even attracted Egyptian merchants who, when visiting Byblos, identified Astarte with their own fertility deity, Hathor, the Cow Goddess. Throughout Phoenicia, celebratory rites honouring Astarte and Baal (Adonis) were held whenever the Goddess appeared as the Morning Star at sunrise in the eastern sky.

> At Aphaca in Syria, where there was a famous temple of Astarte, the signal for the celebration of the rites was apparently given by the flashing of a meteor, which on a certain day fell like a star from the top of Mount Lebanon into the River Adonis. The meteor was thought to be Astarte herself, and its flight through the air might naturally be interpreted as the descent of the amorous goddess to the arms of her lover . . . The appearance of the morning star on the day of the festival may in like manner have been hailed as the coming of the goddess of love to wake her dead leman from his earthy bed.[8]

As the era's most powerful maritime empire, Phoenicia traded with Greece, Crete, Egypt and Babylonia and, by overthrowing Mycenaean strongholds, established strategic trading posts throughout the Mediterranean. From the Levant to North Africa, Astarte was revered as Mistress of Heaven and the Sea by Phoenician sailors who, in their quest for wealth and power, sought her blessing by patronising her temples. At the harbour sites of Kition and Paphos (Cyprus), Mt Eryx (Sicily), Carthage (North Africa), and Sparta, Cythera and Corinth (Greek city-states), Astarte's shrines became sanctified brothels where in-house priestesses fulfilled the needs of sailors, making these shrines tantamount to present-day 'red-light districts'. Although 'sacred harlotry' became their primary function, temples still held initiatory rituals deflowering young virgins and annual rites mourning Astarte and Baal (later worshipped as Aphrodite and Adonis). But the most extensive worship of Astarte outside the

---

*At Byblos, Astarte was also worshipped as Baalat – the feminine derivative of Baal.

Levant took place on the Mediterranean island of Cyprus, whose principal harbour, Paphos, became known as the birthplace of Aphrodite, the Greek Goddess of Love and Beauty.

CYPRUS

Strategically located in the Mediterranean Sea off the coast of Turkey, the independent island of Cyprus (derived from 'kypros', the Greek word for copper) was highly desirable due to its abundance of corn, wine, oil and copper mines. Her natural resources and overwhelming wealth not only contributed to the island's successful entry into the mercantile arena but targeted Cyprus as a haven for foreigners and the object of conquest. Since fertility deities had been idealised on this densely forested island as far back as the Neolithic Era, the Mycenaeans, who settled the island during the Greek Dark Ages, easily incorporated Cypriot images into their own worship of a Minoan-Mycenaean Mother Goddess – early manifestations of Astarte and Aphrodite (see Chapter 1).

Visible from the Syrian Coast, Cyprus was occupied by Phoenician settlers (850-750 BC) who consecrated magnificent sanctuaries and shrines to Astarte throughout the island. Temple priestesses continued to provide sexual favours to honour the love between Astarte and Baal, the Vegetable God, who was also venerated as Adonis, a derivative of Adonai, the Semitic word for 'young lord' and Hebrew name for God. Claiming to be earthly manifestations of Adonis, each Phoenician king who ruled Cyprus appointed himself and his progeny as priests in the service of the Goddess. The sanctuary at Paphos was immortalised by Herodotus, the Greek historian, for its initiation rites (originally held throughout Babylonia and Phoenicia) whereby a young maiden copulated with a stranger and then donated the offerings he had given her to the temple.[9] In fact, mothers often brought their virginal daughters to participate in these initiatory rituals as a preparation for the responsibilities of monogamous marriage and motherhood.

The Mycenaeans, who remained on Cyprus throughout the

Phoenician occupation (850-750 BC), incorporated Astarte's legends, symbols and rituals into the worship of their own Fertility Goddess called Aphrodite (from the Greek root 'Aphros', meaning foam). Just as Astarte was frequently depicted in mermaid form, Aphrodite, dubbed 'protectress of sea animals', was often sculpted throughout Cyprus (and later Greece) atop dolphins* or accompanied by doves, geese and fish – reminiscent of the Neolithic Bird and Fish Goddesses. Scenes of priestesses anointing the Goddess with oils, adorning her with flowers and bearing gifts were depicted on Cypriot vases (725-450 BC) and reflected actual priestesses who, in fact, spent hours primping for the rituals which characterised Aphrodite's worship. It was from this point on that the Goddess, often sculpted gazing into a mirror, became associated with vanity, beauty and indulgence to a far greater extent than had the fertility divinities who preceded her.

After Phoenicia's maritime empire crumbled, Cyprus retained its Greek influence even though she eventually fell to Assyria (750 BC), Egypt (614 BC), Persia (540 BC), Greece (325 BC) and Rome (53 BC). As ruler of the Earth, the Waters and the Heavens, Aphrodite was, like Astarte, patroness of sailors, sanctioning fruitful journeys and protective harbours. Rededicated to Aphrodite, the magnificent sanctuary at Paphos continued to hold preparatory marriage and fertility rituals for young maidens consisting of purifying baths in the sea and guidance from temple priestesses. Men desiring fertility for their land, animals and wives utilised the services of the temple's sacred 'prostitutes', while women wishing to conceive paid homage to Aphrodite with offerings of pomegranates (whose innumerable seeds symbolised fruitfulness), flowers (especially red roses)** and a variety of plants which became associated with the Goddess. One of the most noteworthy icons of this temple was a black meteorite engraved with Aphrodite's image in the form of a 'white cone or pyramid'.

The Romans, who later conquered the region, eventually

---

*Dolphins were often sighted in the Mediterranean Sea where the Goddess was said to have emerged.

**The red rose's affiliation with love and courtship stemmed from its function as a votive offering to both Astarte and, later, to Aphrodite.

converted the temple at Paleopaphos (its Latin name) into a shrine dedicated to Venus (the Roman Aphrodite), whose image continued to be engraved on coins and conical stones. The site of the sanctuary, which Herodotus called the most magnificent shrine of the ancient world, is marked by the 'Rock of Aphrodite' – three large rocks protruding from a small bay in the Mediterranean – the precise location where Aphrodite was said to have emerged from the foam of the sea.

A well-known Greek legend, considered by many mythographers to be an allegory of Astarte's transformation into Aphrodite, concerns Europa's importation to Crete, the slaying of the Minotaur and Ariadne's subsequent journey east. The story unfolds with Zeus' arrival in Tyre, Phoenicia's capital, where he falls in love with Europa, daughter of the king. Disguised as a tame, gentle bull, Zeus completely charms Europa, who playfully mounts him moments before he abducts her to Crete – the place of his birth.[10] Upon their arrival in Crete, Zeus, no longer the mild-mannered bull, rapes Europa. They ultimately marry and she bears him three sons, one of whom is Minos, the future king of Crete. Scenes depicting Europa adorning the bull's horns with flowers – thus associating her with nature – are etched on innumerable Greek vases of the sixth century BC. These renderings are clearly symbolic of the two sides of Zeus in the same way that Baal, the Canaanite Vegetable Lord, was a thunderbolt and fertility God.

Astrologically speaking, the two aspects of Zeus depict the positive and negative attributes of the zodiacal sign of Taurus the Bull and its ruling planet, Venus. Initially, the Bull, radiating an almost magical aura, is charming, gentle, sensual and generous – positive Taurean qualities that link him to earlier vegetable deities. His ugly 'thunderbolt' side exhibits the more problematic Taurean qualities of aggression, violence, uncontrolled sexuality and possessiveness.

The tale then focuses on the Cretan King Minos (son of Zeus and Europa), his wife, Queen Pasiphae, and their beautiful daughter, the princess Ariadne. Like Europa, Queen Pasiphae becomes enamoured of a beautiful white bull; the consummation of their union produces the Minotaur, a monstrous hybrid with a human body but the head of a bull. Because he is so repulsive, King Minos conceals the Minotaur in a labyrinth* from which escape is impossible. To quell the beast's insatiable appetite and assert Crete's supremacy over its rival, Athens, the King demands that seven Athenian children be sacrificed to the Minotaur each year. To end these ritualistic murders, Theseus, Prince of Athens, journeys to Crete. There he falls in love with Ariadne, half-sister of the Minotaur, and promises to marry her once he slays the beast. To direct him through the labyrinth, Ariadne provides a magical ball of thread enabling Theseus to weave through the dark maze, kill the Minotaur and emerge victorious.

In one version of the myth, Ariadne and Theseus marry and set sail for Athens. Detoured to Cyprus by a storm, a pregnant Ariadne goes ashore at Amathus but dies in childbirth and is buried in a grove hear Amathus (a festival commemorating her as Aphrodite-Ariadne is held to this day at her sanctuary on Cyprus).[11] In another version, Theseus leaves Ariadne on the island of Naxos and flees to Athens. When Dionysus arrives, Ariadne marries him and they happily reside on Naxos.

Many mythographers agree that because the legend's locales are Phoenicia, Crete and Cyprus, the myth clearly illustrates the diverse roots of Greece's culture and religion as well as the intermingling of the fertility Goddess myths of Phoenicia, Crete and Greece. Just as the Semitic princess, Europa, was transported to Crete and her granddaughter Ariadne journeyed to Cyprus (where, as mentioned, she was known as Aphrodite-Ariadne), the worship of Astarte was brought over from Phoenicia to Cyprus and, ultimately, Greece (Naxos), where she was venerated as Aphrodite. The motifs of rape (Europa) and abandonment (Ariadne) are repeated throughout patriarchal Greek mythology which, like Hebrew legends, was concerned with mortal women as well as divinities. Whereas the Old Testament lauded their mortal heroines, Greek women were, for the most part, victimised.

The tale of Theseus, the mortal warrior hero, represents

*The labyrinth was modelled after the labyrinthine structure of the palace at Knossos.

another important patriarchal motif – man's need to triumph over nature symbolised by the Minotaur caught in the labyrinth. Whereas matrifocal, agrarian societies identified with their natural environment by worshipping fertility deities, the Greeks, like the Hebrews, emphasised the superiority of the intellect over the natural world. For this reason astrology, which propounded the natural world's influence over human events, was not at first embraced by Hebrews nor by Greek mathematicians and astronomers.

Aphrodite – Greek Goddess of Love and Beauty

Although Aphrodite continued to be revered throughout the Mediterranean as a fertility deity, it was the literary descriptions of early Greek writers such as Hesiod and Homer which ultimately transformed her into a Goddess of Love and Beauty.

As urbanisation accelerated at an alarming rate, Greece, whose agrarian economy hinged upon selling surplus food, colonised Phoenician strongholds to sustain its growing population. Although the Phoenicians retained Carthage and parts of Sicily, the intermingling of Greek and Phoenician languages, customs and religions nevertheless resulted in the rededication of Astarte shrines at Sicily, Cythera and Corinth to Aphrodite – the Greek name for the Phoenician Goddess. Because the temple at Corinth was especially renowned for its priestesses who conducted initiation rites and provided sexual services for incoming sailors, Aphrodite's reputation as patroness of prostitution slowly but surely overshadowed her former role as fertility deity. In Athens, especially, where slaves and immigrants made their living as prostitutes and courtesans, Aphrodite was idealised in the guises of Aphrodite-Porne and Aphrodite-Hetaira (Greek for 'courtesan').*

Due to an extensive affiliation with the Phoenicians, the Greeks, whose only written records had heretofore been the primitive Mycenaean script known as Linear A and B tablets,

---

*By this time Solon, the Athenian administrator, had demarcated housewives as 'good' women and prostitutes and slaves as 'bad' women.

'adapted the Phoenician alphabet [inherited from the Sumerians] to the requirements of the Greek language'.[12] The new alphabet provided a wider forum for Greek bards and storytellers who, prior to this time, were limited to captivating live audiences with their songs and tales. Recording countless oral stories handed down through generations led to the widespread dissemination and popularisation of legends surrounding the Gods and Goddesses who resided on Mt Olympus (located in western Greece). These divinities were honoured throughout Greece with temples, shrines, rituals, seasonal festivities, athletic contests and observances dedicated to the protective deity of each city.

Unfortunately, most of our information about the religious and social climate of Greece stems not from historical records but from the literary descriptions set down by the poets Hesiod (b. 700 BC) and Homer (b. 750 BC), both of who endowed the deities with the anthropomorphisms (later expounded by Greek playwrights, philosophers and historians) by which they are still known.

HESIOD

Hesiod's major works, *Theogony* and *Works and Days*, chronicle the creation of the world and subsequent assemblage of the 12 Gods and Goddesses on Mt Olympus, commanded by Zeus, an Indo-European thunder and wind deity. Because Aphrodite was incorporated into Greek religion by Mycenaeans returning from Cyprus and Asia Minor, Hesiod's account of her birth in *Theogony* metaphorically conveys her transformation from an Eastern fertility deity into a Goddess of Love and Beauty.

Theogony opens as the world emerges from chaos,* followed by the birth of the 12 Titans – 'ancient, primeval, nature powers'[13] – whose parents were Ouranos, the Sky, and Gaia, the Earth. Unprepared for the responsibilities of fatherhood, Ouranos inflicts great pain upon Gaia by hiding their offspring inside her body. Imploring her children for help, it is only Chronos, the

---

*One reason ancient people created elaborate mythologies was, in fact, to make order out of apparent chaos.

youngest, who angrily responds by castrating Ouranos and tossing his genitals into the Mediterranean Sea. All at once, the dismembered organs become enveloped by a mist of 'white foam' from which a beautiful young maiden miraculously emerges. Transported on a scallop shell to the western Greek island of Cythera, where she is called Cytherea, the damsel then journeys to the island of Cyprus (where she was first worshipped) and is named Aphrodite, a name which means literally 'she who comes from foam'. Alighting at the Cypriot harbour of Paphos, where grass springs up under her feet, Aphrodite, whom Hesiod calls 'the foreigner', is affirmed as a Fertility Goddess who revitalises the earth.

Eros (love) and Himeros (longing) – who along with Pathos (regret) make up the three Graces – pamper and groom Aphrodite before escorting her to Mt Olympus to be welcomed into the assembly of deities. By electing the Graces to chaperon Aphrodite to the sacred peak on the Greek mainland, Hesiod emphasises Aphrodite's foreign origins and cites her as the last to join the pantheon of Gods and Goddesses whose roots lay primarily in Indo-European lore.

The violent act of castration has always been associated with ancient fertility rites whereby eunuchs, as a token of eternal devotion, traditionally cut off their sexual organs and presented them to the Goddess. These votive gifts provided the Goddess with life-giving energy and the ability to regenerate the earth. In fact, Chronos' act of throwing his father's castrated organs into the Mediterranean Sea can be viewed as the ultimate devotional gesture and Aphrodite's birth as the supreme act of procreation. This tale also conveys the hope that from violence springs eternal love perpetuated by new life.

Because the foam is symbolic of both the sea and the life-giving sperm from Ouranos' dismembered genitals,* reaffirming both her reproductive and sexual roles, Aphrodite, known as Aphrodite-Ourania ('Queen of Heaven) at Cyprus, Cythera, Corinth and Athens, became the symbolic daughter of the Sky God. By

---

*In Hindu mythology (whose Indo-European roots are similar to those of the Greeks) *Sukra*, Sanskrit for the planet Venus and for the word 'semen', is said to have emerged from the genitals of Shiva, God of Creation and Destruction.

depicting her birth as emanating from both the sky and the sea, Hesiod presents the Greek version of the fertility Goddess who, as Inanna, was Queen of Heaven and Earth and, as Astarte, was Mistress of the Waters.

Another interpretation of this myth lies in regarding Aphrodite as the feminine counterpart of Ouranos and her emergence as the transformation from the lustful, belligerent male into the peace-loving, fertile female. Like Ishtar, Aphrodite was also revered in certain regions as a bearded, androgynous Goddess whose male characteristics stemmed from Ouranos, the Sky God.* Hesiod also reveres Aphrodite-Ourania as the Muse of Astronomy, one of Zeus' nine daughters, or muses who inspired and healed, each from her particular sphere of influence.**

In *Works and Days*, Hesiod describes the assignations of the deities by Zeus, King of the Olympians:

- Hades – Lord of the Underworld
- Poseidon – Lord of the Sea
- Hephaistos – Lord of Metallurgy
- Apollo – Lord of the Sun
- Dionysus – Lord of Wine and Intoxication (?)
- Hera – Goddess of Marriage and Birth
- Demeter – Goddess of Agriculture
- Hestia – Goddess of the Hearth
- Athena – Goddess of Wisdom and War
- Artemis – Goddess of the Hunt
- Aphrodite – Goddess of Love and Beauty

Because these Gods and Goddesses represented archetypes of human nature, their exaggerated behaviour expounded virtuous qualities and exposed human foibles. At the same time, the Olympians personified the disparate roles of the sexes within the framework of a hierarchical Greek society whose attitudes were

---

*Astrologically speaking, this myth reflects the 1993 Uranus/Neptune conjunction which marks the emergence of an era in which women are recognised, once again, for their magnanimity and strength.

**During the Renaissance, Aphrodite-Ourania was frequently depicted in paintings and sculpture as the Muse of Astronomy.

unfavourable to women. Thus the Goddesses were almost always depicted as either subordinate to the Gods or jealous of one another. (Hesiod's unsympathetic attitude towards women was also characterised by his portrayal of Pandora who, like Eve, was held responsible for unleashing evil, suffering and pain upon the world.

Whereas Near and Middle Eastern Fertility Goddesses maintained patronage over multiple aspects of life – such as fecundity, love, marriage, war – each Greek Goddess (and God) was assigned one particular domain and, as a result, became less authoritative and influential. While the fertility Goddesses had heretofore provided fruitfulness *and* sexual services, Demeter was now assigned rulership over agriculture, while Aphrodite was instructed by Zeus 'to shower charm, painful yearning and consuming obsession'.[14]

HOMER

It was Homer, the renowned blind bard, who immortalised the Goddess of Love and Beauty in 'Hymn to Aphrodite', one of the *Homeric Hymns* (a collection of individual odes addressing each deity), and in two narratives first sung to the accompaniment of a lyre: the *Iliad*, an epic about the Trojan War, and the *Odyssey*, the post-war saga of Odysseus' heroism and ultimate return to his wife, Penelope.

In 'Hymn to Aphrodite', Homer renders a different version of Aphrodite as the daughter of Zeus, the Thunder God, and Dione, a water nymph – symbolic of the union of air (Zeus) and water (Dione).

As retribution for the spells she has cast upon her 'fellow' deities, forcing them to bed mortals and bear their children, Zeus curses Aphrodite by compelling her to sleep with an ordinary man. Disguised as a young maiden, Aphrodite travels to Mt Ida in Asia Minor (near Troy) where she seduces the strikingly handsome shepherd Anchises, who does not realise that he has made love with a Goddess until he awakens and recognises her golden aura. Admitting her identity, Aphrodite prophecies that her shepherd-lover will raise their son Aeneas in Asia Minor – far removed from Mt Olympus, where the child risks being kidnapped by nymphs and raised as one of their own. She warns that, should Anchises ever reveal that Aphrodite was the mother of a mortal child, Zeus would surely smite the shepherd with his thunderbolt.*

The unabashed passion displayed by Aphrodite in Homer's 'Hymn to Aphrodite' went far towards transforming her into a carnal deity seen to evoke lust in men and women, both mortal and divine. Furthermore, Homer's references to Aphrodite as 'golden' identified her with the Sun and not with the Morning and Evening Star. In fact, it was not until the sixth century BC that Aphrodite became associated with the Morning and Evening Star as Inanna, Ishtar and Astarte had been.

The Iliad

In a well-known Greek legend, Aphrodite's insatiable need for flattery and recognition leads her unwittingly to spark the Trojan War – an *actual* conflict which pitted a united Athens and Sparta against Troy, a city-state in Asia Minor (1183 BC).

According to Greek lore, Athena, Hera and Aphrodite, Olympian rivals, participate in a beauty contest to be judged by Paris, the son of Troy's King Priam. To win the contest and be awarded the coveted golden apple (the biblical symbol of temptation) each Goddess promises Paris something within her command. Hera guarantees he will possess all the power in the world, Athena vows to give him extraordinary fame and Aphrodite pledges she will secure for him the most desirable and captivating woman in the world – Queen Helen, wife of Sparta's King Menelaus. The Goddess of Love wins and, in return, leads Paris to Sparta where he seduces Queen Helen and carries her back to Troy. (This particular legend, referred to as the 'Judgment of Paris', influenced countless Renaissance paintings of the same name.)

*In the later Roman epic, *The Aeneid*, Virgil recounts how Anchises, after bragging about his exploits, is indeed struck dead by Zeus' thunderbolt as Aphrodite (now called Venus) has promised.

Although the 'Judgment of Paris' is never mentioned in the *Iliad*, it forms the prelude to the events in Homer's epic. King Menelaus of Sparta, with the help of his brother, Athenian King Agamemnon, leads their combined forces into Troy. After 19 years of continuous warfare, the Greeks eventually reclaim Helen. (Through his delineation of Helen, Homer draws attention to the correlation between Helen, the world's most seductive woman and Aphrodite, the spirit world's most beguiling Goddess.)

Aphrodite's role in the *Iliad* extends to the battlefield where her son Aeneas is fighting on the side of his homeland Troy – where he was raised by his father Anchises.

> The noble Aeneas . . . supported himself with one great hand on the ground; but the world went black as night before his eyes. Indeed the prince would have perished there and then, but for the quickness of his mother, Zeus' daughter Aphrodite . . . Seeing what had happened, she threw her white arms round her beloved son, and drew a fold of her shimmering robe across him, to protect him from flying weapons and a fatal spear cast in the breast.[15]

Although venerated as a Warrior Goddess in militaristic Corinth and Sparta, Aphrodite does not possess the deftness of martial deities such as Athena and Artemis. Accused of sympathising with the Trojans, she is an easy target for a Greek charioteer whose 'sharp spear cut her gentle hand at the base of the palm'.[16] Extending comfort, her father Zeus sums up Aphrodite's duties very succinctly: 'Fighting, my child, is not for you. You are in charge of wedlock and the tender passions.'[17] Because she willingly protects Aeneas by shielding his body with her own, Homer also acknowledges Aphrodite's maternal instincts – recognition reserved for Demeter, Goddess of Grain.

As Aphrodite's legends became more enmeshed in Greek literature, she was granted an Olympian mate. Due to her association with Cyprus and copper mining, Aphrodite was linked with Hephaistos (the Roman Vulcan), the crippled but skilled God of Metallurgy – emblematic of the Iron Age. Sanctioned by Zeus, the union symbolically assured her acceptance into the Greek pantheon.

The Odyssey

In the *Odyssey*, Aphrodite is represented as a narcissistic deity whose carnal indulgence wreaks havoc and tragedy. Though married to Hephaistos (the Roman Vulcan, God of Metallurgy), she is passionately in love with Ares, God of War. Meeting in secret at Ares' palace in Thrace, the lovers are spotted by the Sun God Helios, who informs Hephaistos about his wife's deception. Convincing Aphrodite that he will be spending time on his island Lemnos, Hephaistos uses his skill as a master builder to erect an inescapable trap above their bed.

> He set up the great anvil and wrought chains that could be neither torn asunder nor unfastened, but were invisible, delicate as cobwebs. He hung them over the bedposts and departed, or so he pretended.[18]

As Hephaistos predicted, the moment they feel safe, Ares and Aphrodite make passionate love, only to awaken the following morning entrapped by the chains which have closed in on them.* Hephaistos then summons Zeus, Poseidon, Hermes and Dionysus to behold the naked lovers and implores each to help him seek revenge. His scheme backfires, however, and Zeus, embarrassed that the affair has become common knowledge, tells Hephaistos that instead of eliciting sympathy he has made an utter fool of himself. As they view Aphrodite's nude body, Poseidon, Hermes and Dionysus fall in love with the beautiful Goddess and, instead of avenging Aphrodite's unfaithfulness, each God contrives to seduce her.

Aphrodite bears children to Poseidon, Hermes and Dionysus. Poseidon sires their sons, Rhodus and Herophilus; Hermes is the father of Eros (the Roman Cupid) and Hermaphrodite, who is half-male and half-female; Dionysus fathers Priapus, known for his ugliness and enormous genitals (inflicted by the Goddess Hera, who is jealous of Aphrodite and intolerant of promiscuity). Ares

---

*It was Hephaistos who engineered the chains that eternally bound Prometheus to the chair in which he was attacked by eagles (as punishment for attempting to steal fire from the Gods).

returns to his palace on Thrace while Aphrodite then retreats to her temple at Paphos where she is anointed and pampered by the Graces as she had been at birth.

In addition to portraying Aphrodite as a *femme fatale*, these legends also convey her loneliness and isolation; she is often depicted as an outsider, feared and disliked or simply shunned by the other Goddesses.

APHRODITE AND ADONIS

Despite the fact that these literary portrayals cast aspersions on Aphrodite's character, she was none the less venerated throughout Greece as both a Fertility Goddess and a martial deity protecting the districts which bore her patronage. Although certain temples erected to Aphrodite continued to hold fertility rituals, the only Greek *legend* (never appearing in the works of Homer or Hesiod) which linked her to those rites centred around her love affair with Adonis – glorified as a Vegetable God throughout the Mediterranean.

The story of Aphrodite and Adonis begins when Myrrha, the Cypriot king's daughter, invokes Aphrodite's wrath by claiming to have lovelier hair. To retaliate, the Goddess casts a spell under which Myrrha seduces her own father. Discovering that he has slept with his disguised daughter, the king is so appalled and outraged that, in a frenzied moment, he murders her. Shocked that her playful curse has resulted in Myrrha's death, Aphrodite transforms the corpse into a myrrh tree – the fruit of which yields gum resin.* Resurrected in her new form, Myrrha gives birth to the beautiful baby Adonis, her son/brother, whose emergence from the bark of the tree, an archetypal symbol of regeneration, affirms his role as a vegetation deity.

Rumours of Adonis' physical perfection quickly spread throughout Greece and, to ease the burden of her misdeeds, Aphrodite adopts the magnificent baby. Obsessed by his exquisite

---

*To commemorate the great love Aphrodite has for Adonis, Greek brides customarily wear crowns made from the leaves of the myrrh tree, which grows throughout Cyprus, Syria and Asia Minor.

beauty (even today, a strikingly handsome man is referred to as 'an Adonis'), the Goddess falls insanely in love with the boy and conceals him in a box entrusted to her half-sister, Persephone, for safekeeping in the Underworld. Unable to control her curiosity, Persephone opens the box, becomes completely enamoured of Adonis and refuses to part with the boy. Grief-stricken, Aphrodite beseeches Zeus to decide Adonis' fate. Unwilling to take sides with either daughter, Zeus compromises, decreeing that Adonis must spend four months with Aphrodite, four months with Persephone and four months by himself.

During the four-month period when Adonis is alone, Aphrodite, encircled by a magic girdle with the power to bewitch, completely ignores the conditions set by Zeus and seduces the boy – with tragic results. After an envious, obsessed Persephone informs Ares about Aphrodite's love for Adonis, the God of War, consumed with jealous rage, disguises himself as a wild boar and kills the boy. Once again Aphrodite pleads with Zeus to allow Adonis to stay half the year with her and the other half in the Underworld with Persephone – and he agrees.

In another version of the story, Adonis is not resurrected and Aphrodite, stripped of her magic girdle, is banished to an island where she spends the remainder of her life peacefully sewing and weaving. In yet another account, the Goddess' fate was to be worshipped as Aphrodite Genetyllis, Patron Goddess of Childbirth, as a reminder of the pain caused by love.

Just as Near Eastern Sacred Marriage Rites once commemorated the lovers' reunion, the *Adonia*, sorrowful rituals bemoaning separation and unrequited love, were held annually throughout Asia Minor, the Levant and, from the fifth century onwards, at various Greek locales. Celebrated in early spring, these yearly festivals honoured the death and rebirth of the Vegetable God, which coincided with the emergence of the fruitful, growing season. Athenians in particular paid homage to the deceased Vegetable God by planting 'Gardens of Adonis' consisting of lettuce, dill, fennel and other plants. When the plants died, the gardens were discarded into springs and streams.[19] And at Aphrodite's shrine in Corinth, infamous for its temple prostitutes, initiation rites were held where 'women took strangers as lovers only on the feast day of Adonis'.[20]

Although the legendary infusion of Adonis' blood into rivers, streams and flowers symbolised the regeneration of nature, the story may be viewed as both a fertility myth *and* a morality tale which focuses on the tragic outcome of obsessive love and uncontrollable passion. Due to the transformation from a matrifocal to patriarchal culture, unabashed love and sexuality – which once empowered the fertility Goddess – now was seen as the cause of Aphrodite's downfall. While Inanna banned Dumuzi to save herself from death as well as to teach him humility, she also appointed him reigning king and provided him with power, loyalty, sex and love. In the cases of Ishtar and Aphrodite, however, their lovers are killed due to their uncontrollable lust and greed. It is only due to the compassion of Zeus, not the power of the Goddess herself, that Adonis is revived for part of the year.

Because fertility was no longer Aphrodite's primary province, she was transformed by poets and philosophers into the Goddess of Love and Beauty, while the ability to regenerate the earth was appointed to Demeter, Goddess of Agriculture. Although the legend of her love for Adonis still linked Aphrodite to the Eastern Fertility Goddess, Demeter's search for her daughter became the primary myth explaining the distinction between the rainy, growing season and the dry, dormant season. While the Near and Middle Eastern mourning myths associated sexual love with sensual pleasure and the earth's fruitfulness, Demeter's *maternal* love brought forth the corn and revived her daughter. Aphrodite's obsession with Adonis, on the other hand, represented tainted, tragic love – it was the legend of Demeter and her daughter Persephone that came to symbolise the earth's regeneration and the perpetuation of Grecian life.

SAPPHO

Despite Aphrodite's demeaning portrayal throughout Greek mythology, the Goddess continued to embody creativity and feminine strength on the eastern Greek island of Lesbos where women, like their Spartan counterparts, were sexually emancipated, highly respected, vain and enormously proud. Venerated on Lesbos for her passion, tenacity and magnanimity, Aphrodite, whose temple remains are still visible at the site of Mesa, inspired many of the extraordinary love poems written by Sappho, the great lyric poetess who lived on the island *ca.* 612 BC. Although the bulk of Sappho's magnificent verse was destroyed when libraries were burned by invading Romans, extant versions have been reconstructed from quotes by Greek and Latin authors or from remaining fragments.[21]

Many of Sappho's passionate odes allude to women's love for men as well as for one another. Frequently dedicated to Aphrodite, they were used to invoke fertility, love and creative inspiration. In the heartfelt lament, 'A Prayer to Aphrodite' (see page 60) – one of the few original poems found in its entirety – Sappho humbly implores the Goddess for divine guidance so that the poet may recognise and, ultimately, embrace true love.

Due to the proximity of Lesbos to Cyprus and Asia Minor where Adonis was originally esteemed, Aphrodite's love for the Vegetable Lord was also the subject of a number of Sappho's poems. Rather than admonish Aphrodite for Adonis' death, Sappho's lyrical verses praise Aphrodite's devotion and empathise with her loss.

The Death of Adonis

> Our tender Adonis is dying, O Kythereia,
> What can we do?
> Beat on your breasts, my girls, and tear
> your dresses.
>
> Sappho
Translated by Willis Barnstone[22]

Above all, Lesbos was noted for its creative groups which attracted women from far and wide to be instructed in 'dance, music, singing, the care and adornment of the body, and probably the lore and knowledge of sex and motherhood.' Inspired by Aphrodite, these artistic 'sororities', were also said to prepare young girls for marriage. Since most Greeks could not comprehend the concept of friendship or love between women, it was simply assumed that Sappho's poems, which projected female love, were homoerotic. (It is no wonder that Sappho, whose poetry celebrated the strength of women, was an early symbol of the feminist movement.)

PLATO

While Sappho elevated Aphrodite as a positive role model for women, Plato (428-347 BC), the Greek philosopher who advocated personal and political freedom, transformed the Goddess into a symbol of female inferiority. In his well-known essay, *Symposium*, Plato theorised that the Love Goddess, as mythologised by Homer and Hesiod, was, in actuality, two distinct deities who served as paradigmatic models for the two types of love – sexual and non-sexual. Homer's Aphrodite, the daughter of Zeus and Dione, was dubbed Pandemos (literally 'Common Aphrodite') and epitomised erotic heterosexual love which, according to Plato, 'belongs to a much younger goddess, who, through her parentage, partakes of the nature both of the female and the male.'[23] Hesiod's goddess, on the other hand, 'whose descent is purely male' as the daughter of Ouranos, was called Ourania (– also Urania; literally 'Heavenly Aphrodite') and personified spiritual love and friendship – the ideal form of devotion which Plato believed could only exist between men. This devotion often, but not always, extended to homoeroticism – a practice widely accepted in ancient Greece.

Because homosexual love was both physical *and* cerebral, Plato believed it to be superior to heterosexual love which, he theorised, lacked intellectual companionship owing to woman's purely sexual nature. Although 'Platonic love' presently connotes non-sexual affection between two people (regardless of gender), the concept originally described a man's affection for another man – considered the superior expression of love because it need not be sexually motivated. Ironically, Plato's definition of the nature of love generated many of the prevailing attitudes towards women – misconstruing, as it did, the meaning of the terms Pandemos and

Urania. Whereas 'Urania' simply meant 'the Heavenly One', 'Pandemos' referred to any secular Patron or Patroness of a city-state 'who embraces the whole people . . . the common bond and fellow-feeling necessary for the existence of any state'.[24]

While literary images immortalised the Goddess of Love's more irreverent qualities, the Aphrodite actually glorified throughout Greece bore *little* resemblance to the mythological descriptions that ultimately became her trademark. In fact, the diversity of her regional titles and the range of her eclectic functions not only characterised her versatility but emphasised an ability to serve the unique needs of each region where she was venerated.

Exalted in Athens as Aphrodite-Ourania, the Heavenly Goddess, she was also worshipped there as the benefactress of prostitutes in the guise of Aphrodite-Hetaira and Aphrodite-Porne. When Greece was threatened by Persia during the fifth century BC, Aphrodite flourished at the strategic ports of Corinth and Sparta where, as a War Goddess, she was called on to protect her cities by 'haunting cemeteries and slaying men'.[25] At Delphi, the site of the Delphic Oracle, Aphrodite Epitymbia was a patroness of marriage, imparting to wives the secrets of carnal passion.*[26] There was even Aphroditos, a bearded, androgynous incarnation from Cyprus, which represented her asexual birth and descent from Phoenicia and Babylonia where there were bearded Astartes and Ishtars.[27] And in later fourth century Hellenistic Egypt, Aphrodite-Euploia, Goddess of Navigation and patroness of Alexandria, blessed sailors with safe voyages.

SCULPTURAL REPRESENTATIONS OF THE GODDESS

Despite the fact that most of Aphrodite's temples were destroyed by invasions and natural disasters, thousands of miniature terracottas reflecting her patronage of the waters and her affinity

*Hera, wife of Zeus, usually assumed the role of Guardian of Marriage.

with fertility have been uncovered at ancient sites throughout Cypriot and Sicilian harbour towns and agricultural regions of Greece and Turkey. Frequently depicted with motifs of aquatic animals, the bulk of these artefacts show the Goddess accompanied by turtles and bulls or atop swans, geese* and dolphins. Most often, however, she was surrounded by doves, which symbolised passion and fertility long before they became emblems of peace.

One of the most striking terracottas features a stately, sombre deity standing gracefully and proudly atop a giant swan. Casket in hand, she wears a long gown; a tall, vertical crown is placed atop her head. Quite uncharacteristic of the literary Aphrodite, this Boetian sculpture, which embodies her role as Patroness of the Dead and Guardian of Secret Knowledge, represents the nature of her worship throughout agricultural eastern Greece.

The popular legend surrounding Aphrodite's birth also inspired a vast quantity of fifth and sixth-century works including miniature terracottas rendering the Goddess atop a scallop shell, the 'Ludovisi Throne', a late archaic sculpture of the Goddess' head as she surfaces from the water, and Apelles' famous painting, 'Aphrodite Rising from the Sea' (fourth century BC). This latter likeness of the Goddess shaking water droplets from her hair has influenced countless portraits, sculptures and photographs of both the Goddess and contemporary images of femininity.

The daring representation of the nude Aphrodite taking her ritual bath sculpted by Praxiteles (370–330 BC), Greece's most renowned sculptor, redefined the way deities were sculpted and, in particular, how the Goddess of Love and Beauty was perceived. Praxiteles' acclaimed marble statue, 'Aphrodite Preparing for her Bath' (350 BC) projected, for the first time, the sacred and the profane within a single work of art. One of the finest representations of the Goddess ever crafted, the statue, also known as 'Aphrodite of Knidos', was a naturalistic, uncompromisingly sensual likeness of a sacred figure. It featured Aphrodite preparing for her bath with one hand covering her genitals – a posture which ironically drew attention to the concealed area. Although it was

---

**It is quite possible that the fairy-tale Mother Goose descended from the association of this bird with the Fertility Goddess.

quite shocking to view a deity completely undressed, Praxiteles' majestic statue was none the less placed at a shrine atop a cliff overlooking the Greek colony of Knidos, a thriving port in Asia Minor.*

Because the Goddess was worshipped as Aphrodite-Hetaira and Aphrodite-Porne, it was quite appropriate that Phryne, a beautiful Athenian courtesan, was the model for Praxiteles' sculpture, as she had been for Apelles' painting. Inspired by Phryne's flawless beauty and remarkable body structure, Praxiteles, reputed to have been her lover, endowed the statue with the proportions of his curvaceous paramour and unknowingly established the standard measurements for sculpting female nudes – many of which came to be called 'Aphrodites'.

> The canonical proportions for the female nude established by Praxiteles were that the same distance should exist between the breasts from the lower breast to the navel and from the navel to the crotch.[28]

Unfortunately, these 'perfect' specifications not only set the standards for aesthetic superiority but unfortunately became the paradigm for feminine beauty.

Because 'Aphrodite Preparing for her Bath' depicted a *Goddess* participating in a ceremonial rite, Praxiteles' sensually explicit nude was not deemed sacrilegious and paved the way for the sculpting and drawing of nude deities, a practice previously frowned upon in Greek society. Harking back to Sumerian images of Inanna and Dumuzi, this sensual approach was not innovative at all in societies that were more matrifocal and, therefore, less inhibited.

In the wake of widespread destruction and military takeovers, most Greek sculptures were either demolished, partially mutilated or, in the case of bronze works, dismantled and recast as weapons and utensils. Fortunately, Roman art patrons commissioned sculptors to produce hundreds of impeccable

---

*Knidos later became part of modern-day Turkey. The archaeologist Dr Iris Love led an expedition there which uncovered the remains of Aphrodite's temple. In the 1970s, however, the seaport was converted into a military base and declared off-limits to the public.

facsimiles – thus the marble statues of the Olympians displayed in museums throughout the world are, in actuality, Roman copies of Greek originals.

HELLENISTIC ERA (323-30 BC)

Marked by the expansion of the Greek Empire throughout Europe and Asia, the Hellenistic Era began with the untimely death of Alexander the Great in Babylon (323 BC). At its height, Alexander's empire encompassed Egypt, Cyprus, Asia Minor, Babylonia, Persia and, for a brief time, India.* A search for financial, educational and cultural opportunities saw the migration of many Greeks to Alexandria, resulting in an amalgamation of Greek and Egyptian cultures.

Because Hathor, the Egyptian Cow Goddess, was a fertility and sky deity who patronised music, dancing and love, the Hellenistic Egyptians identified her as Aphrodite-Hathor. Worshipped at the Great Temple of Denderah, known for its frescoed ceiling illustrating the zodiac and mythological scenes, Hathor, also associated with cruelty and war, was the daughter of Isis, the Egyptian fertility Goddess who was identified with the Moon. It is quite possible that Hathor's affiliation with Aphrodite influenced astrological interpretations of the Morning and Evening Star – which came to be known as the 'Star of Aphrodite'.

Greek Astrology

While Near and Middle Eastern lore was readily absorbed by Greek culture, astrology – the causal relationship between the heavenly bodies and earthly events – took longer to penetrate Greek consciousness. Though admired for their miraculous splendour and studied for their complex movements, the luminaries were not identified as Gods and Goddesses as they had been in the East.

*Due to the presence of Alexander's armies in the Far East, Mesopotamian and Greek culture exerted a profound influence on Hindu (Vedic) astrology and mythology.

Prior to the sixth century BC, when their scientists first visited Babylon, Greek astronomers considered the five planets to be fixed stars which were labelled according to appearance. Consequently, 'Mercury was named the "Twinkling Star", Mars, because of his red color, the "Fiery Star", Jupiter, the "Luminous Star", Saturn the "Brilliant Star" or perhaps, taking the word in another sense, the "Indicator".'[29] Whereas Mesopotamian religion imposed the designations 'Inanna' and 'Ishtar' to both the luminary *and* the Goddess, the Greeks never regarded Aphrodite (whose epithet 'Ourania' highlighted her as the feminine derivative of Ouranos, the Sky God) as a manifestation of the Morning and Evening Star. While they acknowledged that the two aspects of the planet constituted one celestial body, the Greeks none the less dubbed the Morning Star 'Phosphorus' ('Bringer of Light') and the Evening Star 'Hesperus' ('Vesper').

The Greeks were initially introduced to Babylonian astrology by Pythagoras, the mathematician and philosopher, who spent eight years in Babylon studying Mesopotamian stellar theory. While conceding that Babylonian astronomy was mathematically unsophisticated, Pythagoras was nevertheless fascinated by the notion that the heavenly bodies were sacred objects which influenced mundane occurrences. Upon his return to Greece, he distinguished the *fixed* stars from the Sun, Moon and five planets, introduced early division of the zodiac into 12 constellations and initiated the usage of sexagesimal numbers (that is, 60 seconds = 1 minute, 60 minutes = 1 hour, 360 degrees = 1 circle) – concepts originally used by the Sumerians and subsequently employed by Greek mathematicians and astronomers.

Pythagoras' greatest contribution to the development of Greek astrology, however, was 'The Harmony of the Spheres' – his philosophy expounding the correlation between planetary motions and the notes of a musical scale, each of which results in 'universal symmetry' which pervades and, thus, aligns both heaven and earth. By comparing the perfection of the universe to the flawlessness of a musical composition, Pythagoras initiated the concept that the movement of a heavenly body indicated the quantity of its soul. It was this mode of thinking which led the Greeks finally to view the luminaires as sacred manifestations. But despite mathematical theories which 'combined religious initiation with a scientific quest', Greek astronomers remained reluctant to investigate the possibility of a connection between celestial and terrestrial phenomena.

Plato first introduced the term 'planetes' (Greek for 'wanderers') in his work *Timaios* to describe the Sun, Moon and five stars which were believed to orbit the Earth. While his firm belief in the supremacy of individual will was anathema to the fatalistic premise of Mesopotamian astral divination, Plato none the less acknowledged the luminaries' spiritual omnipresence.[30] It was ultimately the popularity of the Stoic philosophy throughout Greece (fourth century BC) which created the climate in which astrological divination could finally be embraced. Founded by Zeno, an Athenian of Phoenician origin, Stoicism viewed the heavenly bodies as divine manifestations and as a result, 'the Stoics were supportive of astrology and the Babylonian conception of a correspondence between heaven and earth'. Combined with the pre-existing Greek philosophy which espoused the sacredness of numbers (Pythagoras) and the value of the individual (Plato), Stoicism fuelled interest in horoscopic astrology as a means of amassing the personal power necessary to comply with, rather than succumb to, the will of the Gods.

To acknowledge the new religiosity surrounding the astral bodies, the Greeks identified the five planets, formerly named for their physical characteristics, with the Gods and Goddesses most analogous to the Babylonian planetary deities. Like the Mesopotamians who used the same name to describe the planets and their corresponding deities (Nebo, Ishtar, Nergal, Marduk and Ninib), the Greeks designated the planets with the names of Hermes, Aphrodite, Ares, Zeus and Kronos.*[31] Because the imagery, legends and rituals of Ishtar most resembled those of the Greek Goddess of Love and Beauty, the Morning and Evening Star belonged to Aphrodite. Outfitting the luminaries with the anthropomorphic qualities of the corresponding Olympians enabled the rational Greeks to relate to the planets as symbols

---

*When translated into Latin, these names became Mercury, Venus, Mars, Jupiter and Saturn.

of human experience, paving the way for the eventual acceptance of horoscopic astrology.*

The Seleucid Era (312-64 BC), the period of Greek occupation of Asia Minor, Babylonia and Egypt, saw the remarkable growth of mathematical astronomy. Greek scientists perfected Babylonian astronomical data resulting in the precise measurement of the rate of movement of the equinoxes, division of the fixed stars into the 12 equal constellations of the zodiac, the prediction of eclipses and the construction of individual horoscopes. Detailed computations perfected by the Greeks determined the position of the heavenly bodies before and after an event – culminating in the first ephemeris, which gave 'planetary positions for the first year of the Greek kingdom of Babylonia, 312 BC'.[32]

By the third century BC, interest in both the theoretical and divinatory aspects of astrology accelerated to the extent that Greek students travelled to Babylonia to study the science. Simultaneously, Berosus, a Babylonian priest of Marduk, founded the first Greek astrological school (280 BC) on the island of Kos, the site of the Hippocratic School of Medicine. Because Berosus' approach was scientific rather than religious, he taught medical astrology which emphasised the relationship of the planets to healing stones, medicinal plants, herbs and parts of the anatomy.

The tremendous rise in the usage of horoscopic astrology for purposes of divination and self-understanding must ultimately be credited to the Greek astronomers Hipparchus (190-120 BC) and Ptolemy (100-178 AD), whose invaluable discoveries, though more than 200 years apart, formed the fundamentals of the astrological system we use today. A proponent of the Tropical Zodiac which places the beginning of the astrological year at the vernal equinox, Hipparchus calculated the precise rate of the precession of the equinoxes by determining the exact point for 0 degrees Aries.

An Egyptian of Greek descent, Ptolemy (whose full name was Claudius Ptolemaieus) lived in Alexandria during its domination

---

**Because correlating the stars with deities probably did not commence until sometime during the fifth century BC, any mention of the Morning and Evening Star in the works of Homer or Hesiod strictly refer to the heavenly body and not to the Goddess.

by the Romans. Drawing from volumes of Egyptian, Mesopotamian and Persian scholarship housed in the city's university library, Ptolemy produced his classic, authoritative astronomical and astrological texts, *Almagest* and *Tetrabiblos*. Based on Hipparchus' doctrine that the Sun, Moon and five planets revolved around the Earth, *Almagest* was utilised as a reference until Copernicus (1473-1543) adopted a heliocentric view of the universe by determining that the Sun was the centre of the solar system and the planets (including the Earth) revolved around it.* Ptolemy's accomplishments as an astronomer also included the determination of longitude and latitude, the stationary points, the first and last visibilities, and computation of eclipses.[33]

Ptolemy's interest in the fate of the individual and the ability to master one's own destiny resulted in his *Tetrabiblos* (literally meaning 'four books'), the first definitive astrological handbook which exerted such a profound influence that it remains, to this day, the basis of contemporary natal and mundane astrology. Combining the art of divination inherited from Mesopotamian omen literature with the scientific refinement and sophistication of the Greeks, Ptolemy utilised the positions and interrelationships of the heavenly bodies to define the nature of the individual and the cycles of human life. Employing a myriad of interpretive techniques, Ptolemy devised a symbolic language which defined the planets according to both their physical properties and the nature of their namesake deities. One of Ptolemy's accomplishments was in setting down the properties of the planets, including the Morning and Evening Star, in both mundane and, for the first time, horoscopic astrology. It was, in fact, Ptolemy's elucidation of the Star as the Lesser Benefic which set the precedent for the way we view the planetary symbol today.

According to Ptolemy, when it was prominent among the constellations Aphrodite's Star would bestow prosperity, honour, happy marriages, numerous children, glory, joy, profitable and safe voyages and, most important, the proliferation of animal,

---

*Several Greek astronomers, most notably Aristarchus of Samos, had already asserted that the planets revolved around the Sun which, like the fixed stars, remained stationary. Because the dominant theory held the Earth as the centre of the universe, the hypothesis about the Sun was invalidated and discarded.

vegetable and human life. Furthermore, in accordance with its classification as temperate and moist (like the Moon), there would be 'favourable temperature cooled by moistening breezes and frequently refreshed by fertilising showers'.[34] Whereas the aforementioned mundane interpretation of the Star perpetuated its abundant and loving attributes, it veered from the Babylonian mundane interpretation in that it did not apply solely to the harvest. Moreover, the star's belligerent, warlike qualities were thus completely eliminated; military strategies were now the domain of the planet Mars.

Although Ptolemy diligently studied Egyptian and Mesopotamian stellar theory, the Morning and Evening Star's divinatory meaning in the natal chart, garnered in part from purely astronomical observations, included the qualities of Aphrodite and Hathor (love, beauty and creativity) but eliminated the attributes of Ishtar (abundance and hostility), which were reserved for the mundane interpretation.

> When Venus rules alone in a position of glory, she renders the mind benignant, good, voluptuous, copious in wit, pure, gay, fond of dancing, jealous, abhorring wickedness, delighting in the arts, pious, modest, well-disposed, happy in dreams, affectionate, beneficent, compassionate, refined in taste, easily reconciled, tractable, and entirely amiable: but, if contrarily posited, she renders the mind dull, amorous, effeminate, timorous, indiscriminating, sordid, faulty, obscure, and ignominious.[35]

On the heels of Hipparchus' calculation of the precession of the equinoxes, Ptolemy finally adopted the usage of the Tropical Zodiac and divided the stars into 12 signs, each spanning 30 degrees. Although the Babylonians first named the constellations according to their shapes and sizes (e.g. Aries the Ram and Taurus the Bull), it was Ptolemy who designated the months of the year which the zodiacal signs encompassed and assigned qualities that related to their physiognomy. Due to the Greek application of astrology to medicine, Ptolemy also associated different parts of the body with the signs of the zodiac.

While the concept of planetary rulership originated in

Babylonia, Ptolemy's retention of these relationships obviously relied on the similarities between the constellation symbol (e.g. Ram, Bull, Twins) and the planet. In the case of Aries the Ram ('Krios' in Greek), the animal's reputation for aggressiveness was most compatible with Mars, its ruling planet, whose corresponding deity was Ares/Mars, God of War. To investigate Venus' rulership over both Taurus and Libra, it is necessary to examine the symbolism of the Bull and the Scales – from which Taurus and Libra derive their names.

TAURUS (20 APRIL–21 MAY)

From early Neolithic cultures to the Greek and Roman Empires, the bovine has always been a symbol of male potency and a source of empowerment to an array of Fertility Goddesses whose most treasured offerings included bull-shaped figurines and the consecrated horns and organs of the sacrificial animal. While Inanna's husband Dumuzi is described as 'the young bull', Europa, the Phoenician Queen, is enamoured of Zeus disguised as a docile bull – confirmation of the powerful connection between the fertility Goddess and the bovine. This correlation saw its ultimate manifestation in the image of Hathor, the Egyptian Cow Goddess of love, fertility and creativity, worshipped by the Hellenistic Greeks as Aphrodite-Hathor.

Astrologically speaking, the Taurean qualities of patience, productivity, stubbornness and sensuality are descriptive not only of the slow yet steady bovine but of the Age of Taurus (approximately 4000–2000 BC) – an era epitomised by matrifocal, agrarian communities and the worship of Fertility Goddesses. It is not simply by chance that the Sun's annual movement through the constellation of Taurus (literally meaning 'Bull'), from 20 April to 21 May, coincided with innumerable springtime festivals ranging from the Babylonian New Year to the Roman Veneralia and Vinalia. Known for their exuberant and, sometimes, sexual rituals (e.g. Sacred Marriage Rites), these seasonal celebrations honoured the Fertility Goddess for producing a bountiful and profitable harvest. Because the constellation was so closely connected with burgeoning nature as well as male and female sexuality, the symbolism of both Taurus and its ruling planet Venus as they appear in the birth chart incorporated the qualities of the Fertility Goddess as they related to the productive season – patience, passion, determination and abundance.

LIBRA (23 SEPTEMBER–24 OCTOBER)

While the bovine represents fecundity of the womb and the earth, the balancing scales symbolise harmony and justice – aspects of the Goddess that were equally revered but remarkably different from the overt sexuality associated with the Bull. Coinciding with the planting of the harvest throughout the Middle East and Greece, the autumn equinox is the starting point for the Sun's yearly passage through the sign of Libra (literally meaning 'scales') which occurs from 23 September–24 October. Although it is difficult to pinpoint precisely when the planetary rulers of the zodiacal signs were first assigned, Libra's association with the Morning and Evening Star may have stemmed from Mesopotamian Sacred Marriage Rites honouring the reunion of the Goddess (the Star's embodiment) with her consort. These rites were performed around the time of the equinox and not only inaugurated the productive growing season, but consisted of simulated lovemaking between the reigning monarch and temple priestesses, emblematic of the Vegetable Lord and the Fertility Goddess respectively. It is no coincidence, therefore, that the zodiacal sign of Libra, associated with both nature and the institution of marriage, should signify love, relationship, beauty and harmony – traits associated with the early Fertility Goddesses and, especially, Aphrodite.

The Morning and Evening Star's rulership over Taurus and Libra was validated by Plato's distinction between the earthy Aphrodite Pandemos (Taurus) and the heavenly Aphrodite Urania (Libra). As ruler of Taurus, the Star's sensual aspects are emphasised; the luminary's governorship of Libra accentuates cerebral relationships – which Plato equated with 'true' love.

Like rulership, Ptolemy's designation of planetary relationships (exaltation, detriment and fall) is still used in modern horoscope interpretation especially in Hindu (Vedic) astrology which employs these categorisations to determine the strength or weakness of a planet. As a moist planet, Venus is exalted in Pisces since the sign falls during the dampness of spring; Venus is, therefore, fallen in Virgo, the sign of the dry autumn – a reversal of the seasonal makeup of the Near East.[36] It is also no wonder that moist Venus was exalted in the sign of the fish (Pisces) nor that it falls in the opposite sign of the Virgin – who, according to traditional interpretation, has never known the pleasures of passionate lovemaking.

Ptolemy also introduced the concept of the 12 houses – 'imaginary divisions of the Earth's surface projected into the sky, marked by the four angles – ascendant (first house), nadir (fourth house), descendant (seventh house) and midheaven (tenth house)'. When Venus is on the ascendant, it affects one's appearance.

> Venus operates in a manner similar to that of Jupiter, but, at the same time, more becomingly and more gracefully; producing qualities of a nature more applicable to women and female beauty, such as softness, juiciness, and greater delicacy. She also peculiarly makes the eyes beautiful, and renders them of an azure tint.[37]

In addition to using Venus (as the Babylonians did) as a predictor of meteorological conditions and cycles, Ptolemy was one of the earliest to assign planetary rulers to various cities, states and countries in order to 'determine how different parts of the world will be affected by any given astronomical event'.[38] The Cyclades Islands, the coast of Asia Minor and Cyprus were all under the domain of Taurus and 'through the influence of Venus they [residents of those places] are lovers of the arts and sciences, as well as of music and poetry, of public show, and all the refinements of life. They are also voluptuous, fond of elegance, and overstudious in their attention to the body.'[39] Mesopotamian dwellers, on the other hand, were described as 'hot in constitution, amorous and lustful, fond of acting, singing, and dancing, gaudy in their dresses and ornaments; owing to the influence of Venus', while

Persia's inhabitants were affiliated with Venus and Taurus due to their splendid garments, elegance and refinement.

Because *Tetrabiblos* is the earliest extensive compilation, it represents a turning point in the development of interpretive natal astrology.* Its Latin and Arabic translations were disseminated throughout Roman and Islamic society respectively. During the Dark and Middle Ages, the only astrological strides were made by practising Arabic and Hindu astrologers who incorporated Mesopotamian and Greek techniques into their own systems. Because India was far removed from European culture, however, the Renaissance only saw a revival of Greek, Roman and Islamic astrological techniques which originated with Ptolemy's revolutionary insights. For this reason, modern interpretations of the Morning and Evening Star's role in both mundane and natal astrology have not changed much since Ptolemy's original descriptions were first set forth. (The horoscopic interpretation of Venus, Taurus and Libra will be fully discussed in Part II.)

Venus – From Goddess of Love to Divine Mother of Rome

Although Venus, the Roman Goddess of Love, mirrored Aphrodite's appearance, she quickly established her own identity and, at the height of the Roman Empire, was worshipped from the shores of the Atlantic Ocean to the Black Sea under a variety of regional guises. Venus' transformation from Goddess of Love and Beauty to Divine Mother of Rome is rooted on the Italian peninsula, where she was originally esteemed as a regional garden nymph.

First colonised by Central Europeans during the Bronze Era (1600 BC), the Italian peninsula flourished with the arrival of the intellectually and technologically superior Etruscans, under whose regime Rome emerged as a leading cultural force. At the height of their power (fifth century BC) the Etruscans controlled Italy and, owing to an intense commercial relationship with Greek and Phoenician settlements in Sicily, Sardinia and

---

*There are many other influential Greek and Latin astrological texts which are presently being translated and published by Project Hindsight.

Carthage (North Africa), Eastern culture was introduced. This coalescence of Etruscan and Oriental civilisations resulted in the incorporation of popular Greek and Near Eastern mythological motifs throughout Etruscan art.

In the absence of surviving written documentation, what is known of Etruscan religion has primarily been gleaned from the preponderance of images displayed on elaborately sculpted sarcophagi, illustrated vases and finely engraved bronze mirrors. Because she is prominently displayed in scenes depicting both the 'Judgment of Paris' and Aphrodite's love affair with Adonis, Turan, an Etruscan deity, has been deemed the Etruscan Love and Fertility Goddess, with Atunis (the Etruscan equivalent of Adonis) her lover.

When Italy was overrun by Latin-speaking Romans (sixth century), many local Etruscan deities were merged with Roman Gods and Goddesses. Due to Turan's association with fruitfulness, she easily blended with Venus, a Latin garden spirit of neuter gender. Primarily venerated in Rome, Venus (from the Latin root for 'vegetable') was a minor deity affiliated with the city's magnificent gardens and revered for her patronage over aesthetics, growth and fertility.

By the beginning of the fifth century, the Roman Republic's thriving commercial relationship with Greece and Hellenistic Egypt resulted in the 'cultural Hellenisation of the Italic peoples'. Contact between the two cultures led to the integration of their pantheons, resulting in Greek legends affixing themselves to the Roman deities who had previously had no real mythology of their own. By identifying regional Gods and Goddesses with the characteristics and escapades of their Hellenic counterparts, Latin poets incorporated Greek legends into their narratives, hymns and plays – thus imbuing the religion of Rome with the richness of the East. Bronze and marble likenesses of the Olympian Gods and Goddesses poured into Rome, further enforcing the transformation of local Roman divinities into corresponding Greek deities by providing visual images to accompany the legends.

Jupiter was already Zeus. Juno, the power of fertility in women, became Hera with all her attributes and myths. Mars, perhaps a storm god ... became involved with agriculture and war, identified with Ares, and in literature and art though not in ritual was solely associated with war. Minerva, an Etruscan craft goddess, was counterpart to Pallas Athene. Diana, a power of the wildwood, was assimilated to Artemis. Venus, a garden numen, because of her association with growth, was one with Aphrodite, the power of sex. Poseidon became Neptunus and Hephaestus became Volcanus. Mercurius, a mercantile power, was deemed equivalent to Hermes, and so became messenger to the Gods.[40]

It is interesting to note that many of the Roman deities are, in some instances, markedly different from their Greek counterparts. In the case of Venus, there was absolutely no gender identification until she acquired the attributes of Aphrodite and became associated with love, sex and beauty.

VENUS ERYCINA

During the first Punic War between Phoenicia and Italy (264–41 BC) the Romans, occupying Phoenician-dominated Sicily, Sardinia and Corsica, first encountered Astarte, venerated at Sicily's Mt Eryx. The Phoenician Goddess' main function was the sanctioning of Phoenician and Greek mariners by providing them with the sexual services of her priestesses. When Sicily later fell to Rome, Astarte's Mt Eryx sanctuary replete with temple priestesses was consecrated to Venus Erycina (Venus of Eryx) who, in effect, became an amalgam of the Phoenician Astarte, the Greek Aphrodite and the Roman Venus. The temple ultimately served two disparate functions – as a pilgrimage site and a source of entertainment 'to high placed officials and other visitors from Rome who patronized its courtesans'.[41]

The triumphant Romans, whose earliest Goddess temple had been dedicated to Venus Obsequens ('Venus who gratifies'),[42] glorified Venus Erycina as Goddess of Victory and she became a national heroine. Imitating the style of the Phoenician shrine on Mt Eryx, two magnificent temples honouring Venus Erycina were constructed in Rome and filled with icons of the Goddess transported from Sicily. While one temple (181 BC) incorporated sexual rituals, the other sanctuary (215 BC) did not accommodate sacred harlotry and was situated adjacent to the Jupiter (Zeus) temple. Due to this juxtaposition of shrines, both Jupiter and Venus were honoured at the *Vinalia*, a festival held twice a year: on 19 August to commemorate the harvesting of wine-producing grapes, and on 23 April to celebrate the previous year's vintage. To acknowledge Venus' affiliation with gardens and vineyards, her devotees, praying for beauty, charm and wit, made offerings of incense, myrtle, mint and wine.[43]

Another springtime festival was the *Veneralia*, which honoured both Venus and Fortuna Virilis (Fortune), an earth deity glorified for her ability to bestow wealth. Just as the month of March was dedicated to Mars, the Roman God of War, the month of April, which hosted agricultural festivals highlighting the burgeoning of the earth, was associated with Venus as the Fertility Goddess. (This emphasises the assignment of Venus as ruler of Taurus, which spans 20 April–21 May).

Despite the fact that slaves and prostitutes (commonly employed in brothels, inns and the public baths) formed an intrinsic stratum of Roman society,* the need for independent courtesans diminished with the elevated status of wives, who now accompanied their husbands to public functions. While Aphrodite-Hetaira and Aphrodite-Porne was still revered throughout Greece, these aspects of Venus were reserved for just a few sanctuaries in Rome, Sicily and Cyprus which perpetuated the Phoenician/Greek tradition of temple priestesses. In its place, sacred prostitution became the domain of the Vestal Virgins who, in the service of Vesta, Goddess of the Hearth, participated in festivals designed to ensure agricultural productivity.

As early as the fifth century BC, marble likenesses of the Olympian deities decorated palaces, villas and gardens of affluent Roman heads of state, government officials and Patrician nobles.

---

*Under siege by the Romans, Greeks were imported as slaves and labourers. Whereas educated men were utilised for professional skills, Greek women, mostly housebound and uneducated, were often employed as servants.

Although sensual images of Aphrodite were interchangeable with those of the Roman Venus, her sexual identity became secondary to her manifestation as *Venus Genetrix** ('Venus the Mother'), hailed by Julius Caesar as Rome's ancestral mother who led the Republic and ultimately the Empire to her greatest victories. During Julius Caesar's reign (100–44 BC), multitudes of looted masterpieces from Greece, Egypt and Asia Minor were brought home by triumphant Roman generals as mementos of their conquests abroad, thus stimulating interest not only in Aphrodite but in the entire pantheon of deities.

While the aesthetically superior sculptures of Greek deities were initially utilised for adornment, they were eventually placed at shrines and temples honouring corresponding Roman divinities. Due to the profusion of well-proportioned statues which reproduced Aphrodite's image, Venus, too, became identified as the hallmark of physical perfection, in spite of the fact that the functions and qualities of the two Goddesses were often at variance. The quest for perfection – only attainable through art – was recounted in the well-known Roman legend concerning the narcissistic sculptor, Pygmalion, and his love for Galatea – an ivory statue.

As recorded by Ovid in his *Metamorphoses*, Pygmalion, a misogynist artist and bachelor,** becomes wildly infatuated with his own creation – a perfectly formed ivory sculpture whom he names Galatea. Obsessed with the life-size statue, which represents his ideal of womanhood, the artist implores Venus, the paragon of perfect love and feminine beauty, to bring it to life. In the name of love the Goddess complies and even presides over Pygmalion's marriage to Galatea, who later gives birth to Paphos – named for the Cypriot port where Aphrodite/Venus first came ashore. (According to legend, Paphos later fathered the Cypriot king Cinyras, whose daughter Myrrha gave birth to Adonis.)

Despite a happy ending, this parable cites the complex relationship between creator and creation as well as the need to

---

*She was also popularly called *Venus Victrix* ('Goddess of Victory') throughout the military provinces.

**In other variations of this legend, Pygmalion was the king of Cyprus and Galatea was created by the Love Goddess, Venus.

distinguish between art/imagination and reality. Inspired by the legend, George Bernard Shaw's play *Pygmalion* (upon which the Lerner and Loewe musical *My Fair Lady* was based) reiterates the theme of the narcissist who wishes not simply to create/teach but to *control* the destiny of his creation/student, whom he does not recognise for her own unique abilities. (The association of love with possession and control is a recurrent theme of Venus-ruled Taurus and Libra and will be discussed more fully in Part II.)

Although the Romans were long familiar with Greek mythology, it was Ovid (43 BC–AD 18) and Virgil (70–19 BC), Rome's most enduring literary figures, who popularised Eastern legends by recording them in Latin. Their characterisations of the pantheon of divinities influenced Roman religion just as the works of Hesiod and Homer had affected the *actual* worship of Olympian deities. In his *Metamorphoses*, Ovid compiled his own versions of original Greek, Egyptian and Near Eastern tales by inserting Roman cultural details and substituting the names of corresponding Roman deities. Because Venus and Aphrodite shared patronage over love and fertility, Ovid's accounts of Venus' liaisons with Adonis, Vulcan (Hephaistos) and Mars (Ares) veered from the Greek myths in that the Roman Goddess was, for the most part, never belittled or relegated to a position of pure sexuality. Although she is remembered primarily as a Love Goddess, Venus was, in fact, most significant to Rome as Goddess of Victory and Divine Matriarch.

In accordance with Venus' transformation, she was conveyed as both a benevolent figure and an authoritative, jealous and overprotective mother. This latter aspect of her character was most evident in her relationship with her son Cupid, the esteemed Purveyor of Love – a role that his Greek equivalent Eros, one of the Graces, never acquired.* According to the legend popularised by Apuleius (second century AD),[44] Venus, jealous of and threatened by the amazing beauty of the mortal Psyche, beseeches Cupid to strike Psyche with one of his magical arrows so that she may fall in love with the most despicable man on Earth.

---

*The image of Cupid shooting his arrows in the air is practically identical to that of Kama, the Hindu God of Love and son of Lakshmi – the Love and Fertility Goddess equivalent to Aphrodite/Venus.

The scheme backfires, however, and Cupid himself becomes completely enamoured of Psyche. Upon learning of her son's passion, Venus attempts to humiliate Psyche by assigning her impossible tasks and tests of strength which, against all odds, she miraculously accomplishes. In the end Cupid marries Psyche, who is deified by Jupiter (Zeus); no longer a threat to the vainglorious Goddess of Love, the divine couple ecstatically reside on Mt Olympus.

THE *AENEID*

Virgil's glorification of Venus as Mother of the warrior hero Aeneas in his patriotic epic, the *Aeneid*, definitively altered the way the Love Goddess was worshipped throughout Rome. Although the tale centres around Aphrodite's mortal son, Aeneas, originally castigated in Homer's *Iliad*, the story depicts the qualities that make Venus the quintessential maternal figure – overprotectiveness, sacrifice, co-operation and love.

Commemorating the origins of the great Roman Empire, the *Aeneid*, beginning where the *Iliad* ends, opens as Aeneas, aided by the divine intervention of Venus, escapes from the burning city of Troy which has been captured by the victorious Greek armies. Symbolic of ancient Roman filial love, Aeneas, carrying his wounded father Anchises on his shoulders, leads his fellow Trojans to freedom and onward to Sicily (where Venus Erycina is worshipped). En route to the Italian mainland, Aeneas is detoured to North Africa (Carthage) due to a storm brought on by the Goddess Juno (Hera) in an attempt to prevent him from establishing Roman roots. Upon his arrival Aeneas is welcomed by Queen Dido, who is instantly fascinated by the young warrior. Knowing that Dido has the power to entice her son to remain in Carthage, thus avoiding the danger she knows awaits him in Rome, Venus, the loving but manipulative mother, solicits Cupid to cast a spell under which Dido and Aeneas fall madly in love. But their union is short-lived; Aeneas is commanded by the Gods to lead his men onward to Italy to establish the city of Lavinium. Unfortunately, when Dido discovers that her lover must depart, the heartsick Queen commits suicide.

Before reaching the Italian mainland, the heroic Aeneas is transported to the Underworld where he encounters Dido and begs for her forgiveness. Despite Aeneas' heartfelt explanation that he was *ordered* to leave, the unrelenting Dido turns away in silence – reducing her former lover to tears. But the hero is also reunited with his father Anchises, who, as the didactic voice of Virgil, informs Aeneas that his descendants [the Caesars] will one day transform Lavinium into Rome, the centre of the expansive Roman Empire.[45]

Upon reaching Latium's Tiber River, Aeneas and his men are welcomed by King Latinus. The king promises Aeneas his daughter Lavinia's hand in marriage, thereby eliciting the anger of Turnus, a Latin soldier who had expected to marry the princess. To safeguard Aeneas from his enemies, Venus presents him with protective armour and a 'shield engraved with a prophetic series of scenes from Roman history'[46] crafted by her husband Vulcan (Hephaistos). Inflicting the fatal wound on Turnus, Aeneas then leads the Trojans to victory and marries Lavinia; together they reign as king and queen. Because their descendants included Romulus and Remus, Aeneas (and Venus) were honoured as the progenitors of a new Roman race – an amalgamation of Latins and Trojans.*

Throughout Greek legends depicting: Aphrodite's love triangle with Hephaistos/Ares, her romance with Adonis and her seduction of Anchises, the Goddess was seen to 'test' Zeus by deviating from expected moral standards – behaviour for which she was ultimately punished. In the *Aeneid*, however, Venus is keenly aware that co-operation among the Gods is an indispensable key to success, and she is rewarded in her attempts to make peace with Juno and Jupiter.

Written upon the advice of Octavius (Augustus Caesar) who, after the assassination of his great-uncle Julius Caesar (44 BC)

---

*According to legend, Venus and her son Aeneas were direct ancestors of Romulus and Remus, twin abandoned infants who were raised by a she-wolf until shepherds found the boys and brought them up in the hills overlooking the Tiber River. After murdering his brother Remus in a quarrel, Romulus founded Rome (753 BC), which thus bears his name.

transformed the Roman Republic into the Roman Empire, the *Aeneid* celebrates the founding of Rome and establishment of its values. Virgil's literary masterpiece became a national epic, Aeneas a heroic symbol whose sense of duty, loyalty and patriotism embodied the very ideals which made Rome great. At the same time, the popular narrative strengthened Venus' apotheosis as national heroine and giver of life – an identification reminiscent of early Mother Goddesses but withheld from the Greek Aphrodite. The metamorphosis from her earliest incarnation as Inanna, Love and Fertility Goddess, to matriarch of the entire Roman race paved the way for the canonisation of the Virgin Mary, exalted as ancestral mother of the Christian peoples.

As the Empire extended from the Black Sea to the Atlantic Ocean, the worship of Venus spread throughout Roman colonies and influenced the myths of Celtic, Norse and Teutonic Love and Fertility Goddesses. Under the Roman occupation of Cyprus (50 BC–395 AD), the port of Paphos was renamed Paleopaphos and its renowned sanctuary, which glorified Astarte and Aphrodite, was re-dedicated to Venus. During the subsequent Christian and Byzantine Eras, the Cypriots worshipped Mary under the name Panghia Aphroditessa (meaning literally 'Mother Aphrodite'), an amalgam by which she is still revered in contemporary Cypriot villages.

APHRODISIAS

One of the most extraordinary temple complexes honouring Aphrodite was erected by Greek colonists at Caria (present-day southwest Turkey). Once honouring the Neolithic Fertility Goddess, the sacred city – renamed Aphrodisias – remained relatively obscure until the region was conquered by the Romans, who re-dedicated the site to Venus. As the worship of Venus spread throughout Asia Minor (formerly Anatolia), the sanctuary at Aphrodisias became a major religious centre attracting Roman emperors, each of whom claimed direct descent from Aeneas and prayed to Venus for fortune and power. In addition to her roles as Goddess of War and Divine Matriarch, Venus, 'Goddess of spring, blossoming nature, fertility, and of exuberant vegetation',[47] was exalted for filling Aphrodisias with abundant orchards, vines and life-giving springs. By the third century AD, Asia Minor (including Aphrodisias) fell to the Christian Byzantines who incorporated many of the qualities of Venus into their veneration of the Virgin Mary.

Rome's gradual change from Republic to Empire was accompanied by a 'revolution in man's intellectual and spiritual outlook' which sought to find meaning and individual salvation in a world dominated by the state and its conquests. Consequently, many Romans embraced astrology and Eastern 'mystery religions' honouring the Egyptian Isis, the Phrygian Cybele and the Persian Sun God Mithras. Although these cults had loyal followers, Rome's militarism and gradual transformation to Christianity forced their rituals, primarily fertility rites, to be practised clandestinely.

MITHRAISM

Mithraism flourished in Rome (first century BC) and extant wall reliefs, mosaics and paintings juxtaposing constellations with ruling Gods and Goddesses tell us that astral divination was a part of Mithraic doctrine. In fact, this mystery cult was so popular that relics commemorating the Bull Slayer were discovered in the ruins of Roman settlements as far afield as the Scottish Highlands and the Sahara Desert.[48] Whereas the Persians regarded Mithras as a fertility God whose capture and sacrifice of the sacred bull regenerated the earth, the Roman armies coveted Him as the warrior Sun God possessing inordinate strength and courage. Because the Mithraic Mysteries of ancient Rome were practised only by men, the slaying of the bull may have even symbolised the demise of the power of Goddess-worshipping cultures.

CYBELE

Since Venus' primary role was empowering her sons to march into battle, Roman women found solace in the worship of Ceres (Demeter), Isis and, especially, the popular Cybele who, like Venus, was venerated for her maternal attributes.

Originally revered by the Indo-European Phrygians in Asia Minor (1000 BC), Cybele was the fertility Goddess whose legendary love affair with Attis inspired the tale of Aphrodite and Adonis. Her shrine at Ephesus, one of the wonders of the ancient world, was re-dedicated to Artemis (Greek Goddess of the Hunt) by Greek colonists during the Hellenistic Era. The Romans adopted the worship of Cybele after annexing the region in 204 BC – just as Aphrodite/Venus entered the Roman pantheon of Gods and Goddesses. Cybele's epithet 'Mother of the Gods' correlated with that of Venus Genetrix ('Mother Venus'), and she became the centre of a mystery cult whose clandestine fertility rituals were practised only by women.

These popular mystery religions prevailed until Christianity swept the Roman Empire. The fanaticism and barbarism with which Christian zealots attempted to convert all peoples to their faith resulted in the expulsion of the Jews and the destruction of all vestiges of pagan worship. The eradication of any form of 'heathenism' included the banning of the study of astrology.

Although Christianity was declared the official religion of the Eastern Empire (ca. 300–700 AD) by Emperor Constantine the Great (312–337 AD), it was not until the fifth century that Mary, mother of Jesus, was assimilated into the religion and proclaimed Divine Mother and Holy Virgin by the Council of Ephesus (431 AD) in Asia Minor – the very region in which Cybele and Venus had also been enshrined as Mothers of Gods.[49] Replacing the plethora of female divinities honoured in Rome, Mary's iconography and legendary history incorporated the maternal qualities of the Empire's most popular Mother Goddesses – such as Cybele, Isis, Ceres and Venus (Aphrodite) – each praised for her devotional strength while mourning the loss of a loved one. In fact, Christ's crucifixion, resurrection and ultimate deification evolved from the legends of Dumuzi, Tammuz, Baal, Attis and Adonis who, like Jesus, were each killed, revived and immortalised.

As a result of Mary's glorification as both Mother and Virgin, copulation, no longer an acceptable expression of love, was deemed to be a purely procreative act. (While Mary inherited the matriarchal functions of the Roman Goddesses, their sensual qualities were transferred to Magdalene, the maligned prostitute to whom Jesus first appears after being resurrected.) Also called 'Queen of Heaven', Mary was far removed from Inanna – the passionate Love and Fertility Goddess who had bore that title three millennia earlier.

ROMAN ASTROLOGY

Although the art of divination was an intrinsic feature of Etruscan culture, the Romans were first exposed to the science of astrology during the second century BC, when Roman armies annexed the Greek settlements of southern Italy and Hellenistic Greece (including Babylonia, Persia and Egypt). At the height of their Empire the Romans, influenced by Stoicism, adhered to a sidereal philosophy which propounded the concept that the soul, born of the constellations, cascades to earth with a particular mission to accomplish. After divesting itself of the passions and faculties which it has acquired during its descent to earth, the soul dies and returns to the stars.[50] Furthermore, the Oriental belief that the Gods and Goddesses resided in the heavens was bolstered by Ovid's version of the legend of Phaethon who, with his sisters, ascended to the sky as the planet Venus and the constellations respectively. As in the Greek legend of Phaethon, however, it was he, not Aphrodite/Venus, who became the Morning and Evening Star. The Goddess was portrayed as a lover of Phaethon's rather than as a manifestation of the star itself.

Like the Greeks, the Romans originally referred to the stars by their physical descriptions, only later substituting the names of the corresponding deities. These are the names by which we know them today. Not only was the Morning and Evening Star – known to the Romans as Lucifer* ('light') and Vesper respectively – renamed Venus, but the 'stars' of Hermes, Ares, Zeus and Chronos became Mercury, Mars, Jupiter and Saturn respectively. In addition, Helios became the Sun (Sol) and Selene became the Moon (Luna).

Among those who adhered to astrological beliefs were Augustus Caesar, who attempted to predict the certainty of conquest, and the poet Manilius, whose pre-Ptolemaic writings included the designation of completely different planetary rulers to the zodiacal signs. Although Venus was still assigned rulership of Taurus, he linked Vulcan with Libra. While astrology was indeed practised among the Romans and even advanced by Firmicus Maternus (fourth century AD), who 'tried to accept both free will and the rule of the stars',[51] astral divination never really gained any firm hold among the intelligentsia, nor did it pervade everyday life.[52]

Because Latin translations of Ptolemy's *Tetrabiblos* became the standard astrological text, the symbolism of Venus as Divine Matriarch and Victory deity was never woven into Roman astrological thought. Although Ptolemy's work was disseminated throughout the Empire, adherence to Christian doctrine resulted in the text's suppression during the repressive European Dark Ages.

After Mohammed's rise to power (622 AD), astrology flourished throughout the Islamic world and was especially popularised by the Vedic Hindus in India, where Babylonian and Greek horoscopy had long been assimilated into their astrology (known as *Jyotish*). The translation of the *Tetrabiblos* into Arabic stimulated the Islamic astrologers Albumasar (786–886 AD) and Al-Biruni (*ca.* 1030 AD), whose writings resurfaced, along with Ptolemy's, during the Italian Renaissance, when the art of horoscope interpretation was once again revitalised and taught at European universities.

---

*It is quite likely that designating Lucifer as the name of the Devil originated with the Morning Star's association with sexual temptation.

4

THE RENAISSANCE VENUS

REDISCOVERING THE GODDESS AND HER PLANET

> The change of the times is evident in the Renaissance picture of Venus. With the development of the patriarchate the Great Goddess has become the Goddess of Love, and the power of the Feminine has been reduced to the power of sexuality.
> *The Great Mother*, Erich Neumann[1]

Throughout the Dark and Middle Ages, Christian religious motifs dominated Western art and literature to the total exclusion of any theme that did not propound the conscious pursuit of a devout existence leading to salvation and redemption in the hereafter. For the first time in almost 1,000 years, European popular culture was concerned with the question of earthly love and its place in man's life - a theme that first materialised in the lyric poetry, troubadour ballads and Arthurian legends of twelfth-century Britain.

Although the great literary figures of the early Italian Renaissance reintroduced the subject of human love into popular Italian culture, their female protagonists were still idealised as the essence of beauty and perfection - offering not the fulfilment of sexual desire but the attainment of heavenly bliss. Petrarch cites his eternal love for Laura in his sonnets, and Dante, in *The Divine Comedy*, relentlessly pursues Beatrice, the epitome of spiritual perfection, through Hell, Purgatory and Heaven, where they are finally united. It is only Boccaccio, author of *Decameron*, an epic noted for its frank treatment of sex, who utilises Venus to represent, as Plato had centuries before, the two types of love - spiritual and physical - and it is this theme which came to dominate Italian Renaissance art and to alter the image of the Goddess of Love.*

---

*An in-depth study of Boccaccio's interpretation of Venus as a symbol of love can be found in *Boccaccio's Two Venuses* by Richard Hollander.

The Italian Renaissance (1350-1520)

Literally meaning 'rebirth', the Renaissance (fourteenth-seventeenth centuries) reflected the natural evolution of man's changing beliefs in relation to his environment, resulting in the desire to set higher values upon personal experiences.

Originating in Florence, the Renaissance was a thriving period of ingenious creativity and economic wealth marked by the rediscovery of suppressed classical Greek and Latin manuscripts which unveiled a myriad of epics, plays and philosophical treatises. These manuscripts enabled Renaissance scholars to reconstruct the ancient world. The works of Ovid, Virgil, Horace and Cicero, either translated into Italian or studied in the original Latin (mastery of the Greek vernacular did not commence until the late Renaissance), were once again taught as part of the Humanities – a new curriculum which encouraged the pursuit of languages, literature, history and philosophy.

This new Humanism promulgated the exploration of philosophical and political beliefs based on the ascendancy of individual will and an enjoyment of the physical world within a secular framework – and thus veered from the Christian ethic which emphasised a disciplined, spiritual life as preparation for the hereafter.[2] Most important, the introduction and reinterpretation of dormant Roman and, later, Greek legends revealed a pantheon of pagan deities whose complex characteristics, love affairs and escapades were utilised by Renaissance writers, painters and sculptors as allegories for the human condition.

In addition to the reappearance of inspirational legendary themes and characters, the recovery of Greek and Roman paintings, marble statues and illustrated vases aroused an aesthetic fascination with the human anatomy – inconceivable during the preceding epoch – which was eagerly replicated in painting and sculpture. Utilising biblical scenes and figures to convey the spiritual world and mythological deities to signify the human condition, the Renaissance artist could strike a balance between religious and secular motifs. For the first time Jesus, Mary and other biblical figures were portrayed as mortals with naturalistic physical attributes and human emotions rather than as stylised caricatures. By the same token, mythological figures, modelled after the rediscovered classical nude, presented master sculptors and painters with their greatest challenge – portraying sensuality in an acceptable and even desirable fashion without seeming lustful or sinful, as the nude had theretofore been viewed.[3]

MARSILIO FICINO (1433–1499)

Due to the emergence of Florence and Venice as prosperous trading centres, the desire for profitable works of art led to the patronage of some of the most brilliant sculptors and painters who ever lived.* To this end, Cosimo de' Medici, head of Florence's wealthy ruling family, patronised the Platonic Academy where the most ingenious humanistic philosophers, scholars, artists and writers met to discuss their consuming passion for Greek and Roman culture. While the most profound influences on the members of the Florentine Academy were undoubtedly Plato's philosophical, social and political ideals, it was the Florentine philosopher, poet and astrologer Marsilio Ficino who commanded the greatest admiration and respect among his peers. As mentor to this intellectual circle of 'Neo-Platonists', Ficino instructed and guided them in their application of Platonism to Humanist philosophical thought.

Because intellectual purity and the quest for love constituted the paramount debated issues, Plato's two Aphrodites – Heavenly Urania who was born from the sea and Earthy Pandemos, daughter of Zeus and Dione – were once again employed to represent spiritual and physical love, respectively. In his revamped, somewhat optimistic translation of Plato's *Symposium*, Ficino eliminated the sinful aspects of the earthy Venus by placing equal value on both aspects of love and no moral judgment upon those who partook of either.[4]

From the standpoint of an astrologer, Ficino used the Heavenly interpretation of the Goddess to convey Venus' function as a planetary symbol. In a letter to Lorenzo de' Medici, Ficino described the Goddess:

*These artists included Donatello, Michelangelo, da Vinci, Raphael, Botticelli, Giorgione, Titian, Veronese and Tintoretto, to name but a few.

Luna (the Moon) should fix her eyes on Venus herself, that is to say on humanity. For humanity herself is a nymph of excellent beauty, born of heaven and more than all others, beloved by God all highest. Her soul and mind are Love and Charity, her eyes Dignity and Magnanimity, her hands Liberality and Magnificence, her feet Comeliness and Modesty. The whole then, is Temperance and Honesty, Charm and Splendour. Oh, what exquisite beauty. How wonderful to behold.[5]

Inasmuch as Venus continued to symbolise fecundity, heavenly grace, love and beauty, the maternal attributes for which she was once exalted now belonged to Mary, while her heroic, almost belligerent qualities had virtually disappeared.

Ficino's descriptions of the heavenly bodies in *The Planets* went further than simply serving as reinterpretations of Ptolemy's writings. By setting forth 'instructions on how to make an archetypal model of the universe',[6] Ficino concluded that, in addition to indicating the future, the planets were significators of spiritual possibilities. These revolutionary theories uncannily foreshadowed the humanistic psychological astrology pioneered by Marc Edmund Jones and Dane Rudhyar in the 1930s, who stated that the horoscope was 'the mirror of the soul' – not unlike Ficino's vision of the natal chart six centuries earlier.

Perceived to be the personification of both intellectual and physical love Venus* became one of the most commonly portrayed mythological figures throughout Renaissance art and literature. To explore how Venus embodied the pervasive theme of love during the Renaissance, I have focused on the Florentine Botticelli and the Venetian Titian – two painters whose dissimilar but equally valid delineations of the Goddess exemplify perfectly the polarity between sensual and cerebral love, as well as the distinction between Taurus and Libra respectively. Although the extent to which these two painters were familiar with astrology is uncertain, it is documented that Botticelli based his portrayals of Venus, in part, upon the mythological and astrological

---

*Because recovered visual images of the Goddess were based on translated Greek and Roman legends, the generic word 'Venus' here refers to both the Greek Aphrodite and the Roman Venus – considered by this time to be interchangeable deities.

teachings of Ficino – whose influence was felt throughout Florence's intellectual and artistic community.

SANDRO BOTTICELLI (1445-1510)

Sandro Botticelli, the ingenious Florentine painter patronised by the de' Medicis, gave Venus her most renowned visual interpretation based on the Neo-Platonists' view that ideal beauty was of utmost importance. Knowledgeable about Ficino's theory on the equality of spiritual and physical love, Botticelli combined Venus' ethereal and sensual qualities by celebrating her body as well as her spirit. In fact, his ability to place sensual and reverential imagery successfully side by side supports the esteem in which Botticelli held both classical mythology and religion.

'Primavera' (1478)

Commissioned by Lorenzo de' Medici, art collector, poet and student of Ficino, the 'Primavera' (Italian for 'spring') with its intricate composition and complex mythological allusions portrays Venus as an amalgamation of Heavenly Urania and Earthy Pandemos. Prominently positioned amid a burgeoning meadow in springtime, the beautiful, sensual, ethereal and stylised deity is fully clothed and clearly in the latter stages of pregnancy – linking her with procreation of both womb and earth. The painting is inundated with mythological scenes and characters – from the blindfolded Cupid shooting arrows of love overhead to the rejoicing three Graces who welcome the Goddess ashore to Paphos. As the title of the painting indicates, who can better personify the growing season than Venus, the fertile ruler of Taurus (20 April–21 May), who was honoured at ancient Rome's springtime celebrations of the wine harvest?

Adhering to Ficino's promulgation of Venus and Mary as equal symbols of divine love and beauty, Botticelli created a visual image of Venus whose physical features were practically interchangeable with his depictions of the Madonna. These divine mothers not only shared highly stylised, delicate facial features but were both associated with the star, rose, garden, shell, mirror and dove. Although Venus is pregnant, she is encircled by two angels affirming the epithet 'Goddess of Heaven' – a title shared by the earlier Goddesses Inanna, Aphrodite/Venus and by the Virgin Mary.

'Birth of Venus' (ca. 1485)

One of the most recognised images, 'Birth of Venus' is a magnificent visual rendering of the Goddess' emergence from the sea and subsequent transportation from Paphos to Cythera atop a scallop shell. Instead of recreating the Greek legend, however, Botticelli allegorised Venus' birth in the light of Renaissance Humanism and, as in the 'Primavera', juxtaposed the celestial Goddess with the world of the senses. Although the painting depicts the nude Goddess arising from the water and being greeted by the three Graces (depicted as two nude angels and a fully clothed maiden), its serene seascape and forested environs symbolise universal procreation and fruitfulness.

Because pagan deities were once again acceptable subjects in art, Renaissance painters and sculptors often reproduced the poses and dimensions of recovered Greco-Roman statues while preserving Christian idealism. Although Venus' slender form and angelic face 'invoked an interchangeability between the celestial Venus and the Virgin Mary',[7] her nude figure – positioned with one hand over her breast and the other covering her genitalia – replicated Praxiteles' 'Aphrodite of Knidos'.

TITIAN (1490–1576)

Although the term 'Italian Renaissance' implies that this cultural revival penetrated the entire Peninsula, the flowering of genius centred, for the most part, in the populated city-states of Florence and Venice. A major harbour linking trade between Europe and the East, Venice attracted wealthy merchants who commissioned its artists to produce aesthetically superior and commercially viable works of art. Venetian painting became noted for its marketable 'naturalistic' portraiture, while Florentine painting, patronised by art collectors who preferred idealism to realism, was characterised by philosophical themes and stylised images.

Tiziano Vecelli (better known as Titian) became one of Italy's most highly regarded artists – his naturalistic style ranging from contemporary portraiture to mythological and religious panoramas. Due to the importance placed upon individual values, it was Titian's realistic portraits, particularly his nudes, which dominated the art of sixteenth-century Venice and, at the same time, satisfied that city's mercantile population and cultural elite.

The majority of Titian's masterful nudes depict sensual full-bodied women with luxurious tresses, bedecked with exquisite jewellery and reclining in compromising positions on lush fabrics as well as on wrinkled sheets. Praising earthy sensuality rather than vilifying it as lustful led Titian to apotheosise these likenesses as the Goddess of Love in his masterpieces 'Venus and the Lute Player' (1560s), 'Venus with the Mirror' (1567) and 'Venus of Urbino' (1538). By presenting the pleasures of the flesh in a tasteful and appealing manner, Titian inaugurated the acceptance of the full-bodied frontal nude as a new form of aesthetic beauty and sensuality. Although reclining Venuses had been painted by earlier artists such as Giorgione and Campagnola, it was Titian's incomparable craftsmanship (particularly his manipulation of colour and light) that set apart his portraits and revolutionised the portrayal of the nude.

While Botticelli and Titian both glorified the Goddess of Love, the former idealised her while the latter aimed to demythologise her. Rather than being motivated by ardent philosophical beliefs and lofty intellectualism, as was Botticelli, it was the desire for aesthetic perfection that influenced Titian's paintings. Rather than allegorise the meaning of love (as did Botticelli), Titian called his contemporary portraits 'Venuses' to draw attention to their beauty. His paintings may have even represented marital bliss and procreation; in fact, throughout the Renaissance, the figure of Venus often adorned marriage chests which served as talismans for both brides and grooms in order to promote fertility.[8]

Due to the revival of Latin literature, Titian painted Venus against a background of Roman, rather than Greek, mythology.

As a result Venus, like Mary, was idealised as the model of heavenly bliss and perfection – unlike Aphrodite, who was castigated for falling prey to her emotions. Titian's 'Venus and Adonis', for example, depicts a human, grief-stricken Venus pleading with a strong and commanding Adonis to stay with her; instead, the young lord willingly goes off to die in battle. Titian based his interpretation on Ovid's version of the myth (which attributes Adonis' death to impetuousness) rather than on Greek versions of the tale, which recount the young lord being murdered by a jealous Ares (Mars) blinded by his passion for Aphrodite. Because she was heroically revered by the Romans, it is understandable that Ovid, and hence Renaissance artists, render Venus blameless.

'Sacred and Profane Love' (1515)

While it may not have been Titian's original intention, his 'Sacred and Profane Love'* exemplifies perfectly the marriage of spiritual and physical love. This exquisite painting depicts two women, identical in form and colouring, who personify two separate but equal forms of love: the Sacred – represented by a fully clothed woman, and the Profane – symbolised by a semi-nude woman about to remove her velvet robe. Although these two figures seated at opposite ends of a fountain are not necessarily Venus *per se*, they are nevertheless symbolic of the heavenly love and sexual passion which the Goddess evokes. To emphasise this point, Titian surrounds the two women with mythological symbols of passion: Cupid hovering over a fountain, 'profane love' holding a rose, and the myrtle tree – the plant Venus used as a shield when she first arose from the sea.

Although Venus was a most compelling and fascinating subject for many Italian Renaissance artists, the renditions of Botticelli and Titian, in particular, not only depict the 'two' Aphrodites but personify the Venus-ruled zodiacal signs, Taurus and Libra. Whereas the qualities of the fertile sign of Taurus are easily embodied by Titian's sensual, earthy Venuses (Plato's Pandemos),

---

*It is important to note that the title 'Sacred and Profane Love' was first applied to the painting during the seventeenth century.

the attributes of the idealistic sign of Libra are identifiable in Botticelli's celestial Venuses (Plato's Urania). Considering the fact that he did not set out to personify the zodiac, Titian none the less captures the raw sensuality, materialism, luxuriousness and placidity of Taurus, while Botticelli focuses on the delicacy, beauty, perfection, tranquillity and ethereal qualities inherent in the sign of Libra. While Botticelli's portrayal of Venus was based on his knowledge of mythology and astrology, there is no evidence that Titian was ever schooled in the art of star-gazing.

Although Italy's influence waned, its cultural legacy endured as the Humanism of the Italian Renaissance spread to sixteenth-century Germany, Scandinavia and the Low Countries where art, literature, philosophy and even astrology were taught at these nations' universities. While the Protestant Reformation (1519) that swept through northern and western Europe no longer elevated the Virgin Mother and other female saints (their worship being deemed 'flagrantly excessive'), Venus none the less remained an oft-portrayed mythological subject.

Botticelli's ethereal images stimulated a series of highly stylised 'Venuses' by the German painter, Lucas Cranach the Elder (1472-1553). Displaying a graceful, slender body and delicate facial features, Cranach's erotic and often sophisticated portrayals of the Goddess – set against pastoral landscapes – are almost interchangeable with his portraits of Eve in the Garden of Eden, due in part to their association with sexual temptation. While Venus embodies what is desirable and acceptable in the flesh, Eve represents what is desirous and dangerous in the flesh.[9]

While Botticelli influenced the stylised figures of Cranach, Titian's acknowledgement of full-bodied sensuality paved the way for painters such as Rubens (1577-1640) and Renoir (1841-1919) – known for their erotic, favourable portrayals of well-developed women. In fact, 'the series of nudes produced by Renoir between 1885 and his death in 1919, one of the most satisfying tributes ever paid to Venus by a great artist, knits together all the threads in this long chapter. Praxiteles, Giorgione, Rubens and Ingres, different as they are from one another, would have recognised him as their successor.'[10]

PART 2
The Planet

THE ASTRONOMY OF VENUS

Rotation on its axis: 243 days
Orbital or sidereal period: 225 days
Synodic period: 584 days
Distance from sun: 67 million miles or ⅔ of the distance between the Sun and the Earth
NASA missions: Mariner, Pioneer and Magellan

While Venus is called the sister planet of the Earth due to their similarity in size and mass as well as their relative proximity, their differences are far more dramatic. Unlike the Earth, Venus has no Moon, very high surface temperature and no water in its atmosphere which consists of almost 95 per cent carbon dioxide as compared with less than 0.1 per cent carbon dioxide in the Earth's atmosphere. Its two main mountainous regions, or continents, were named after Aphrodite and Ishtar and its rocky surface consists of a series of active giant volcanoes. Because it reflects the light of the Sun, Venus is, next to the Sun and the Moon, the brightest object in the sky. While Venus often appears as a bright white light, photographs taken by NASA's Pioneer and Magellan missions at close range reveal that Venus creates an orange cast (see cover photo).

As stated in Chapter 3, it takes Venus approximately 225 days to orbit the Sun but the longer time of 584 days to go from superior to superior conjunction with the Sun (from a geocentric framework). Superior conjunction with the Sun occurs when Venus is farthest from the Earth and the Sun lies directly between the Earth and Venus. Inferior conjunction occurs when Venus is closest to the Earth and lies directly between the Earth and the Sun (see Fig. 2.1, page 56). Although each conjunction occurs at different zodiacal positions, it takes five synodic periods or, eight years, for the Sun-Venus conjunction to return to approximately the same zodiacal sign and degree. This caused the Mesopotamians to liken Venus' journey through the sky to a five-pointed star, or pentagram (see Chapter 10).

Retrogradation – the process by which Venus (or any planet) appears to slow up and move backwards as seen from the Earth – occurs for a period of 41-42 days with inferior conjunction to the Sun occurring midway through the cycle. After inferior conjunction, Venus emerges as the Morning Star in the East until it reaches superior conjunction when the planet's view is obliterated by the Sun for up to two months depending on the particular season. After superior conjunction, Venus then emerges as the Evening Star in the West and begins its journey towards retrogradation and inferior conjunction once again. Venus' last setting before and first appearance as Morning or Evening Star after conjunction are known as the planet's heliacal settings and risings. While the Babylonians noted that periods following heliacal risings were marked by periods of hostility and abundant harvests, Mesoamericans also noted that political upheavals occurred during those same times. Astrologer Bruce Scofield has observed that heliacal risings often signal air disasters as well as the decline of a political leader and his policies.

5

THE PLANET AS SYMBOL

♀ Venus

Rules: Taurus and Libra
Exalted: Pisces
Fall: Virgo
Detriment: Aries and Scorpio
Keywords: love, beauty, aesthetics, prosperity, fertility, abundance

Body Parts: skin, kidneys, throat, eyes
Gems: emerald, diamond, lapis lazuli
Professions: therapists, mediators, salespeople, politicians, show business personalities, models, cosmeticians, bankers, financial planners

In the preceding chapters I have attempted to correlate the changing face of the fertility Goddess with the evolution of Venus as a planetary symbol. Because the Mesopotamians (the earliest known astrological practitioners) worshipped the Morning and Evening Star as an omen of peace, hostility and agricultural cycles, Inanna/Ishtar, the Goddess of Love, War and Fertility, was viewed in the same manner. During Babylonia's occupation by the Persians and, ultimately, the Greeks (to whom the fate of the individual was paramount), the prominence of mundane forecasting was replaced by a person-orientated system which charted the lives of individuals – most notably the ruling family whose fate represented that of the nation and its people.

Although the Babylonians constructed the earliest natal (birth) charts, the Greeks furthered the art of interpretation and prediction resulting in the widespread utilisation of individual horoscopes among noblemen and commoners alike. A fusion of Egyptian, Mesopotamian and Greek principles converged in

Ptolemy's *Tetrabiblos* – which, through Latin and Arabic translations, became the standard guide for horoscopic delineations throughout Greece, Rome and the Islamic world. Moreover, its influence on Hindu (Vedic) astrology is evident from classical Indian scriptures, whose descriptions of the planets, signs and houses are, at times, almost interchangeable with those of *Tetrabiblos*.

Following the suppression of Western astrological writings during the dogmatic and repressive Dark and Middle Ages, the Renaissance ushered in a new era marked by the rediscovery of Greek and Roman classical texts and artefacts. Not only was the visual image of Aphrodite/Venus the most commonly reproduced mythological figure, but Ptolemy's standard work was once again taught throughout European universities. This text, coupled with Islamic writings which filtered to the West after the breakup of the Byzantine Era, influenced the development of Renaissance astrological thought and served as the model for modern horoscopic delineations which, in some cases, have not strayed far from Hellenistic descriptions.

As perceived by most contemporary astrologers, the planet Venus – which alongside the Moon represented the Mother, or feminine, principle – was painted as a symbol of love, charm, beauty, fertility and creativity. While this definition mirrored the attributes of Aphrodite, the Greek Goddess of Love and Beauty, it unfortunately omitted the victoriousness, power and often belligerent qualities associated with the long-forgotten pre-Grecian fertility Goddesses whose artefacts and legends were recovered and translated during the nineteenth century.*

By tracing the lineage of the Goddess Venus – from the Paleolithic Era to the present – through her visual images, literary portrayals and complex rituals, I have endeavoured to capture the complete range of qualities and depth of emotion evoked by the Goddess/planet. If successful, this exploration will deem it impossible to envision Venus as the paragon of love, sexuality and

---

* Although it is unclear where the Venus symbol actually originated, the consensus is that it is a representation of Aphrodite's hand mirror.

beauty without equally viewing her as the harbinger of fruitfulness, prosperity and personal strength.

While the mention of Venus has always conjured up an image of two passionate lovers (herself and Ares) ensnared within the chains of deceit, the Goddess should also invoke pictures of a regal and benevolent Inanna locked in an erotic embrace with her husband, Dumuzi. Because the definition of the horoscopic Venus has always reflected how the Goddess and, thus, women are revered in a particular culture, it is vital to reinterpret the planet as an eclectic, multi-dimensional symbol to reflect the rich, complex condition of modern women.

The recent resurgence of interest in matriarchal societies and their worship of the fertility Goddess perfectly complements women's tireless efforts over the last 25 years to regain the respect and strength they were once afforded as leaders, workers, lovers and mothers. In her groundbreaking book, *Goddesses in Everywoman*, Jean Shinoda Bolen, the well-known Jungian analyst, has successfully correlated a woman's multi-levelled personality with feminine archetypes as personified by the Olympian Goddesses – Artemis, Athena, Hestia, Hera, Demeter, Persephone and Aphrodite.

> The Aphrodite archetype governs women's enjoyment of love and beauty, sexuality and sensuality. The realm of the lover exerts a powerful pull on many women; as a force with a woman's personality, Aphrodite can be as demanding as Hera and Demeter. Aphrodite impels women to fulfil both creative and procreative functions.[1]

But while Bolen declares that Aphrodite represents the urge to reproduce, she contends that it is only 'because of a desire for a man or her desire for the sexual or the romantic experience'.[2] The unselfish, maternal longing for children, according to Bolen, is still undeniably the domain of Demeter, Greek Goddess of Agriculture. Although Bolen's book certainly provides women with a range of roles and experiences, the qualities of Aphrodite's predecessors (Inanna–Astarte) must also be incorporated into any explanation of the archetype. Until these early Fertility

Goddesses are, in fact, assimilated into the paradigmatic model of Venus, the artistic, psychological and astrological symbol will continue to evoke images of love, beauty and sexuality, failing to add fertility, productivity, strength and economic prosperity to her roster of attributes.

Viewing Aphrodite/Venus as the archetype of a 'new' and powerful woman can be traced to Hesiod's myth recounting how Chronos (Saturn) castrated Ouranos (Uranus) and ejected his genitals into the sea (Neptune). Out of the foam emerged the beautiful Aphrodite, whose role as a powerful procreative deity was affirmed by the grass which immediately sprung up under her feet. Just as the confrontation between Ouranos/Uranus, the Sky God, and Poseidon/Neptune, the Sea God, resulted in the emergence of the powerful fertility Goddess, the 1993 Uranus/Neptune conjunction, a planetary combination occurring only every 171-2 years, signified the advent of an era in which women are to be recognised, once again, for their magnanimity and procreative strength.* Furthermore, the myth indicates that violence and chaos (symbolised by the act of castration) can be transcended through compassion and understanding (symbolised by the woman who is washed ashore).

It is quite appropriate that during the 1993 Uranus/Neptune conjunction, Bill Clinton, whose horoscope is Venus-dominated, should be elected President of the United States, and that his wife Hillary, known for her toughness and compassion, should set a new precedent by combining traditional First Lady functions with her role as policy administrator. (The conjunction may also indicate that the recognition of women's nurturing, powerful qualities may be our only hope for a co-operative, peaceful and productive future.)

Translated into a horoscopic symbol, Venus represents the self-

---

*The association of this conjunction with the birth of Aphrodite was derived from various discussions with astrologer Edith Hathaway. It seems quite fitting that a book reassessing Venus as a planetary symbol should be finished during the same year as the Uranus/Neptune conjunction (1993). Interestingly, the first women's university (Troy Female Seminary) was founded in the United States in 1821, coinciding with the last Uranus/Neptune conjunction.

esteem and empowerment (or lack thereof) that directly affects the individual's capacity to form creative, loving and compassionate relationships with family, friends, colleagues or lovers. Because Inanna (Venus) was the sister of the Sun God, the astrological Venus defines how we apply love, beauty, creativity and procreative strength first to ourselves (the Sun) and, ultimately, to others (Venus). Although the astrological Moon has always represented emotional nourishment, it is actually Venus that epitomises reproduction not merely as a sexual act but as the ultimate form of creativity – the birthing and nurturing of a life from conception to adulthood. Consequently, the contentment and empowerment garnered from the fruition of a creative project – whether it be child-rearing, a successful marriage, decorating a house or planting a vegetable garden – is also signified by the horoscopic Venus. This is evidenced by the fact that while Inanna was portrayed as an Earth Mother who bestowed fruitfulness and wealth upon her subjects, while Dumuzi was described as her son/lover, she was never portrayed with children. Aphrodite, who was not primarily portrayed as a maternal figure, did, in fact, have many children by various Gods. Rather than use this information to illuminate Aphrodite's fecundity and adoration as a regional fertility deity, the Greek poets, with whom we are most familiar, utilised it to emphasise her promiscuity.

To this end, a positively placed Venus in a horoscope indicates that the individual's capacity for self-love (affected by the adulation, admiration and/or sexual validation of others) allows him or her to give and take love freely. Moreover, a harmonious Venus signifies the creative desire and empowerment attained from the respect and support of friends, family and colleagues which inevitably leads to sustained productivity and prosperity. On the other hand, an inharmonious Venus precipitates low self-esteem and an inability to commit to long-term personal and professional relationships or to sustain creative projects. Once the struggle for self-acceptance is achieved, however, these individuals can experience the planet's full impact.

These characteristics are especially apparent when Venus is dominant or, as they say in the East, in a position of strength in the horoscope. As opposed to a system like the Hindu (Vedic)

'Shad Bala', which assigns a numerical rating to determine planetary strength and weakness, there are a variety of methods employed to ascertain whether a planet (in this case, Venus) is emphatic in a Western birth chart:

1. Taurus as the Sun, Moon or ascending sign
2. Libra as the Sun, Moon or ascending sign
3. Venus conjunct one of the four angles (the ascendant, immum coeli (i.c.), descendant or midheaven)*
4. Venus in aspect to four or more planets
5. Stellium** in Taurus, Libra, the second house or seventh house.

If the planet is dominant in a horoscope, it must then be assessed whether that manifestation is primarily beneficial or detrimental. Oftentimes an overpowering Venus, though well aspected, may overemphasise an individual's hedonistic tendencies, focusing on the need for instant gratification or constant admiration and validation from others. To this end, a dominant Venus may be just as detrimental as an underemphasised or difficultly aspected planet.

In assessing the role of Venus in a particular horoscope it is also noteworthy to take into account whether Venus is manifesting as the aggressive Morning Star or the tranquil Evening Star. When Venus appears as the Morning Star, it can be seen in the horoscope clockwise from the Sun, indicating that it rises and sets first. By the same token, when Venus emerges as the Evening Star, it is viewed in the anti-clockwise position from the Sun, signifying that it rises and sets later. Although the effects are subtle, an analysis of Venus as a planetary symbol will usually reveal that if it appears in the horoscope as the Morning Star it is more likely to convey her jealous, possessive aspects as well as the proud, victorious qualities that, for the most part, have been omitted from

---

* For more information about the angular Venus in the birth chart, one is referred to 'The New Astrology' by Ken Irving in *American Astrology*, August, 1992.

**A *stellium* is defined as four or more planets occupying the same sign and/or house.

traditional horoscopic interpretations. The Evening Star, on the other hand, signifies the more passive, peaceful and loving Venus noted for her sensuality, beauty and facility for co-operation and harmony (for an example of Venus as Morning Star, see Gloria Steinem's horoscope, Fig. 6.2, and for Venus as Evening Star, see Bill Clinton's horoscope, Fig. 6.1, page 135).*

Dual Rulership

Prior to the discovery of Uranus (1781), Neptune (1848) and Pluto (1930), each planet – except for the Sun and the Moon – governed two zodiacal signs:

- Sun – Leo
- Moon – Cancer
- Mercury – Gemini and Virgo
- Venus – Taurus and Libra
- Mars – Aries and Scorpio
- Jupiter – Sagittarius and Pisces
- Saturn – Capricorn and Aquarius

The discovery of Uranus, Neptune and Pluto, however, led to their assignment as planetary rulers of Aquarius, Pisces and Scorpio, respectively. While Saturn, Jupiter and Mars still retain co-rulership of these three zodiacal signs, the trans-Saturnian planets undoubtedly evoke an entirely new dimension of Aquarius, Pisces and Scorpio nonexistent in the ancient world.** But while numerous asteroids (Chiron, Persephone, Demeter, etc.) have proven significant in the individual horoscope, two new planets which would relieve Mercury and Venus of their dual rulership have not yet surfaced, though scientists are convinced that additional planets lie beyond the orbit of Pluto.

*For a detailed description of these two personality types, one is referred to *An Astrological Study of Psychological Complexes* by Dane Rudhyar.
** The astrological examples frequently cited are the fields of psychology and nuclear science, which come under the domain of Pluto and which emerged during the twentieth century concurrent with the planet's discovery by Percival Lowell.

Although Venus' rulership of Taurus has never been disputed, it has none the less caused a great deal of consternation among those astrologers who are desirous of allocating one planet per sign and who therefore reject Venus' rulership of Taurus in favour of Vulcan – an undiscovered planet named for the Roman God of Metallurgy (the Greek Hephaistos). (Still other astrologers believe that Vulcan is perfectly suited to govern Virgo. Interestingly enough, Manilius, the Roman astrologer, assigned Vulcan as ruler of Libra.)

It was this astrological debate which, in part, prompted the need to reaffirm the multi-faceted nature of Venus epitomised by its dual rulership of Taurus and Libra. Whereas earthy Taurus – reminiscent of the pre-Grecian Fertility Goddesses – highlights fruitfulness, productivity, wealth and sensuality, ethereal Libra – perfectly exemplified by Aphrodite – accentuates the ability to love, create, harmonise and socialise. The descriptions of Taurus and Libra in Chapter 6 will hopefully provide an in-depth understanding of the multi-dimensional Venus and its manifestation in the natal horoscope.*

---

*Note: While these characteristics can also be applied to mundane, electional and horary charts, the focus of this particular volume will be geared to natal astrology – the astrology of the individual.

6

TAURUS AND LIBRA

♉ Taurus

Taurus, or To Have, To Hold and – Not Always Let Go

> Hanging-jowled bovine,
> savoring goodies, munching cuds,
> sniffing the flowers:
> inalterable budgelessness,
> all gorged with sensuous delights.
>
> Ken Negus

Ruling Planet: Venus
Exalted Planet: Moon
Fallen Planet: Pluto
Detrimental Planet: Mars
Element: Earth
Modality: Fixed
Sign Keywords: perseverance, stubbornness, sensuality, conventionality (habit-forming nature), gentility, jealousy, materialism (material security), possessiveness, sexuality, indulgence

House Keywords: finances, attainment of wealth, resources, talents, skills, assets, speech
Body Parts: throat, neck, thyroid gland, eyes, skin
Gems: diamond, emerald*, lapis lazuli
Professions: the creative arts (especially singing [throat], sculpture [form] and music), economics (banking, accounting, etc.), agriculture, commerce and collecting

To examine the influence of Taurus as it relates to both the second sign of the zodiac and the corresponding second house, it is beneficial to review briefly the symbolism of the Taurean Epoch

---

*Diamonds and emeralds are the birthstones for April and May, respectively, the two months that encompass Taurus (20 April–21 May).

(4000–2000 BC).* Like the Age of Aries (2000 BC–0 AD), the Age of Pisces (0–2000 AD) and the forthcoming Age of Aquarius (2000–4000 AD), the Taurean Epoch was marked by corresponding 'archetypal images and motifs projected collectively in myth and symbol' – that is, sacrificial bulls and rams during the Ages of Taurus and Aries respectively. Because there is no apparent causal reason why an agricultural era should be accompanied by the Sun's journey through the constellation of Taurus,** or why a militaristic era should be marked by the Sun traversing the constellation of Aries, the appearance of these archetypal themes in their corresponding Eras is best attributed to synchronicity – Jung's term for a series of 'acausal coincidences which take place simultaneously within the psyche and outwardly in the world'.[1] (Jung has also credited synchronicity, rather than causality, with the validity of astrology – the occurrence of planetary patterns in conjunction with particular events.)

Although synchronicity is one explanation for the occurrence of astrological phenomena, it should not to be confused with the fact that various agrarian cultures associated fertility deities with the planet Venus due to its observed effect on planting cycles.[2]

The Taurean Era (which encompassed the Bronze Age) was marked by the flowering of Goddess-worshipping, matrifocal agrarian communities (such as those of Crete, Egypt and Sumer) whose productivity, prosperity, self-sufficiency and creative ingeniousness are characteristic of both the sign of Taurus and the fertility deities that dominated the Epoch. While Taurean qualities of perseverance, craftsmanship, precision and planning are particularly apparent in the innovative and lasting accomplishments of these civilisations – Sumerian gem-cutting, the Egyptian pyramids – the Taurean insularity, stubbornness and resistance to change were also reflected by the decline of the Epoch's dynasties. The complacency of these self-sufficient agricultural societies and their denial that the threat of invasion was imminent paved the way for Arian civilisations (that is, those

*These figures are rounded-off approximations. In actuality, each planetary epoch encompasses about 2,150 years.
**The actual physical constellation of fixed stars must be distinguished from the zodiacal sign of the same name.

of Babylonia, Persia, Greece and, ultimately Rome), each more powerful than the last, systematically to destroy them.

Because the agrarian Fertility Goddess, the embodiment of the Morning and Evening Star, dominated the epoch, Taurus, the second sign of the zodiac and its ruling planet Venus represented (and continues to represent) fecundity, productivity and victory as well as the more obvious love and creativity. On the negative side, however, personality traits associated with this sign include jealousy, possessiveness, indulgence and belligerence – the latter quality inherited from the martial Inanna, Ishtar and Anath, who led the battle-cries of their peoples.

Because Taureans are consumed with building and sustaining a self-contained environment where they can closely monitor or control the course of their lives, the speed of the outside world often outstrips the slow but steady pace with which the Taurean personality* feels comfortable.

The most stubborn, possessive and often inflexible sign of the zodiac, Taurus is quite content to proceed at its pace. Unless Taureans are self-employed or entrepreneurial, they prefer to work for an organisation in which they can perform their duties in a relatively autonomous manner. Since they are not born leaders, it is vital for these individuals to learn to delegate responsibility. Their inability to trust others leads to an overdeveloped sense of duty and responsibility and a tendency to 'bite off more than they can chew'. It is, in fact, the desire for certainty and predictability in their lives that fuels their most noteworthy character traits – attachment to the patterns and habits that yield increased creativity, productivity and/or profitability. Secure with their own methodology, they become resistant to change and find it extremely difficult to embrace new ideas or take advice – however sound. In fact, the only reasons a Taurean or second house personality will contemplate change are: 1) if it is practical and logical, and 2) by discovering it him-or herself. Although slow in making major transitions, once a

---

*The Taurean personality may be defined as having the Sun, Moon or Ascendant in Taurus or a concentration of planets in Taurus or the second house. By the same token, the Libran personality has the Sun, Moon or Ascendant in Libra or a concentration of planets in Libra or the seventh house.

decision has been made, Taureans never look back.

Like the fertility Goddess whose sexual passion ignited a bountiful and prosperous harvest, Taurean personalities are motivated by the need for physical pleasure, productivity and economic well-being, often going so far as to associate love with money. This often translates into a preoccupation with the acquisition of material assets or the accumulation of personal resources, talents and skills with which they hope to attain financial and emotional security by attracting a business partner or spouse with common goals. Unwilling to relinquish anything they may have earned or 'acquired', Taureans can become financial wizards, ruthless competitors or, on a personal level, possessive, jealous partners and overprotective, controlling parents.

Although an accentuated Taurus and/or second house endows an almost obsessive fixation on finances, this emphasis can just as easily incite constant money problems. Because financial success is the yardstick by which these people measure their own worth, individuals with afflicted planets in Taurus or the second house are more concerned with the image of success and the accumulation of wealth rather than the disciplined means by which they may attain it. Impatience coupled with the feeling they are being judged in terms of their earning capacity can lead them to borrow or go into debt in order to give the illusion that they have reached their goals. It is important for those who are prone to indulgent spending to focus on the patience, persistence and financial planning that Taurus and the second house are capable of achieving. On another level, afflicted Taurean or second house planets may give low self-worth leading to the feeling that they do not deserve success or wealth.

Classified as a fixed, earth sign, Taurus' affinity with nature translates not merely into a desire to live in a rural environment (though this is certainly indicative of the Taurus) but represents a dependable approach to life enhanced by the enjoyment of physical pleasure. Best suited to working in areas where calculated courses of action generate predictable results, Taureans are drawn to any line of work that provides economic security and fits neatly within the practical scope of their everyday lives. If they are artists, for example, they may excel in portraiture or landscapes rather than abstract drawings for which their ideas must emanate from their imagination. Professions with which there is an affinity include singing (throat), sculpture (form), classical music, economics, agriculture, commerce, construction or art collecting.

Coarse when compared to the more refined Libran, the Taurean personality, though often too brusque and forthcoming, can never be accused of being dishonest or formulating opinions to suit particular situations. Like the Goddess who was alternately loved and feared for her power, Taureans are benevolent, creative, loving and extremely sensual. Though stubborn and wilful in their determination to express themselves, they are extremely balanced and completely reliable so long as they are respected for their lifestyle choices and can remain autonomous. Generous to a fault, they can be unforgiving – even vengeful – should they feel betrayed, manipulated, taken advantage of or have their freedom and/or authority challenged – like the wrathful Goddess who banned Dumuzi when he countermanded her authority.

While Taureans are noted for their coolness, gentility, smooth features and stately charm, outward vanity often conceals an insecurity which can culminate in an obsessive need to be fawned upon for their beauty and desired for their sexuality. The corpulent yet erotic images of Venus portrayed by Titian, Rubens and Renoir embody the carnal yet desirable Taurean whose need to possess may, at times, dominate the timbre of his or her relationship towards work, friends, family, spouses and even the body. While their purely excessive and sensual nature can extend to hedonism and a craving for satiation in the form of overeating, promiscuity and overspending, these tendencies come to the fore only if Taureans feel neglected or unfulfilled. When feeling inadequate or confronted with what seems to be an insurmountable obstacle, rather than 'taking the bull by the horns' (which should come easily to Taureans), they may indulge in excessive behaviour patterns or neglect their finances, possessions and/or appearance. As inflexible creatures of habit, they often sink into depressions from which they do not easily arise. As with any situation or relationship, however, when they move to the next plateau, they do so without a backward glance.

Extremely practical concerning their finances, the temptation to overspend is ever-present, and even the most disciplined Taureans must constantly fight the tendency towards extravagance – often a lifelong struggle. Due to the Taurean and second house affiliation with money, sexuality and appearance, indulgent behaviour may be expressed in terms of overspending, borrowing, gambling, overeating or promiscuity. It would be extremely helpful to Taureans, who rely on their possessions for self-definition, to practise a philosophy of non-attachment similar to Zen Buddhism, to dissociate themselves from materialism and identify with their inner strength and beauty. When serenity and clarity of purpose are attained, the balance and harmony which Venus so relentlessly seeks can be achieved.

It is interesting to note that, according to Hindu (Vedic) astrology, the second house, in addition to signifying money, assets, talents and skills, is indicative of early education. While this definition may at first glance seem far off the beaten track, it does not really stray from the Western astrological delineation of the second house, since our early schooling shapes our learning habits – second house concerns. The talents and skills developed in the formative years are quite frequently the ones that enable us to fulfil our goals. To this same end, if planets ruling or occupying the second house are well placed, there is an ability to listen, concentrate, acquire and perfect the tools one needs in order to succeed. Because the Hindu (Vedic) second house also rules the eyes, afflicted planets ruling or occupying the second house may cause a lack of concentration, an inability to listen, nearsightedness and, at its most extreme, learning disabilities and dyslexia.

Libra

Libra, Relating or Sharing in the Aquarian Age

> On silvery chains
> a perfect balance of the
> golden weighing pans
> shows occasionally a wave
> of thoughtful uncertainty.
> Ken Negus

Ruling Planet: Venus
Fallen Planet: Sun
Detrimental Planet: Mars
Element: Air
Modality: Cardinal
Sign Keywords: relationships, harmony, poise, partnership, diplomacy, co-operation, aloofness, dishonesty, manipulativeness
House Keywords: marriage, partnerships, co-operation, open enemies, contracts

Exalted Planet: Saturn
Body Parts: diaphragm, kidneys, adrenal glands, abdomen, skin
Gems: sapphire, opal
Professions: counselling, therapy, social work, mediation, the creative arts; receptionist, personnel, public relations, advertising, politics, cosmetics – anything involving glamour and the creation of an image

Just as mythographers overlooked Aphrodite's heritage as an earth and sea deity by designating her the Goddess of Love and Beauty, so traditional astrologers, also unaware of the planet's original embodiment as the agrarian Fertility Goddess, have labelled the horoscopic Venus the symbol of love, sex and relationships. Because of this affiliation, the planet Venus has always been readily acknowledged as the ruler of Libra – a sign that evokes the tranquillity, harmony and angelic beauty of Botticelli's Venus. It is, in fact, these enduring Renaissance images of the Goddess which have not only influenced modern likenesses but have helped reinforce the belief among many astrologers that Libra is the 'true' domain of Venus, even though the uncovering of Neolithic and Bronze Age relics prove that Taurus is just as suitable a ruler.

Because the Libran Epoch, marked by the Sun's traverse through the constellation of the same name, occurred approximately 14,000–12,000 BC, the era's patterns and motifs still remain untraceable and, therefore, unidentifiable. Unable to derive the sign's symbolism from its planetary epoch, Libra's definition as a sign of harmony, justice and tranquillity has been garnered primarily from the constellation's literal meaning and identifying symbol – the balancing scales. It is also significant that the autumn equinox, when day and night are of equal length, not only commences the Sun's yearly passage through the sign (23

September–24 October) but was the time of year when the Sacred Marriage Rites were celebrated and the fertility Goddess, an incarnation of the planet Venus, was honoured for inaugurating the harvest and boosting the economy.

Classified as a cardinal, air sign, Libra is the only zodiacal sign represented by an inanimate object – a fact often noted in many astrological texts. The fact that the symbol is neither human nor animal motivated by the will to survive provides a clarity of vision, objectivity and reasoning not accessible in the remaining zodiacal signs.

Projecting aloofness, outward calm and sociability, Librans, like Venus-ruled Taureans, are also concerned with harmony, creativity, sensuality and relationships. Unlike Taureans and the agrarian fertility Goddess whose need for sexual fulfilment, control and loyalty invoked her procreative powers, Librans and seventh house personalities, like the Roman Venus who led Aeneas to victory, are gifted with the capacity for co-operation, mediation, diplomacy and, most important, the intrinsic awareness that sharing adds to, rather than detracts from, their strength. In fact, their purpose in life is not, like Taureans, to maintain control but, instead, to delegate responsibility and lessen the burden of the decision-making process. Librans' innate recognition that 'two heads are better than one' never interferes with but instead enhances their facility for understanding diverse viewpoints, being empathetic and pleasing others which, in turn, elevates their self-esteem.

While the sign of Libra perfectly corresponds to Plato's Aphrodite Urania, the symbol of spiritual or platonic love, I do not subscribe to the philosopher's contention that the respect and love which results from 'the marriage of two minds' can only occur between men. I do agree, however, that the Libran or seventh house personality places as much value on this type of mutual love and respect as Taureans place on passion. If the partner cannot provide both sexual and intellectual stimulation, the Libran or seventh house personality will seek mental communication through a colleague or friend.

With a strong Libran emphasis in his horoscope, Bill Clinton*

---

*Due to President Clinton's overwhelming Venusian emphasis, his horoscope will be used as an example throughout these latter sections of this book.

Taurus and Libra

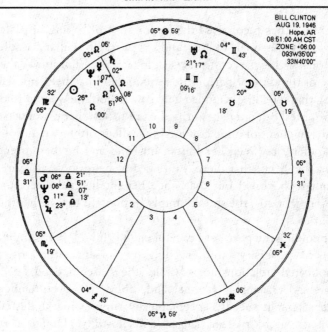

Figure 6.1: Bill Clinton's horoscope.

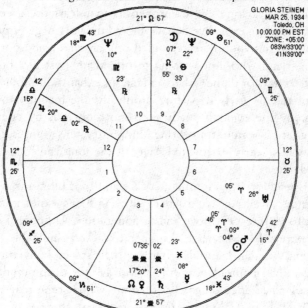

Figure 6.2: Gloria Steinem's horoscope.

(Figure 6.1) has recognised the importance of having his wife as his closest personal advisor and, as a result, Hillary Rodham Clinton is a vital part of his success. In fact, Mr Clinton was always aware of the type of partner he required and has been quoted as saying that when he attended Yale Law School he wanted to date the brightest but not necessarily the prettiest student. Conversely, a Taurean client of mine confided that she is often envious of the camaraderie between her Libran husband and his best friend. I have assured her that there is no need to be jealous (as Taureans are apt to become) but that since her intellectual interests are different than his, she should simply be content that he has found an outlet.

Upholding the need for peaceful equilibrium, Librans shun any form of adversity, thus evading unpleasant situations and complicated relationships. While they are, indeed, gentle, courteous, charming, rational and, above all, even-tempered, Librans remain socially acceptable by suppressing 'undesirable' emotions such as fear, anger and hostility. Under certain circumstances and stressful situations, however, Librans – reticent and polite for so long – have a propensity to unleash these feelings, thereby fuelling explosive behaviour and the very negativity they had hoped to avoid. I am reminded of a charming and outgoing Libran friend who, not wishing to offend his host and hostess, agreed to stay for dinner when, in fact, his exhaustion should have precipitated an early departure. Ironically, the inability to relax and enjoy the evening (made even more obvious by continual glances at his watch) transformed him into a tense, unresponsive guest whose early exit would have, in the long run, been more considerate.

This reaction is symptomatic of a significant Libran trait – the tendency to act in accordance with another's expectations in order to gain respect, love and/or admiration. Although Librans are extremely impartial, co-operative and amicable, they frequently remain neutral by stifling their strong convictions or masterfully manipulating their words to accommodate a particular audience or given situation. While some may regard this as dishonest, Librans do not feel that there is anything particularly wrong with appeasing others by telling them what they wish to hear, or withholding information which might precipitate discord.

Although it may appear contradictory for a sign so prone to the formation of relationships to be viewed as somewhat detached, it must be remembered that airy Librans are neither motivated by passion nor their emotions. Whereas earthy Taureans and second house individuals garner self-assurance and comfort from financial security, material possessions and physical appearance, Librans and seventh house people revel in companionship, the world of ideas, image and approval from others. Due to an innate feeling that they are always being judged and evaluated, Librans, like all Venusian types, are extremely concerned with what others think about their appearance, manners and opinions. While co-operation, empathy and the ability to understand the viewpoints of others are virtues, they must develop more reliance on their own opinions rather than forever asking for advice.

Like Venus-ruled Taureans, Librans are prone towards laziness, extravagance, excess and indulgence. Priding themselves on a love of refinement, artistry and aesthetic harmony, these eclectic, cultured and *bon vivant* Librans derive as much pleasure from a heated political discussion or an exhilarating performance as Taureans do from walking in the countryside, eating a good meal or making passionate love. Because their detached yet engaging manner attracts, humours and comforts, Librans often become successful counsellors, therapists, mediators, salespeople and public relations specialists. Concerned with their public images, they are often drawn to politics, show business or other fields where glamorous façades do not necessarily reflect the private individual.

While the 'scales of justice' imply that Librans make excellent litigators, I have not found this to be the case. Usually ethical and fair, they are best suited to public interest, contractual or constitutional law, or any type of law where they can apply their keen intellect, powers of persuasion, mediation and counselling skills. Martian or Jupiterian individuals are more likely to welcome the opportunity to vent aggression and hostility in the courtroom arena.

Due to the Libran penchant for viewing the world through the eyes of others, it is no wonder that the seventh house (whose cusp is the descendant) represents marriage and partnerships (personal and professional), contracts and disputes. Furthermore, an accentuated Venus or preponderance of planets in Libra/the seventh house endows a charm and social awareness which attracts partners, followers, admirers and friends who may help Librans attain their goals – easier achieved with a partner than alone.

Although they usually have a wide circle of friends and acquaintances, Librans prefer relating on a one-to-one basis (with friends, colleagues or partners) rather than in a group where they tend to be overpowered. While their external Venusian placidity and the ease with which they relate may give the impression of stability, Librans are, actually, often plagued with self-doubt. They rely on the reassurance and steadfastness of a professional and/or personal partner. To preserve their relationships, jealous, insecure and indulgent Librans may even resort to immoral or unethical acts of desperation such as emotional blackmail, manipulation, lies and deceit.

A prime example of the sign's insecurities is a client of mine – a therapist with four Libran planets in the third house (an air house) who was completely obsessed with a man she had been involved with for 10 years until he finally married someone else. His insensitive behaviour unleashed such jealousy and uncontrollable rage that, like the rejected Goddess, she resorted to humiliating and threatening her ex-lover and his new wife, thus obliterating her Libran sense of fairness, honesty, gentility and diplomacy – qualities which make her an excellent counsellor.

It is vital that Librans strengthen their self-esteem to preclude total reliance on a partner for their sense of purpose and feelings of self-worth. Once they do become more self-reliant and fulfilled, the possibilities for an interdependent relationship replete with 'true' sharing, exhilaration and complete freedom will begin to emerge.

7

VENUS THROUGH THE SIGNS

In this chapter and the one that follows, I attempt to define the behaviour of Venus as a symbol of self-worth, love, abundance and prosperity when placed in a particular sign and house. Although the characteristics of the zodiacal signs are similar to their corresponding numerical houses (that is, Aries/first house, Taurus/second house, Gemini/third house, etc.), there are none the less subtle distinctions. While the sign of the zodiac that Venus occupies describes *how* one loves and values the self and, ultimately, others, the house inhabited or ruled by the planet reveals *where* (that is, in which area of life) one can best experience creativity, love and prosperity. Consequently, the placement of Venus in its corresponding sign and house will, in some instances, render the same results; at other times the outcomes will be completely different.

It may be beneficial to envision the planet as the Goddess herself in order to understand how the position of Venus in a zodiacal sign and house can affect someone's self-esteem and therefore the ability to express love, form relationships, initiate creative enterprises and accumulate wealth. By ascertaining if the planetary symbol is exemplary of the earthy, Taurean Venus (reminiscent of Inanna) or the ethereal, Libran Venus (exemplified by Aphrodite), one can surmise how the Goddess and, therefore, the planet may have behaved had she forayed into a particular region represented by the zodiacal sign and/or house.

Whether the position helps or hinders Venus (by empowering or denying self-esteem) is further determined by planetary aspects, midpoints and a range of other astrological interpretive devices. If Venus is positively situated, the attributes of the sign and house it occupies and/or rules will enhance self-esteem and, consequently, relationships; if Venus is afflicted, the individual will search for these qualities – which are less accessible to them – in others. The timing and description of the circumstances by which the particular issues affecting Venus are activated are then determined by planetary cycles such as transits, progressions and solar returns.

I have ascertained the following delineations by observing the manifestations of Venus in the horoscopes of innumerable clients, students, family members and friends as well as notable personalities. Although each segment describes a wide range of possibilities relating to each position, it is the skilled and intuitive astrologer who must ultimately synthesise each astrological factor affecting Venus before concluding which facets of the definition apply to a particular individual. Above all, it is important to remember that these definitions are general and will always be modified by other indications in the horoscope.

Venus in the Signs

Due to the multi-dimensional nature of Venus as ruler of both Taurus and Libra, it may be helpful initially to categorise the planet according to the element of the sign and house in which it is placed.* In general, Venus in fire signs and houses desires passion, admiration and respect; Venus in earth signs and houses yearns for material security and loyalty; Venus in air signs and houses craves intellectual stimulation and mobility; and Venus in water signs and houses wishes to love and be loved. It can also be said that Venus in fire and earth signs may be likened to the Taurean Venus, while Venus in air and water signs mirrors the Libran Venus.

Fire and earth Venuses tend to be more assertive and self-centred concerning affairs of the heart. Like the earthy Taurean Venus, they are often motivated by passion, sexuality and success but have more difficulty recognising and, thus, adhering to the

---

*The signs and corresponding houses are categorised according to element as follows: *Fire*: Aries/first house, Leo/fifth house and Sagittarius/ninth house; *Earth*: Taurus/second house, Virgo/sixth house and Capricorn/tenth house; *Air*: Gemini/third house, Libra/seventh house and Aquarius/eleventh house; *Water*: Cancer/fourth house, Scorpio/eighth house and Pisces/twelfth house.

needs of others. Air and water Venuses are more relationship-orientated and understand the importance of sharing. They know instinctively that personal and professional achievements often require the love, support and co-operation of colleagues, friends and family. Like the cerebral, Libran Venus, these people are inspired by the need for love, partnership, harmony, creativity, friendship and intellectual exchange. While Venus in fire and earth signs may question 'what the relationship can do for me', Venus in water and air signs will ask 'what can I do for the relationship?'

VENUS IN ARIES (DETRIMENT)*

Keywords: passionate, headstrong, self-centred, independent

Because fruitful, harmonious and relationship-orientated Venus is inimical to self-willed, aggressive and impetuous Aries, the placement of Venus in the Mars-ruled first sign of the zodiac has traditionally been labelled 'detrimental', that is, in an environment that inhibits the planet's expression due to its antithetical nature. Symbolic of Aphrodite's ill-fated entanglement with Ares (Mars), God of War, this placement according to classical astrology was unable to nurture the planet's sweetness, beauty or diplomacy – qualities inherent in what was then considered the ideal woman. Although the Greeks certainly honoured Aphrodite's beauty, sensuality and fertility, they treated the independent, passionate, sexual and manipulative aspects of the Love Goddess with disdain.

While this position does not necessarily enhance Venus' soft-spoken and gentle side, it does foster passion, pride and assertiveness – traits regarded as heroic by the armies who cherished Inanna, Ishtar, Anath and the Roman Venus.

The combination of Venus in Mars-ruled Aries replicates the tempestuous, adulterous relationship between Aphrodite/Venus and Ares/Mars, whose recipe for love included unabashed

---

*Whereas the planet's fall position is the sign opposite its exaltation, the planet's detrimental position is always opposite the sign it rules. Because Venus is exalted in Pisces, it is fallen in Virgo. Since it rules Taurus and Libra, it is detrimental to Scorpio and Aries.

sexuality and narcissism. Because individuals with Venus in Aries demand approval, they tend to view love as a competition rather than as a team effort, too often asking 'what is the relationship doing for me?', the quintessential Venus in fire question, rather than 'what can I do for the relationship?' In actuality, these individuals are as vulnerable and insecure as they are impetuous, egocentric and childlike; though frequently chastised for demanding centre-stage, their 'performances' are, in fact, pleas for reassurance that they are attractive, creative and well-liked. If, however, recognition and admiration are not forthcoming, there is a tendency to seek 'a quick fix' via compulsive behaviour patterns ranging from extravagant spending to overeating and promiscuity – each of which supplies them with a sense of well-being, albeit temporary and false.*

Impatient and desirous of instant gratification, these individuals tend to lose interest in projects and romantic liaisons once the initial challenge is met and the excitement subsides. Because they lack the patience and foresight necessary to invest time and effort in projects that do not bring immediate results, they fall short on long-term financial planning. If, instead, they focus on their positive Venusian traits – finesse, patience, co-operation and diplomacy – they may learn that creative ventures and loving relationships require nurturing and the ability to overcome obstacles. While severing problematic relationships or discarding projects midstream may be the initial tendency for these easily frustrated folk, the true challenge lies in the ability to rejuvenate rather than destroy and start anew.

These passionate, highly sexed people often confuse love (Venus) with sex (Aries) and become infatuated with the excitement and sensual pleasure offered rather than with the person him- or herself. Unless they learn to distinguish between love and sex, they run the risk of consistently forming highly sexual, emotional, volatile and problematic relationships based purely on physical gratification which, more often than not, become completely self-destructive. In fact, according to Dr Susan Forward, author of *Men Who Hate Women and the Women Who*

---

*Venusian indulgences usually relate to a person's physical well-being (food), beauty (shopping) or prosperity (gambling).

Love Them, it is not uncommon for dynamic, accomplished women, like those with Venus in Aries,* to become involved with ambitious, egotistical men who offer excitement but are, in reality, threatened by the competition.[1] Once Venus in Aries people (both men and women) desist from linking self-worth with sexual attention, they will no longer require constant reassurance from self-serving romantic liaisons which provide a temporary sense of well-being.

While it has always been 'acceptable' for men with Venus in Aries to exhibit egocentric and often insensitive attitudes, this assertive placement is still stigmatic for women, who are frequently admonished for demonstrating those very same qualities. Even today, ambitious, forthright women are alternately feared and rebuked for initiating relationships, directing motion pictures, seeking political office or invading other traditionally male-dominated arenas which call for visibility, responsibility and leadership – attributes for which men are not only lauded but which they are acutally encouraged to possess.

Isadora Duncan (Venus in Aries in the first house), Elizabeth Taylor (Venus in Aries in the seventh house) and Marilyn Monroe** (Venus in Aries in the ninth house) are three women whose beauty, magnetism, innovation and sex appeal revolutionised their respective professions. Duncan, an independent spirit who transformed dance with her innovative free expression and sensual movements, was daring in her role as single parent to several children – the products of assorted lovers and failed marriages. She was even an early influence on Martha Graham, who is *usually* credited with founding modern dance. Taylor and Monroe, two of the most beautiful women ever to grace the silver screen, were idealised to such an extent that they could not distinguish between love and admiration, resulting in a string of unhappy, failed marriages. These larger-than-life, dynamic women could not place the needs of their partners above the self-gratification and excitement provided by fame.

*This also applies to women with Venus in Scorpio, the other detrimental position of Venus.

**Although there are many aspects of these celebrities' lives to which we are not privy, I am making an educated guess as to their motivations, behaviour patterns and personality traits based on an examination of their horoscopes and established facts about their lives.

Other well-known figures with Venus in Aries past and present include Michelangelo, Queen Victoria, Tchaikovsky, Harry Houdini, Mary Pickford, Lawrence Olivier, Henry Fonda, Fred Astaire, Rudolf Nureyev, Shirley Temple, Dane Rudhyar, Jeremy Thorpe, Jayne Mansfield, Edward Kennedy and Liza Minelli.

VENUS IN TAURUS (RULERSHIP)

Keywords: possessive, determined, jealous, materially secure, practical in love

The comfortable and beneficent position of Venus in its own sign of Taurus brings out the attributes that align the planet with the great agrarian fertility Goddess. According to Sumerian legend, it was only when Inanna derived sexual pleasure and loyalty from Dumuzi, the Vegetable Lord, that she was capable of watering the earth – thereby providing a surplus of grain from which the Sumerians could profit and prosper. This fortuitous position supplies the talents, skills and 'lucky' circumstances necessary to attain the prosperity and respect by which these individuals gauge security and self-worth. Like the Sumerian Inanna, Plato's Aphrodite Pandemos and Titian's luxuriating women, these people do not live in the world of ideas but utilise their strong Venusian magnetism, sensuality and power to attract people who will provide the lifestyle they require.

Just as the egocentricity of Venus in Aries prevents individuals from maintaining harmonious, co-operative relationships, Venus in Taurus is completely geared towards amassing affluence and assurance from lovers, friends and colleagues. Due to an obsession with material security and maintaining control over their own lives, individuals with Venus in Taurus guard their assets and, like Inanna, can be as possessive, jealous and wrathful as they are generous should they sense that they've been neglected or betrayed. Just as Venus in Aries people are inspired by constant change, excitement and passion, Venus in Taurus individuals are pragmatic rather than romantic. They can only begin to express themselves lovingly and creatively in an environment that provides economic security and the certainty of partners, friends and family. Given the devotion and trust they demand, these people are, in return, generous, loving and dependable friends, colleagues, spouses and parents.

If Venus is positively aspected, their fruitfulness, sensuality, practicality and perseverance are qualities to which they aspire and, as a result, they are innately drawn to relationships that will provide them with a secure environment in which these attributes can flourish. Their monetary acumen and foresight allow them to manage their finances successfully and attain the level of prosperity that provides costly, beautiful possessions, a luxurious lifestyle and, most important, autonomy. If this goal cannot effectively be reached, they will use every wile at their disposal to attract a partner who can guarantee success and its accompanying comforts.

If Venus is poorly aspected, however, they may doubt their own appearance, earning capacity and/or creative abilities. Operating from a position of insecurity, they may alternately exhibit obstinacy, indulgence, jealousy and bossiness resulting from an inordinate need for control.

Because this placement emphasises the quintessential Taurean Venus, it is obviously one of the most sensual positions in the zodiac as well as the most stubborn, controlling and inflexible. Obsessed with beauty and economic security, they are methodical, patient and persevering in pursuit of a romantic or business partner with whom they can share their financial or creative goals and, as a result, afford them the lifestyle they so desire. Due to their steadfastness and intensity, these people have the potential to summon all their resources to reach their objective – whether it be the attainment of prosperity, commitment to a loved one or the fulfilment of their creative dreams.

Just as Venus in Aries associates love with passion and independence, Venus in Taurus links partnership with sensual enjoyment and financial security, commonly appearing in the charts of those who marry established – sometimes older – partners. Charming, sensual, sophisticated and attractive, Venus in Taurus also appears in the charts of people who make excellent escorts or are used as ornaments to aid their partners in their business dealings.

An example of Venus placed in its ruling sign, Taurus, is Princess Diana, whose aristocratic and sexually inexperienced background qualified her to be the wife of Prince Charles. It has been rumoured that this was a role she consciously sought and, to that end, persisted with until her dream became a reality. Sacrificing passion for a position of affluence and respect, Diana's popularity soared due to the power and confidence she exuded through her impeccable appearance, poise, demure beauty, affinity for motherhood and compassionate advocacy of charitable causes. If press reports are true (and they concur with what one would expect of Venus in Taurus), it was not the lack of passion that destroyed her marriage but Prince Charles' inability to remain completely loyal – behaviour Venus in Taurus demands – which was a major factor in their separation.* While this Venus in Taurus lady certainly knew exactly how to attain the affluence she sought, her insecurity and intense public scrutiny precipitated eating disorders – the dark and vulnerable side of this placement – one of many possible indulgences that beset individuals with an afflicted Venus in Taurus.

Other notables with Venus in Taurus include Karl Marx, Jean Cocteau, Charlie Chaplin, Salvador Dali, Adolf Hitler, Robert Maxwell, Doris Day, Glenda Jackson, Henry Kissinger, Paul McCartney, Eric Clapton, Nancy Reagan, Jessica Lange, Michael J. Fox, Prince Philip and Paloma Picasso.

VENUS IN GEMINI

Keywords: creative (particularly in writing), non-committal, enjoying multiple romances, loving variety

When placed in Mercury-ruled Gemini, a mutable air sign, Venus equates love with friendship, deriving endless pleasure and fulfilment from the intellectual stimulation of people, novel ideas, the media and travel. Since Hermes/Mercury was an asexual God in Greek/Roman mythology and the only planet not assigned a gender in Hindu (Vedic) astrology, this Venus does not crave sexual power and expression as much as a regeneration of ideas

*This was written in December, 1993.

and feedback. Self-worth is not measured in terms of sexual or romantic reciprocation but affability and the facility for conducting constant exchanges of information, ideas and opinions with a diversity of people. In fact, the requirements for partnership are based less on romantic love and physical passion and more on friendship, communication and mobility.

It is important for Venus in Gemini people to choose mates who respect their convictions and, most important, their need for a variety of activities outside the home. The comfort that Venus in Gemini people seek in a multitude of friendships, cultural activities, educational courses, travelling, etc. does not necessarily stem from an unhappy home life and should not be interpreted as a desire to be unfaithful. Because these individuals do an incredible amount of networking, often serving as go-betweens and, if need be, mediators, it is indeed likely that they may be attracted to people outside their relationships if only as a result of the variety of individuals with whom their paths cross. Unfounded jealousy, however, may be the force that drives these freedom-loving people to contemplating an affair, since Venus in air signs are by nature detached and sex is often regarded as a means of communication rather than an expression of love.

Like Plato's Heavenly Urania, honoured for her cerebral qualities, individuals with Venus in Gemini place a higher value on the intellect than on physical desire; due to their own emotional detachment they often do not take commitment as seriously as they should. Due to this placement's lack of physical passion and genuine restlessness, astrological texts have described this position as aloof, fickle, promiscuous, uncommitted and insensitive to the needs of others. Since Venus in Mercury-ruled Gemini, the sign of restlessness and perpetual youth, tends to be somewhat detached towards their loved ones, they may be unable to settle into a monogamous relationship until later in life, after they have 'sown their wild oats'.

If Venus is well aspected, they possess a wealth of cleverness, wit and spontaneity of expression. Due to Gemini's impeccable timing and remarkable ability to replicate sounds, the creative influence of Venus lends itself to outstanding improvisational musicians and performers, ventriloquists, mimics and comedians/

comic actors. Because Gemini rules the lungs and the ability to communicate, a dominant Venus prefigures eloquent speaking voices and the power of persuasion. These people are filled with a plethora of artistic ideas and, rather than direct their passion towards romantic involvements, their fervour is often apparent in the media arts such as film-making, photography, writing, advertising and public relations.

If, on the other hand, Venus is afflicted, these people are insecure about their opinions and rather than look to others for stimulation they validate themselves by mimicking and/or stealing original ideas and presenting them as their own. Additionally, it is difficult for them to commit to a lasting relationship due to an inability to follow the dictates of their hearts. As they mature, they will be less likely to seek validation from others around them and more apt to become good partners who are creative, stimulating and encouraging.

The actress Candice Bergen exemplifies how Venus in Gemini affected her career as well as her intimate relationships. Due to the impeccable timing that Mercury-ruled Gemini brings to Venus and, therefore, creativity, Candice Bergen's career blossomed when her remarkable flair for comedy came to light, first in the film *Starting Over* and later in the television series *Murphy Brown*. Bergen had drifted through several unfulfilling and non-committal relationships before she met and married Louis Malle, the dynamic French film director, who provides intellectual stimulation and a transatlantic lifestyle with homes in New York, France and California. Although her career keeps her in Hollywood a good portion of the year, holidays and summers are spent in France and, according to Bergen, she and her husband maintain a wonderful relationship due to his unconditional support of her success even though it keeps them apart a great deal. While Bergen has said that it would be preferable for Malle to spend more time with her and their child, Venus in Gemini allows her the flexibility to adjust to this unusual way of life. Ironically, it may be their separations that make the marriage interesting and successful.

Other celebrities with Venus in Gemini include William Shakespeare, Albrecht Durer, Johannes Brahms, Alfred Lord

Tennyson, Rudolph Valentino, John F. Kennedy, the Duchess of Windsor, Gerald Ford, Yehudi Menuhin, Ringo Starr, Jackie Onassis, Tony Curtis, Cher, Harrison Ford, Randy Travis, Bob Dylan, Coretta Scott King and Anita Hill.

VENUS IN CANCER

Keywords: imaginative, home-loving, warm and caring, supportive, sensitive

When Venus is placed in the cardinal water sign of Cancer, an inordinate need to love and be loved fuels an immense insecurity from which most of their actions emanate. Since Cancer is ruled by the Moon, the maternal principle dominates the way they perceive themselves and the nature of their relationships. On the positive side, these nurturing individuals provide others with a strong, secure emotional cushion as well as a comfortable, flourishing home environment. Endowed with emotional strength and the ability to hold things together, they often attract individuals in need of intellectual, spiritual and/or financial support.

Amazingly loyal and attentive, these generally insecure people will stop at nothing to keep their families intact and, in the process, frequently become unnecessarily overprotective; if Venus is poorly aspected, they can even be secretive, controlling and manipulative. Often defensive, pessimistic and, at its most extreme, paranoid, they often live in constant fear that they will be deserted by loved ones, lose their money or that their creativity will dissipate. Instead of being secure in the knowledge that they are loved simply for who they are, these people often try *too* hard to create the type of environment from which their partners dare not leave. To solidify a marriage that was already on the rocks, one client with Venus in Cancer even installed a music studio for his wife, a singer, in their beautiful home, only to be totally devastated when she eventually left him. When I pointed out to him that his own insecurities actually prevented him from being sensitive to his wife's real needs, my explanation fell on deaf ears.

This co-dependent behaviour,* in that one person controls the emotional climate by making another person completely dependent on him or her, is typical of Venus in each of the water signs – especially if afflicted. Because it is often simpler for Venus in Cancer people to be caretakers rather than seek assistance (which would reveal their own neediness), they tend to excuse rather than strengthen the character weaknesses of their partners and/or their children.

While romanticism is indeed an asset to their creativity, it may also be responsible for their completely unrealistic attitudes concerning those they love. A desperate need to form a family unit coupled with a lack of faith in their capacity to maintain relationships frequently precipitates idealisation of the partner and the creation of an unequal partnership. While placing someone on a pedestal may seem complimentary, it often becomes manipulative and overly possessive, causing the partner to flee from the very situation Venus in Cancer people have tried so hard to perfect. Although Cancer is known to be an extremely emotional sign, their feelings are often directed inwards towards defensive behaviour; the true compassion of Venus in Cancer can only manifest when it is realised that a healthy relationship is founded on two individuals who are secure within themselves.

Unlike Venus in Gemini, the creativity of introspective Venus in Cancer is marked by romantic idealism and a vivid imagination. Due to an affinity with the home as well as the intricacies of computer technology, they have a talent for real estate, interior design, computer graphics and programming. Because they constantly question their talents, they are overly sensitive to the opinions of others and, as a result, Venus in Cancer people are often very secretive about their work and creative ideas until it is certain they will be met with approval.

Because this placement represents the attainment of self-esteem through their roles as spouses and parents, Venus in Cancer men – whose attributes include fierce loyalty, dependability and devotion to their loved ones – have heretofore been admonished as 'unmanly'. With the distinction between male and female roles

---

*For more detailed descriptions of co-dependent behaviour, I refer the reader to *Co-dependent No More* by Melody Beattie.

narrowing, these sensitive and artistic men may soon be admired and even envied for their emotional attachment and compassion, in much the same way that women with Venus in Aries or Scorpio will no longer have to defend their dynamic personalities or fight for creative autonomy.

Best known for her illustrious career as the greatest ballerina of the twentieth century, Dame Margot Fonteyn's personal life, far removed from the stage, made full use of her compassionate and devoted Venus in Cancer. After her retirement, she chose to live with her invalid husband (a former diplomat who had been shot and paralysed by political enemies) on a sprawling but isolated plantation in Panama. This allowed her to be both devoted wife and nurse (Cancer). Hemmed in by the Central American jungle, she and her husband were shielded from the demands of an adoring public.

Joyce Carol Oates, the prolific fiction writer and Professor of English Literature, is another example of the creative mind produced by Venus in Cancer. Her astonishingly prodigious output of novels written while fulfilling her teaching obligations at Princeton University requires a tremendous amount of discipline and an almost reclusive lifestyle. Perfectly in line with expressing creativity in a Cancerian manner, her complex Gothic-like plots almost always revolve around the dark side of family dynamics – secrets, intrigue, misplaced love and emotional blackmail, to name but a few.

Other notables with this placement include Dante Alighieri, Mary Cassatt, Robert Schumann, Leo Tolstoy, Robert Browning, Alan Leo, Carl Jung, Benito Mussolini, Errol Flynn, Judy Garland, Ernest Hemingway, Harry Truman, Lyndon Johnson, Liberace, Mae West, Fidel Castro, Robert Redford, Dustin Hoffman, Arnold Schwarzenegger, Jerry Hall, Princess Anne, Barbara Cartland, Clarence Thomas and George and Barbara Bush.

VENUS IN LEO

Keywords: flamboyant, generous, self-serving, amorous, domineering

Its most individualistic placement, Venus in the fixed fire sign of Leo is, when positively aspected, flamboyant, magnanimous, generous and extremely loyal to friends, colleagues and loved ones. Once committed to a relationship or project, it is undertaken with such intensity that Venus in Leo people are, in fact, a constant source of amazement to partners and colleagues alike for the seriousness and zeal with which they approach their endeavours.

Obsessed with being noticed, these ostentatious and often outrageous individuals are capable of using friends and lovers as stepping stones to advance their careers. They are attracted to people whose unconditional love, tireless support and endless flattery help to maintain their egos, thus reaffirming their belief in themselves (not to mention conceit).

Like the fertility Goddess whose sexual pleasure ignited her ability to awaken the dormant earth, this placement – more than any other position of Venus – fosters individuals who approach life with unabashed passion, spontaneity and joy. While they are known for their affability, leadership qualities and facility for entertaining others, they are, first and foremost, motivated by a desire to be acknowledged for their talent, sexuality and/or compassion. Although their humanitarian and philanthropic gestures often yield altruistic results, these individuals almost never extend themselves unless they get praise in return. Because they enjoy being the centre of attention as well as being admired for their beauty, Venus in Leo people frequently don bright colours and outlandish outfits or display shocking, unique behaviour.

While self-centred and domineering Venus in Leo forms relationships in which their own needs come first, this placement is, at the same time, indicative of attentive, loving and passionate individuals who will do anything to preserve that romantic feeling. Motivated by a need to impress others, their choice of partners consists of people whom they can boast about.

It is difficult for these people who crave centre-stage and a sense of excitement to make the transition from romantic love to a long-term, committed relationship where everyday realities must be confronted. It is recommended that those with Venus in Leo search for heightened experience through the performing arts, competitive sports, strenuous exercise or an active social calendar to escape boredom. If they release their creative and competitive juices through these types of activities, they will not have to seek drama in their personal relationships. If Venus in Leo is poorly aspected, the need for excitement can result in passionate liaisons inundated with emotional conflict and an inability to distinguish love from sex.

Due to the fact that Leo is a fixed sign, it is vital that those with Venus placed there strike a balance between the pursuit of popularity and the need to dominate and control both personally and professionally. By the same token, they make wonderful teachers and enjoy displaying their talents to appreciative audiences as well as encouraging students to develop their own skills. Although they feel a sense of accomplishment when one of their protégés succeeds, Venus in Leo people can find themselves resentful that a former pupil might become a rival; to enhance the compassion of Venus they must swallow their pride and be happy for others' success.

One example of Venus in Leo was the legendary actress Greta Garbo, who was not only enamoured of herself but transformed her reclusiveness into a lifelong mystique which provided the drama she sought first as a film star and later when she retired from the screen.

Another Venus in Leo personality is Geraldo Rivera, the flamboyant television talk show host who often gives the impression of being captivated by his own words. Never shy about seeking publicity, his nose was broken attempting to break up a fight on his talk show which was induced by the explosive combination of guests. While his countless affairs and marital infidelities were well-documented in a brazen autobiography, the entire proceeds from his book were contributed to a charitable project which Rivera himself initiated, exemplifying the magnanimous though self-congratulatory facet of Venus in Leo. Since we grow into our Sun signs, Rivera (whose Sun sign is Cancer) seems finally to have settled into a faithful relationship (of which he is extremely proud), has gained the coveted respect for his work and appears to have attained the peace of mind which often accompanies maturity.

Venus in Leo celebrities known for their flamboyance and/or

individuality as much as for their creativity include King Louis XIV of France (known as the Sun King), Mike Todd, Leonard Bernstein, Mick Jagger, Madonna and Whitney Huston. Other notables past and present include Claude Debussy, Percy Bysshe Shelley, Georges Sand, Sir Walter Scott, George Bernard Shaw, Françoise Sagan, Ross Perot and Jimmy Carter.

VENUS IN VIRGO (FALL)

Keywords: critical, self-conscious, modest, kind-hearted

Categorised as its 'fall' position, the placement of Venus in the austere, critical and self-conscious sign of Virgo tends to impede the planet's customary warmth, sensuality and creativity. Whereas sexual passion, abundant conviviality and spontaneity may indeed be tempered by this position, Mercury-ruled Virgo, a mutable earth sign, nevertheless anoints an individual with kindness, loyalty and a strong sense of responsibility. Because meticulous and methodical Virgo is ruled by Mercury – a communicative, nervous planet – the power of Virgos lies in their ability to be verbally expressive rather than physically demonstrative. In fact, their idealistic view of the perfect relationship involves mutual respect of ideas, opinions and professional goals rather than the ardour that characterises other placements. The influence of Mercury also causes these people to analyse their feelings, emotions, finances and creative impulses endlessly – so much so that romantic, vocational and monetary opportunities are often overlooked. Due to their quest for purity and simplicity, they may wait until they are certain of how they feel before plunging into love or expressing their true creative strength.

Devoted and practical, these individuals often form relationships based on shared work or a common sense of duty and responsibility to others. Often accused of being 'cold fish', they are cautious, inhibited and often unable to display affection spontaneously or openly. But once they feel secure, familiar and trusting, the earthiness and sensuality of this placement will be expressed.

Because these people are verbal rather than physical there is a great deal of humility in their displays of affection, expressions of creative power and relationship to money and possessions – and the latter are acquired strictly for the security and utilitarian function they fulfil. Rather than spend on ornately decorated homes or invest in land or expensive clothing, they are more likely to put their money into safe investments that yield slow but steady profits. Their love of animals could even make them avid contributors to or supporters of animal rights groups, Greenpeace or other environmental organisations whose goals are to improve the quality of life – all Virgo concerns.

Due to a propensity for modesty, self-consciousness and, if Venus is poorly aspected, self-deprecation, they must learn to be less critical and not expect always to achieve the standard of perfection they have set for themselves and others. Their own harshest critics, they are often inhibited in love as well as in creative expression for fear that others will be quick to denigrate their talents, sensuality and, most important, their procreative strength. It is quite common, however, for these individuals to commit to an intimate relationship out of a sense of responsibility, obligation or friendship, suppressing the love and sexual attraction that they are afraid will not be returned. Because true intimacy is difficult for them, they may even regard the sexual act as just another skill that they must perform methodically without getting close to another or expressing their deepest feelings.

Professing to be a perfectionist, Michael Jackson is a fitting example of Venus in Virgo, epitomising the legendary Pygmalion who implored the Love Goddess to create Galatea, a statue come to life which represented flawless beauty. As are many people with Venus in Virgo, Jackson is highly critical of his appearance and television interview even professed to being such a perfectionist that he has had innumerable cosmetic surgical operations to mould the features of his face. Although he vehemently denies the rumours that he has bleached his skin (attesting the skin-lightening condition to a genetic disease), he has, in fact, admitted to never being satisfied with his appearance and even hating the way he looks.

With Venus in Virgo, Eleanor Roosevelt was not primarily known for her passion or exuberance but rather for her sense of duty, compassion and a true desire to improve the world. On the other hand, beautiful sex symbol Sophia Loren, who probably could have attracted any man she wanted, remained loyal to her mentor/husband Carlo Ponti, the director who made her a star. Not surprisingly, Robert De Niro, a Leo Sun with Venus in Virgo, is somewhat reticent about appearing in public and rarely grants interviews. He is, at the same time, an impeccable, methodical actor and relentless perfectionist noted for researching his roles to a fault. In fact, he intentionally gained quite a bit of weight – despite the health hazards – to portray the aging, retired boxer Jake La Motta in the film *Raging Bull*. It is this meticulous, intelligent and calculated (Virgo) approach to his craft (Venus) that distinguishes this placement.

Other notables with Venus in Virgo include Guy de Maupassant, Goethe, Friedrich Nietzsche, Henry Ford, Pierre Trudeau, Ken Kesey, Jason Robards, Robert Mitchum, Mitzi Gaynor, Mark Knopfler, John Lennon, Bob Geldof, Julio Iglesias, Chevy Chase, Patrick Swayze and Anjelica Houston.

VENUS IN LIBRA (RULERSHIP)

Keywords: co-operative, aesthetic, needing harmony, seeking partnership

The placement of Venus in its own sign of Libra accentuates its manifestation as Heavenly Urania in much the same way that the planet's position in Taurus emphasises the attributes of Earthy Pandemos. While I do not subscribe to Plato's assertion that the cerebral, Libran Venus is *superior* to the sensual, Taurean Venus, I do concede that there is a difference. Whereas Venus in Taurus represents the passionate, sexual and practical ramifications of love, Venus in Libra signifies its more intellectual, spiritual, aesthetic and romantic aspects. This is not to say that individuals with Venus in Libra are asexual; sex is simply not the main issue in their relationships, which they believe should ideally manifest as a 'marriage of true minds'.

The Libran quest for beauty, harmony and perfection extends to their aesthetic preferences, vocation and their choice of friends/lovers. In addition, there is a distaste for 'unpleasantness' and a distinct sensitivity to brashness, argument and disorder. Confident of their own allure and ability to be convincing, these harmonious people make wonderful counsellors, therapists, advisors, directors, colleagues, friends, mentors or simply helpmates who are devoted to the goals of their partnership. There may be, however, a negation of the self and too much dependency on a partner's desires and points of view. Because these people have an empathetic gift that enables them to understand fully how another person thinks and feels, if Venus is afflicted this potential for healing may be transformed into manipulativeness, particularly of others' feelings, dishonesty, superficiality and, at its most extreme, megalomania.

While it is easy to fall in love with these placid, charming, engaging people, it is essential to distinguish between what the Venus in Libra personality really feels and the image he or she projects. This quality is apparent in the charts of politicians, models or film stars whose careers hinge on their facility for projecting glamour and/or illusion; the placement also appears in the charts of fashion designers, cosmeticians, hairdressers and landscape gardeners – all of whom are concerned with beautification.

Because Venus, a creatively expressive planet, is comfortable in its own sign, these individuals often exhibit truer Libran attributes than those who have their Sun or Ascendant in Libra. Whereas Venus in airy Gemini and Aquarius describes one's need for group relationships, Venus in Libra functions best when relating one to one. Unable to spend extended periods alone, if people with Venus in Libra do not have an outlet for their affections or a sounding board for their ideas they will seek out new friendships, cultural activities or even indulgent behaviour to fill the void. Just as Inanna was enraged when Dumuzi functioned independently, individuals with Venus in Libra truly love teamwork and being needed, even if it means working behind the scenes as a silent partner.

A perfect representation of Venus in Libra is evident in the horoscope of Bill Clinton, who not only epitomises the ability to sell himself to the American public but whose relationship with his wife Hillary is the quintessential, interdependent Libran partnership. President Clinton has always admitted that his wife, an accomplished attorney, is his closest advisor and, as a politician, knows instinctively that he is only as good as the partnership. In fact, one of his campaign slogans 'Elect one, get one free' could not describe Venus in Libra more precisely.

Epitomising the mesmerising appeal of Venus in Libra, Princess Grace (Grace Kelly) could have been the model for Praxiteles' statue or Botticelli's paintings. Her angelic yet regal beauty, delicate features, poise and self-assurance captured the hearts of movie fans, co-stars and, ultimately, Prince Rainer of Monaco, who married her in a lavish, romantic Libranesque ceremony. As Princess of Monaco, Grace's accessibility, family devotion and involvement in charitable fundraising endeared her to the citizens of the principality – an example of the hypnotic allure of Venus in Libra.

A somewhat different manifestation of Venus in Libra is Woody Allen, with his obsessive quest for aesthetic perfection in his films. Most fascinating, however, is the Svengali-like effect he wields over his leading ladies for whom stardom – something they may not have otherwise accomplished – is assured. (Although Mia Farrow, for example, was well known prior to meeting Allen, her versatility as an actress was never fully explored until he directed her.) By offering actresses the opportunity to realise their aspirations by believing in themselves, Allen seemed to fill a gap that these women, whom he lived with or married, depended on. I can only speculate that these creative and loving partnerships may have ended when these women went on to pursue independent projects. It would be difficult for an individual such as Allen (with Venus in Libra) to maintain a relationship with a woman who was not intrinsically involved in his creative projects either directly or emotionally. Because Venus is in his Second house, his partnerships are intertwined with his money-making abilities.

Other personalities with Venus in Libra include Queen Elizabeth I, King Louis XVI of France, D. H. Lawrence, Annie Besant, Helena Blavatsky, Aleister Crowley, F. Scott Fitzgerald, Pablo Picasso, Peter Sellers, Mickey Rooney, Frederick Forsythe,

Shelley Winters, Sean Connery, Billie Jean King, k. d. lang, ⌐
Derek, Jacqueline Bisset, Christopher Reeve, Michael Douglas
and Prince Charles.

VENUS IN SCORPIO (DETRIMENTAL)

Keywords: sexual, jealous, demanding, powerful

Because Pluto-ruled Scorpio (the sign opposite Taurus) is detrimental to Venus, the planet's loving, co-operative, creative and productive attributes are not always accessible due to the excitement and fervour (Scorpio) that these individuals crave.

Possessing the capability of getting to the 'heart' of the matter and finding the root of any problem, Venus in Scorpio people possess boundless energy, personal magnetism and disciplined creativity that they use to influence and attract others. Because they demand so much from themselves and others, their personal and professional relationships must be emotionally, sexually, creatively and financially fulfilling to keep their interest.

At times temperamental and overbearing, their dynamic, intense and demanding personalities will attract friends, lovers and business partners who recognise that beneath the need to be the centre of attention there is a compassionate and generous heart. Their attention to detail, leadership qualities, laserlike intensity and powers of concentration make them wonderful stage and film directors, choreographers, mystery writers, private investigators, attorneys, psychiatrists and composers. They will also excel in any field where they can explore the underside of interpersonal relationships or the intricacies, mysteries and hidden depth of the human heart and mind. If, however, Venus is poorly aspected, their insecurity and need for control may lead to compulsive, competitive relationships that can erupt in jealous rages and, at its most extreme, abuse, cruelty and violence.

Due to their strong sexuality and charisma, they often attract powerful and influential people who provide the encouragement and resources necessary to fulfil the goals Venus in Scorpio individuals have set out for themselves. If afflicted, there may be a tendency to attract power struggles rather than supportive, co-operative relationships – the domain of Venus in Libra – and, as a result, they are quite often disappointed and frustrated. It is important for Venus in Scorpio individuals to let go of brooding or anger and move on to the next activity or relationship – difficult for Venus in the fixed signs. Rather than filter their creative and complex attitudes through relationships, these people are advised to use their intense energy towards creativity and money-making ventures to avoid pent up anger and emotional outbursts.

While Venus in Scorpio people need to feel that they have a hand in their partner's success, they refuse to take a back seat; instead they wish at least to be credited for having made an equal contribution. Though they certainly take pride in their abilities to abet their mates, children and employers, this is, in the long run, never enough. Unless they put their own unique abilities to the test, their frustrations may be taken out on their children, their partners or, ultimately, themselves.

Due to the aggressive, destructive and regenerative nature of Scorpio, these people often begin, end and begin again personal and professional relationships over and over without learning from past mistakes. They have even been known intentionally to provoke and challenge the authority of others just to obtain a reaction, thereby finding a release for their own intense emotional energy, which would be better channelled creatively or physically.

On the other hand, Scorpio's fixed quality lends itself to dominance and control – often attracting lovers and friends who rely on them for intellectual, emotional, economic or moral support. If they do not employ their take-charge abilities in a professional sphere, they may formulate 'co-dependent' relationships – consistent with Venus in water signs – by seeking emotionally dependent and needy partners as a means of elevating their own esteem, resulting in control over another's life. Unfortunately, by encouraging dependency Venus in Scorpio individuals simply maintain the status quo by preventing others' recovery from addictions, problems and weaknesses.

Agatha Christie, Anne Rice (author of *The Vampire Chronicles*) and Harold Pinter are prime examples of creative writers whose Scorpionic subject matter includes calculated mysteries, vampires and absurdist black humour, respectively. Each writer has specialised in an area that explores the underside of life, forcing the reader and/or audience to discover the underlying layers that, once revealed, unravel the mystery or expose life's harsh realities.

On the other hand, Hillary Rodham Clinton (Figure 10.1, page 261) and Ted Turner (owner of the CNN news empire) are two creative, powerful, compassionate and, to some extent, dictatorial people who not only thrive on challenge but possess the vision and resourcefulness to take charge of exceedingly difficult situations and bring them to successful conclusions. They accomplish this by meeting challenges head-on, setting new precedents and crossing new frontiers. They are also both married to powerful partners (President Clinton and Jane Fonda respectively) with whom they can hold their own and need not compete. While people with this placement thrive on competition and possess brilliance and charisma, Scorpio is also a vulnerable water sign and it is vital that they receive emotional support; without it they might not be able to achieve their goals.

Other well-known personalities with Venus in Scorpio include Jane Austen, Dr Edith Cavell, Gustav Von Holst, Franz Liszt, Marie Curie, Katherine Mansfield, Mahatma Gandhi, John Paul Getty, Graham Greene, Spiro Agnew, Charles Manson, Uri Geller, Jack LaLanne, Edward Vilella, Patty Duke, Jodie Foster, Meg Ryan, Oliver Stone, Chris Evert, Steven Spielberg, Linda Evans, Phil Donahue and Marlo Thomas.

VENUS IN SAGITTARIUS

Keywords: freedom-loving, passionate about learning and knowledge, philosophical, visionary

Symbolised by the archer shooting his 'idealistic' arrows into the sky, Sagittarius, a mutable fire sign, provides Venus with the quest for knowledge and the love of freedom. When Venus is placed in the ninth sign, individuals derive much of their self-esteem from the knowledge they have acquired through higher education, independent research, foreign travel or their association with a religious organisation or system that best expresses their points of view.

Steeped in philosophical, religious and/or metaphysical pursuits, Venus in Sagittarius people yearn for personal and/or professional partnerships that stimulate these interests. I have found that their passion for learning is so great that these individuals are attracted to personal and professional partnerships that mirror the student/teacher relationship. If Venus is well situated they are attracted to partners who envy their knowledge and encourage their pursuits, which may entail taking prolonged journeys. In fact, it is not unusual for these individuals to marry their teachers, guides, directors, editors, etc. – only to dissolve the union when the student 'graduates' and the two must relate as equals. If Venus in Sagittarius people can withstand this change in the relationship, the partnership has a chance to endure. Quite frequently, however, neither party is capable of making the transition successfully and the union ultimately fails.

This placement is often found in the charts of travel writers, journalists, book publishers, editors, academics or other professionals who can pontificate about their experiences or simply voice their strong opinions, especially concerning love, art, money or other Venusian concerns. Because they place such value on impressing others with their worldliness, individuals with Venus in Sagittarius are avid social butterflies, party-goers and name-droppers – anything to keep them from staying at home.

As much as they love being admired for their worldliness (exhibited by their travel experience, linguistic abilities and social skills), Venus in Sagittarius people are certain to be drawn to those who can teach them or guide them through what they wish to learn or need for their work. While Venus occupying or ruling the ninth house is traditionally representative of marrying foreigners or falling in love while travelling, Venus in Sagittarius is indicative of being attracted to people who possess exotic qualities or attributes that are simply unfamiliar to them. These individuals also express their love quite flamboyantly and, in true Sagittarian fashion, like to be right about what they feel they have mastered. Anything they do not know about they make sure to learn (and master) in due course.

Like all fire signs, Sagittarius endows Venus with the need to be admired and respected by personal and professional partners. And, like Venus in Aries and Leo, relationships can also be exciting, passionate, romantic and, at the same time, completely self-centred. While their creative thinking and financial attitudes benefit from their ardent philosophical and/or religious convictions, their fanaticism about their beliefs can just as frequently interfere with their ability to be objective, thus endangering their work, creative projects and even relationships. At a moment's notice, their flamboyance, magnanimity and happy-go-lucky outlook can just as easily turn to an overly serious, judgmental and dictatorial attitude. If the rest of the horoscope adds confidence, Venus in Sagittarius will be at its most benevolent, creative and encouraging to those who admire their skills and emulate their belief system.

Michael, an American client with Venus in Sagittarius, moved with his wife to London, where he focused on meeting gallery owners who would exhibit his controversial sculptures and drawings. Although his work was impressive, attracting many buyers, he suddenly became overly smug and rather than alter his style to please his patrons, made his art even more subjective. Ultimately both his work and his marriage suffered and his wife and he split up. After moving to yet another country, Michael gave up painting and became involved in a spiritual movement that seemed to accentuate his newly found non-materialism. At the same time he met and married a younger woman who regarded Michael as her spiritual guide and was enamoured of his talent and worldly experience. They too eventually divorced. According to his ex-wife, Michael resented the fact that she stopped regarding him as a teacher and simply related to him as a man.

With Venus in Sagittarius, Jane Fonda is a perfect example of the different manifestations of this placement. Readily admitting to being bulimic and insecure as a teenager, Jane Fonda illuminated her self-worth (Venus) by moving to France and marrying Roger Vadim, the French director who had earlier married Brigitte Bardot and made her a star. Doing the same for Fonda, Vadim transformed her into the sexy 'Barbarella', providing her with the beautiful image she had lacked. Like most people with Venus in Sagittarius, Fonda eventually found it necessary to express her creativity in a more serious and meaningful manner. Politically active and extremely outspoken about the Vietnam War, she married Tom Hayden, a fellow political activist who shared (Venus) her political philosophy (Sagittarius). When Fonda became a successful businesswoman and entrepreneur through the marketing of her fitness tapes, she once again needed someone from whom she could learn and be challenged. It took the confident and successful Ted Turner, self-made businessman and wealthy owner of several cable television stations, to provide Fonda once again with the creative challenge and excitement she requires for inspiration.

Celebrities past and present with Venus in Sagittarius include Rudyard Kipling, Robert Louis Stevenson, Jonathan Swift, Christina Rosetti, Mark Twain, Winston Churchill, Charles De Gaulle, Dwight D. Eisenhower, Douglas MacArthur, Barry Goldwater, Dr Jonas Salk, Albert Schweitzer, Michael Landon, Jimi Hendrix, the Kray twins, Alexander Solzhenitsyn, Angela Davis, Margaret Thatcher, Bill Wyman, Joan Baez, Sally Field and Farrah Fawcett.

VENUS IN CAPRICORN

Keywords: steadfast, creative, ambitious, image-conscious, responsible

Capricorn, the cardinal earth sign symbolised by a goat ascending a mountain, is, along with Scorpio, the workaholic of the zodiac. Just as the persevering, goal-orientated mountain goat climbs slowly but surely until it reaches the top, people with Venus in Capricorn leave no stone unturned in their never-ending exploration of their creativity and money-making potential. Because Saturn-ruled Capricorn represents discipline, structure and the foresight needed to bring budding ideas to fruition, Venus will add creativity and co-operation to whatever they attempt, be it in the corporate, governmental or artistic arena.

Since their self-esteem is intrinsically rooted in the successful fulfilment of their ambitions (to be president of a company or to buy a beautiful home), marriage is often postponed until they feel themselves well established. Conversely, they may choose emotionally supportive, financially comfortable or socially connected partners to help them to achieve their goals. Due to the single-minded sense of achievement that Venus in Capricorn people demand of themselves (and, as a result, of others), they usually do not rush headlong into a relationship. In fact, they devote so much time and energy to building a career that their partners must recognise that success is essential for their self-esteem and, therefore, their capacity for love.

Serious and dutiful, Venus in Capricorn individuals require professional and personal partners who will provide the support, devotion and security they need to continue climbing the ladder of success. Because Capricorn is such a conservative and prudent sign, men with this placement still exhibit many traditional attitudes towards women's roles in both the workplace and at home. By the same token, Venus in Capricorn women may be attracted to strong, successful and protective men.

If Venus in Capricorn is well aspected, these individuals are quite confident and place enormous value on friendships and relationships. While not always verbally expressive, they are none the less loyal and offer unconditional support to their loved ones – and expect the same in return. If Venus is poorly aspected, there may be an insecurity regarding their position or ability to fulfil ambitions, thereby placing a strain on their home life. Their expectations of complete loyalty from personal and professional partners coupled with their obsessive drive to succeed can make them resent any time not utilised in their behalf or in pursuit of common goals.

At times, students of astrology tend to forget that, like all earth signs, sober, judicious Capricorn is also sensual and, as a result, Venus in the sign of the mountain goat represents one of the most ardent positions of the zodiac. It obviously takes a long time for individuals with this placement to fall in love as they are preoccupied with their careers and/or do not approach any facet of their lives – especially love and commitment – lightly or superficially. When these perfectionists ultimately surrender to love, they will not settle for anything less than a long-term commitment – unlike, for instance, Venus in Aries people, who half expect their relationships to fail. In fact, Venus in Capricorn people have feelings that run so deep they can even lead to obsession and jealousy – in extreme cases. While their public displays of affection are minimal, their sexuality is, in fact, exceedingly intense and their commitment to relationships is loyal and steadfast.

The intensity, devotion and pervading sexuality of Venus in Capricorn is typified by show business personalities Paul Newman, Richard Burton, Elvis Presley and Frank Sinatra – each in his own way charismatic and talented. Sinatra and Presley, two of the most popular American singers, each dominated the entertainment industry in his particular era and continue to arouse Capricornian loyalty among their fans – in the case of Presley, even many years after his death. In the early 1940s Sinatra's concerts at New York's Paramount Theater attracted diehard teenage fans (bobby-soxers) who queued up – sometimes overnight – to buy tickets to performances that left them screaming, sobbing and panting in ecstasy. Now over 75, Sinatra, no longer the velvet-throated crooner he once was, still plays to standing-room-only audiences. Teenage hysteria replayed itself in the 1950s with the arrival of guitar-playing, hip-swaying Elvis Presley, whose frenzied fans sobbed uncontrollably when their idol was drafted into the United States Army and sent off to Germany.

Interestingly, the similarities between Sinatra and Presley extend to their very public, obsessive marriages – to Ava Gardner and Priscilla Presley, respectively. While each preferred ornamental wives, the marriages ended, in part due to the inability of their wives to fulfil their assigned roles. Though Presley did not compete with a successful wife, as did Sinatra, his need to dominate was so great that, according to biographer Albert Goldman, he selected Priscilla's wardrobe, hairstyle, makeup and perfume. Like Pygmalion, Presley created an image; but when she came to life there was no Aphrodite to bless them. Richard Burton's obsession with Elizabeth Taylor and Aristotle Onassis' tempestuous affair with Maria Callas and controversial marriage to Jackie Kennedy are other examples of passionate but ultimately destructive relationships between Venus in Capricorn men* and women who are almost mythical in stature. Although each of these men should have been able to internalise his enormous success, it appears that each nevertheless doubted his self-worth. Fuelled by insecurities, their attraction to dynamic women who could not provide the encouragement and confidence they lacked only resulted in obsessive relationships that were doomed to failure.

Very often, however, Venus in Capricorn people who have truly obtained self-worth from their careers do have committed, long-term relationships founded on love and admiration for their partner, both personally and professionally. This certainly seems to be true in the case of Paul Newman, one of America's most charismatic and talented actors, whose marriage to respected actress Joanne Woodward, apparently based on devotion, friendship and mutual respect has endured for over 30 years. It also appears that their creative collaborations, which align love (Venus) and work (Capricorn), have helped preserve this union.

Other notables with Venus in Capricorn include Johann Kepler, Fyodor Dostoevsky, W. H. Auden, Noel Coward, Indira Gandhi, Albert Einstein, James Dean, Jane Wyman, Rock Hudson, Princess Stephanie of Monaco, Alan Alda, Burt Reynolds, Caroline Kennedy, John F. Kennedy, Jr., Goldie Hawn and Danny DeVito.

VENUS IN AQUARIUS

Keywords: charitable, sociable, detached, needing to be part of a creative group

The need to be affiliated with political, social and/or religious groups or causes that reflect one's ideals is one of the hallmarks of the fixed air sign of Aquarius. When Venus is placed in this social, eccentric and often highly-strung sign, individuals crave the excitement and creative stimulation that cannot be obtained from romantic or even sexual love alone. Their self-esteem and

*The sensuality and intensity of this placement is shared by women as well; it is only due to familiarity with their public personae that I have chosen these men as examples.

thus their ability to contribute to a personal and professional relationship are derived from participation in group activities, from which they develop a uniquely personal and oft-times non-traditional outlook on life.

Although they place an enormous emphasis on creative self-expression, it must always be in pursuit of a cause, even if that cause is self-promoting. A longtime client with Venus in Aquarius viewed her photography not simply as an expression of her artistic talent but as a means to penetrate the minds of people she admired in different walks of life. Once she became a well-known photographer, she lent her services to many women's groups and other organisations whose political beliefs were either similar to or sympathetic with her own. In addition, she found that because so much time was spent away from home on shoots or at exhibits, it was important to involve her spouse in her work either as the subject of some of her photos or as manager of her finances. In the end, her husband knew that his wife, though away quite often, was more content, loving and, by far, more interesting and exciting to be with than anyone else.

Some people with Venus in Aquarius prefer not to make statements through their creativity but through their lifestyle choices, which are sometimes non-traditional and even what might be called radical. Any choices they do make, however, whether conformist or non-conformist, are made only if they feel that they are backed up by a support system of friends, an organisation, political party, etc. Whereas the individualism of Leo comes straight from the heart, the uniqueness of Aquarius is never expressed in isolation and can take the form of artistic group collaborations, communal living or sexual experimentation.

Like Venus in each air sign, these people wish to be respected and, to maintain a long-lasting personal relationship, should be encouraged to participate in group activities outside their home since the more outside stimulation they have, the more they will be able to give to the relationship. In fact, people with Venus in Aquarius are often accused of being detached when it comes to their romantic and sexual relationships; though quite verbal in their political and social beliefs they are hopelessly unable to tap into and ultimately share their feelings. Often accused by their partners of being insensitive to their needs, those with Venus in Aquarius simply retort that their partners' needs are trivial compared to those of the community at large.

Because Aquarius is the sign representing groups and friendships, these people ultimately offer themselves to their partners, first and foremost, as friends, and seek out relationships with people who share their point of view. While Uranus-ruled Aquarius is an eccentric sign vacillating between wishing to be alone and yearning for the crowd, its co-ruler Saturn accentuates the need for structure. Although individuals with Venus in this fixed air sign wish to be free, they also wish to have a reliable home to which they can return to share their accomplishments with a chosen mate.

The detachment, social idealism and individuality of this placement is exemplified in the chart of Gloria Steinem, whose Venus in Aquarius also happens to be in the third house of writing and communications. An investigative journalist by profession, her dedication to social causes is legendary, as is her notoriety as co-founder and editor of *Ms*, the first feminist magazine, and as a leading spokesperson of the women's movement. In fact, her best-selling book, aptly entitled *Revolution from Within: A Book of Self-Esteem*, describes her inward journey in pursuit of self-worth. Although she admits searching for acceptance and self-esteem (Venus) through social activism (Aquarius) and, like Aphrodite Urania, platonic, spiritual relationships formed with other feminists (Aquarius), she ultimately discovered that true self-love comes from within – thus the title of her book. As is often the case with Venus in Aquarius, Steinem readily admits to having devoted so much of her life to the women's movement that she was left with little time or energy for long-term intimate commitments – though she does not deny there were numerous love affairs. On the creative level, Wolfgang Amadeus Mozart, Lord Byron, James Joyce, Rudolph Steiner and Walt Disney were each innovators in their chosen fields – and in each case the term creative (Venus) genius (Aquarius) has often been applied.

Other celebrities with Venus in Aquarius include Tycho Brahe, Paul Cezanne, Lon Chaney, Carlos Castaneda, Henri Matisse, Meher Baba, Franklin Delano Roosevelt, Charles E. O. Carter,

Janis Joplin, Aretha Franklin, Mel Gibson, Cybill Shepherd, Vanna White, Morgan Fairchild, Clint Black and Garth Brooks.

VENUS IN PISCES (EXALTATION)

Keywords: self-sacrificing, compassionate, reclusive, sensitive, escapist, deceptive

One of the most compassionate placements in the entire zodiac, Venus is exalted in the sign of Pisces – a position that nurtures the planet's most beneficial qualities. The empathy and unselfishness that guides the behaviour of people with Venus in Pisces is so enormous that they will literally give you 'the shirt off their backs'. In fact, the difficulties confronting these individuals stem from a willingness to give and to sacrifice and an inability to say no.

Just as Venus in Aquarius people feed their egos by participating in idealistic and inspiring group activities and causes (usually political or social), Venus in Pisces will, if humanly possible, offer financial or emotional support to anyone in need. If they have bettered the life of even one individual they are fulfilled. Yet they often confuse sympathy with love, and the belief that emotional strength and/or financial assistance is the means to attract others can be a fatal flaw leading them away from developing a strong sense of self.

Although this is a truly benevolent and compassionate placement, these individuals are oft-times compelled to sacrifice their own agendas to win love and affection. Due to misplaced sympathy they attract needy people, thus forming co-dependent relationships and preventing their true creative strength from shining through. Should their partner recover or become too strong the relationship often disintegrates since it has been based not on love but rather on the need to help and support. It is important for these sensitive, sensual, creative and loving individuals to believe that someone will love them for who they are and not for what they have to give. If they exercise professions or volunteer for work where they can help others, they will have an outlet for their compassion so they will not feel a duty to be caretakers at home.

Incredibly kind, gentle, affable and liked by everyone they meet, these sensual individuals are usually motivated in everything they do by the sheer need to feel good. Since they simply want to love and be loved, feeling good can mean being paid attention to, sexual enjoyment or the elation that comes when they feel they are helping someone get back on their feet. Like Pygmalion, the sculptor in Ovid's myth, people with Venus in Pisces have a strong fantasy life and are quite often unable to cope with life's harsh realities. While romanticism is a wonderful attribute by which a relationship may be kept alive, it is imperative that they view partners with a discerning eye rather than with fanciful expectations. They can misread the object of their affections.

It is not recommended that individuals with this placement follow Pygmalion's lead, falling in love with someone whose image they wish to make over completely; more positive, however, are the sculptor's highly creative and imaginative aspects. Accordingly, Venus in Pisces is found in the charts of many romantic writers, dancers, musicians and painters. It is to the world of the imagination that these people often run when they wish to re-establish their self-worth and discover their hidden voice.

Due to the ability to project an image (Venus) of illusion (Pisces), this placement as well as Venus Neptune aspects frequently appear in the charts of politicians, movie stars, artists and religious figures. What each group has in common is the ability to instil fantasy, hope and/or compassion into the lives of those who need to believe in something beyond their reach. The danger arises when these people, capable of lifting others' spirits, forget the border between fantasy and reality and, at its most extreme, believe in the illusions they have created.

Venus in Pisces is found in the charts of Martin Luther King, Ronald Reagan and Richard Nixon, each of whom expressed this placement quite differently. In the case of Dr King, minister, orator and pioneer of the American Civil Rights Movement, his compassionate plea for equality tugged at the heartstrings of the American people, making enormous inroads into the unfair treatment of all minorities. His most quoted words, 'I have a dream,' epitomise the idealistic, visionary, humanitarian and 'dreamy' quality of exalted Venus in Pisces. Ronald Reagan used his affable personality to provide hope and optimism by supporting unrealistic economic policies that benefited the public for the short term. Though strengthening the economy turned out to be an illusion that eventually fizzled and caused more harm than good, the American public rewarded Reagan by making him one of the country's most popular presidents.

Richard Nixon, on the other hand, suffered from this placement's negative qualities of insecurity, low self-esteem and the feeling that he was constantly under attack, resulting in defensive, paranoid behaviour. It was this sense of paranoia that provoked the dirty campaigning he used to defeat Helen Gahagan Douglas, his first senatorial adversary, as well as his participation in the Watergate break-in. By the time he was indicted, Nixon had become almost completely delusional, continuing openly to deceive the public until the truth was finally revealed. Like all Venus in Pisces people, Nixon was obsessed with being loved – in his case, with being loved by the American people.

Other notables with Venus in Pisces include Henry Fielding, Charles Dickens, Victor Hugo, Frederick Chopin, Franz Schubert (these two were truly romantic composers) Thomas Edison, Hans Christian Andersen, Alfred Adler, Martin Buber, Edgar Cayce, Clyde Barrow, Nijinsky, Anais Nin, Queen Elizabeth II, Betty Ford, Patty Hearst, George Harrison, Quincy Jones, Tom Selleck, Betty Ford, Barbra Streisand, Erma Bombeck and Shirley Maclaine.

8

VENUS THROUGH THE HOUSES*

Keywords for the Houses

First House: The body, personality, constitution
Second House: Money, possessions, values, assets
Third House: Communication, mobility, siblings
Fourth House: Family, domesticity, emotional stability
Fifth House: Creativity, speculations, love affairs, children
Sixth House: Health, work, service
Seventh House: Marriage, partnership, contracts
Eighth House: Sexuality, partner's assets, emotional power
Ninth House: Foreign travel, higher education, philosophy
Tenth House: Profession, authority, conscious image
Eleventh House: Friendships, group activities, ideals
Twelfth House: Isolation, compassion, spirituality

The 12 houses of a horoscope are defined as the imaginary divisions of the ecliptic at the moment of someone's birth. Commonly referred to as spheres of influence, the houses, whose definitions correlate to their corresponding numerical signs (for example, Aries/first house, Taurus/second house, etc.), determine how we approach different areas of our lives. As stated in Chapter 7, the sign in which Venus is placed describes *how* love is expressed, while the house describes *where* we search for love and the experiences we bring to our relationships.

Like the signs, the corresponding houses are also categorised according to their element: Fire houses: first, fifth and ninth; Earth houses: second, sixth and tenth; Air houses: third, seventh and eleventh; Water houses: fourth, eighth and twelfth. And

*Some of this chapter appeared in *Aspects* magazine, published by Aquarius Workshops, Los Angeles, California.

similarly, when Venus is placed in a fire or earth house, the planet may react like the Taurean Venus; when placed in an air or water house, it may react like the Libran Venus. If we categorise Venus according to the element of both the sign *and* house it occupies, the significance of the planet becomes more evident.

For example, if Venus is in a fire or earth *sign* but an air or water *house*, there is a balance between the assertive Pandemos and the cerebral Urania. If, however, Venus is placed in Cancer (water) in the seventh house (air), the planet will more than likely exhibit Libran traits, such as the pursuit of successful relationships which are, above all else, paramount to this person's self-esteem. If, on the other hand, Venus is positioned in Capricorn (earth) in the ninth house (fire), the planetary symbol will manifest in an earthy Taurean capacity, that is, the person's *own* sense of achievement and self-gratification will provide the self-worth necessary to formulate successful partnerships. In short, air and water Venuses are empowered through their relationships; conversely, fire and earth Venuses must first feel worthy before extending themselves to others.

Another equally important means of discerning the significance of Venus in the natal horoscope is to view the planet as the *personification* of the house it governs, that is, whose cusp is occupied by Taurus or Libra. For example, if Venus rules the third house in a particular horoscope, the planet is seen as 1) the harbinger of love, creativity and prosperity (Venus); *and* 2) the symbol of one's siblings, communications, learning, mobility (third house) (see the list above). Going one step further, if this particular Venus is placed in the seventh house, it not only means that one's partnerships are prosperous (Venus in the seventh house) but that opportunities for travel, learning and media contacts are stimulated through the choice of a partner (third house ruler in the seventh house). This method, utilised in both classical Western and Hindu (Vedic) astrology, places equal importance on the planet's role as house occupant *and* house ruler.* To this end, the following interpretations of Venus in a

---

*According to Hindu (Vedic) astrology's equal house system, which deems certain houses good and others evil, each planet becomes benefic or malefic with a particular ascendant depending on which house it rules.

particular house can also be applied to the planet's rulership of that very same house. (For example, if Venus *governs* the third house, the description pertaining to 'Venus *in* the third house' is also applicable.)

Venus in the First House

Keywords: affable, charming, attractive, well-liked, manipulative

Because it is the sign appearing on the eastern horizon at the moment of birth, the ascendant, or rising sign, marks the beginning of the first house and symbolises one's initial contact with the external world. Setting the mood for the entire horoscope, the first house determines one's personality, physical appearance and general constitution. Representing the first breath we inhale, the ascendant and the first house reflect *inherited* traits rather than learned habits and patterns. Whereas the midheaven signifies the way we consciously wish to be viewed and how we strive towards achieving that image, the ascendant represents the way others take us into account based on our mannerisms, choice of clothing, hairstyle or any other external attribute which becomes an identifying feature. It is the characteristics of the ascendant and planets situated in the first house that colour all our activities, ranging from the clothes we wear to our facial expressions to our social skills.

Because the ascendant describes inherited and often unconscious personality traits, it reveals the type of life's journey we will embark on, how we view the world and how we are, in return, viewed by others. In his now classic description, astrologer Alan Oken refers to the ascendant as 'the projected image, the door through which we express and activate our inner motivations and psychological needs in the immediate environment'. He goes on to explain that 'if you were to spend your life in a room with only one window and that window were tinted blue, no matter what the inside of your room looked like to you, people on the outside would only see you and the contents of your room through this blue tint. In the same way, you would see others and the world outside your room through this same blue tint.'[1]

Although it describes the ascendant, Oken's explication can also be applied to a description of the first house even though it sometimes comprises two zodiacal signs – the rising sign and the subsequent one. To this end, the placement of Venus in the first house – especially if it is conjunct the ascendant – transforms an individual into a 'Venus-tinted window' whose poise, passion, conviviality and seductive charm are sources of strength and confidence. Like the agrarian fertility Goddess, those with Venus in the first house know that by pleasing others they will, in return, be offered loyalty, support, prosperity and love.

Because the first house represents one's appearance and outward behaviour, the influence of Venus in this region of the horoscope reveals the enormous value people with Venus in the first house place on being well-liked. Convinced they are being judged by first impressions (since they view others this way), individuals with Venus in the first house are often preoccupied with the way they look, dress and behave. While not always classically beautiful, those with Venus in the first house, ruling the first house, or aspecting the ascendant possess both attractiveness and great charisma – that indefinable something that endears them to families, friends and colleagues. Like a magnet, these sensual and exciting people attract those who wish to absorb their infectious energy simply by being around them. Confident that they can call upon their immense sex appeal, charming personality and beautiful appearance to 'open doors' gives them the incentive to embark upon endeavours that others might find intimidating. (Success will depend on whether Venus is positively or negatively aspected.)

Overly enthusiastic and extremely impetuous when positioned in the dominant first house, Venus wields enough charm, magnetism and charisma to attract supporters and attain certain goals. An overwhelming sensuality and the desire for self-aggrandisement can be so powerful at times that lust is often mistaken for love, precipitating ill-fated romances founded on physical attraction rather than deep commitment. Like Aphrodite, these people are admired for their attractiveness, independence and affability, yet disdained for their indulgences, provocation, overt sexuality and egocentricity.

The planet's position in the first house also offers a sense of self-importance that, at its most extreme, allows individuals to use their allure to manipulate others and, as a result, get what they want. If positively aspected, Venus in the first house will, like the beloved agrarian fertility Goddess, attempt to grant prosperity and pleasure with the stipulation that she receives loyalty, respect, sexual fulfilment and/or love. If afflicted, the planet will manifest the worst aspects of Aphrodite and behave like a spoiled child. People with an afflicted Venus in the first house may be insecure and self-indulgent and may have difficulty being tactful and diplomatic. They may indulge in lies, manipulation or emotional blackmail to satisfy their own whims and attain a false sense of power. Their quest for constant approval will lead these people to employ their Venus-tinted window to project a loving, beautiful, charming and compassionate image – sincere if Venus is well aspected, but a façade if the planet is afflicted.

Although traditionally this placement has been interpreted as captivating, soft-spoken, friendly and having an affinity for the creative arts, it is just as responsible for indulgent behaviour, laziness and complete self-absorption. Because it is prominent in the horoscopes of individuals drawn to the creative arts, cosmetics, modelling, design, clothing, sales or any field that utilises seductive charm, this placement was once considered difficult for men who were not 'one of the boys' or who did not actively participate in sports – the outlets for so-called traditional male bonding.

A perfect example of Venus in the first house is Bill Clinton (see Figure 6.1, page 135), whose Venus is placed not only in the first house but in its own sign of Libra. Because it is also conjunct the Libra ascendant, the planet is quite dominant (notoriously so) in his personality.* During the course of one of his political campaigns it became evident that Clinton had an ability to supply just the right answers to each audience, thus acquiring the nickname 'Slick Willie'. Although Clinton is extremely intelligent, his turbulent youth as the child of an alcoholic makes it extremely

---

*Although Clinton has three planets in Leo (including his Sun), as well as Venus, Mars and Neptune conjunct his Ascendant in the first house, this particular description is only applicable to Venus.

important for him to be well-liked and praised for his achievements. With Venus in an air sign in a fire house, it is apparent that he prides himself on his ability to exchange ideas with a wide public (air) who return to him the admiration and respect (fire) he desperately seeks. Because the American people have given their seal of approval by electing him president, he will attempt to reward them by stimulating the economy – just as Inanna granted prosperity to the Sumerians.

This desire to please everyone can become so overwhelming that it leads to vacillation and an inability to take a decision. In Clinton's case, his inordinate need to be popular and praised for his achievements is both an asset and a liability. Although his ability to win over the public has certainly worked in his favour, his desire to please has unfortunately resulted in too many compromises and broken promises, and, as I write this (December 1993), the public's disfavour – exactly the opposite of what Clinton anticipated. My advice for anyone with as overwhelming a Venusian influence as Mr Clinton's would be, above all, to be direct and honest. If promises or good intentions cannot be fulfilled, do not wait too long before divulging the truth or you will most certainly appear deceptive.

Other notable personalities with Venus in the first house include King Louis XVI of France, Jean Cocteau, Judy Garland, Gerald Ford, Paul Newman, Danny DeVito, Margaret Thatcher, Ethel Kennedy, Ingrid Bergman, Dyan Cannon, Lynn Redgrave and Eartha Kitt.

TAURUS AND LIBRA AS ASCENDANT
(FIRST HOUSE CUSP)

If Taurus is the sign of the ascendant, the course of life is directed towards achieving the complete autonomy that is provided by economic well-being. These people will be good listeners and only speak when there is something to say. They are patient, persevering, sensual and, at the same time, jealous, possessive, lazy and excessive. In addition they are productive, relentless, inflexible and need to be in control. When things do not go according to plan, they find it difficult to bounce back. Solidly built with round faces and thick necks, they have a tendency to put on weight. Since the first house rules physical appearance and, according to Hindu (Vedic) astrology, health, they may be prone to difficulties concerning the thyroid, swollen glands, sore throats, stiff necks, poor eyesight and bad skin.

If Libra is the sign of the ascendant, those born at this time will place the highest priority on being involved with partnerships. Attempting to achieve harmony in their lives and pleasing those close to them makes it difficult for these people to exercise their decision-making abilities. When they do decide to take action it is often prompted by what is expected of them rather than what emanates from their heart and soul. They are artistic, charming, peace-loving and friendly as well as lazy, excessive and manipulative. They may be prone to kidney ailments, bladder infections, bad skin and digestive problems.

Venus in the Second House

Keywords: materialistic, possessive, jealous, aesthetic, practical, devoted, indulgent

Because Venus is the natural ruler of the second house, this placement brings out the best and worst qualities of the planet, ranging from practicality, prosperity, sensuality and an eye for beauty to laziness, indulgence, jealousy and greed. As stated in Chapter 6, the second house is not only indicative of material security but the personal resources – talents, skills and assets – with which we attain our goals and maintain control over our lives. Planets in the second house describe precisely which types of resources (for example Venusian, Martian, Jupiterian) are readily accessible. As a result, the traditional interpretation of Venus in the second house has always been 'making money (second house) through love, beauty and creativity (Venus)'. While this description is still applicable, the definition must be expanded to include the utilisation of social skills, diplomacy and inner confidence to attain economic well-being and its accompanying stability.

Because the second house has traditionally been an indicator of how income is acquired, this placement may indeed foster visual and performing artists, interior designers, clothing manufacturers, cosmeticians, models, salespeople and politicians – all Venusian professions. Like Venus-ruled Taurus, the second house corresponds to the throat, making this placement common in the horoscopes of singers, among them Enrico Caruso, Jessye Norman and Edith Piaf.

Frequently consumed with financial security, these people favour long-term investments such as mutual funds, real estate or art collecting. Due to their powers of persuasion and innate understanding of economics, they can also be successful financial advisers, stock brokers, investment bankers or in any profession in which one assists others in making money. If these people are unable to achieve monetary success on their own, it will likely be pursued through a relationship, thus confirming the position's traditional interpretation. While this placement does indeed indicate a conscious search for affluence, strength and stability in the choice of partner, those with this placement must be cautioned not to regard the partner as another business associate, 'acquisition' or financial conquest, and must never take him or her for granted. Since for these people financial and emotional security are completely intertwined, they often become jealous and possessive about what they could lose (companionship, money and property) should the relationship ever dissolve.

Because self-esteem is based on economic and/or creative success, a positively aspected Venus may ensure financial acumen, prudent monetary planning and wise investment skills. An afflicted Venus, on the other hand, can encourage indulgent, wasteful spending to satisfy opulent tastes and, if the level of material prosperity to which these people aspire is not attained, it will be sought through personal and professional relationships. Due to the desire to maintain an affluent lifestyle, ordinarily good business sense can be transformed into manipulative, ruthless and unethical practices, including the use of sex to get what they want.

These fair-minded, stubborn people are not only proud of their own accomplishments and procurements but are eager to support artists and charities by providing subsidies, loans and employment opportunities whenever possible. Very rarely are they generous, however, unless a personal benefit can be derived. Should they feel betrayed or not afforded the respect and/or gratitude they deem was earned, their benevolence can turn into resentment and hostility – typical of the fixed signs (Taurus, Leo, Scorpio and Aquarius) and houses (second, fifth, eighth and eleventh). While they can be amazingly devoted, responsible and committed partners and parents, their insecurity, possessiveness and/or jealousy often thwart their ability to command respect.

While the Libran-influenced Venus is known for co-operation and diplomacy, the Taurean-inspired Venus (descriptive of this particular placement) cannot accept any challenge to their authority. Loving, proud, magnanimous and extremely sensual, they must (as employers, partners and parents) learn to delegate responsibility and trust the decisions of others – otherwise they run the risk of becoming complete workaholics bent on control. Because their self-esteem is based on economic and/or creative success, they are wary of being taken advantage of and can recognise instinctively ambitious social climbers.

If the second house (as it is in Hindu [Vedic] astrology) is defined as an indicator of one's early education, the planet occupying this region signifies how our learning habits provide the skills and talents that enable us to earn a living and pursue our goals. For people with Venus in the second house, there may be great artistic talent and they tend to learn creatively rather than intellectually. If Venus is afflicted, this placement may contribute to laziness, poor learning habits and an inability to concentrate.

Most important, the placement of this fruitful and sensual planet in its own house bestows the unique ability to create, nurture, and finalise goals. In fact, the acquisition of property, the accumulation of profits or the conception of a child often occurs during transits and progressions to the second house cusp, its occupying planet or planetary ruler.

We have already seen how Venus in Libra is expressed in the chart of Woody Allen. Let's further analyse how this behaviour is affected by the placement of Venus in the second house. Strengthened by its position in the sign it rules (which signifies relationships) and its own house (which represents finances), this

Venus – which is also the subject of a t-square with Mars and Pluto – reaffirms the planet's association of love with money. Not only has Woody Allen been abetted personally and professionally by his leading ladies, but his ability to make or break their careers gives him a certain amount of power and control over them. An exaggerated need for autonomy and control is also exemplified by Allen's afflicted Venus in the second house. Even after his public custody battle with Mia Farrow, in which his behaviour was condemned by the presiding judge, Allen still affirmed his affair with Farrow's adopted daughter. Other notables with Venus in the second house include Queen Elizabeth I, James Joyce, Ross Perot, Joanne Woodward, Rosemary Clooney, Francis Ford Coppola, Diane Keaton, Patricia Neal, Erma Bombeck, Phyllis Schafly, Caroline Kennedy, Johnny Carson and Merv Griffin.

TAURUS AND LIBRA ON THE SECOND HOUSE CUSP

Those with Taurus on the cusp of the second house are obsessed with the attainment of financial security and enjoy accumulating collectibles, especially works of art. Though they may be extravagant, they usually make wise investments – often in conjunction with a partner.

Those with Libra on the cusp of the second house may form business relationships with their spouses or with a trustworthy partner who is also a friend.

Venus in the Third House

Keywords: creative (particularly with regard to writing), media-orientated, detached, talkative, eager to share ideas, desiring freedom in love

When Venus occupies the intellectual and communicative third house, there is an enormous passion for learning that is usually satisfied through travelling, devouring books, magazines and newspapers, attending media events (theatre, film, concerts, lectures) and, most significantly, by observing and conversing with others. Empowered by constant intellectual exchanges and the wealth of information amassed therefrom, people with Venus in the third house revel in the creativity and productivity that these interchanges stimulate. Particularly suited for professions that encompass communications (oral and/or written) and the media arts, these individuals are drawn to writing, journalism, filmwork, public relations and advertising – third house fields that may provide the artistic fulfilment and potential economic stability craved by Venus. Possessing eloquent speaking voices and powers of persuasion, they are as comfortable with the sales and marketing end of these professions as they are with the creative aspects. Influenced by the versatility intrinsic to the third house, such individuals also have an enthusiasm and willingness to share ideas and work towards a common goal, making them adept as team players where communication and co-operation are of the essence – for example on the editorial staff of a magazine, as a member of a film crew, etc.

Because their self-confidence hinges on peer approval, these individuals, unwilling to fight adversity, usually form friendships and partnerships with those who can provide intellectual stimulation and instruction as well as encouragement and support. Due to an innate restlessness, they often choose vocations that do not require being chained to a desk and partners who share their passion for mobility and are willing to travel or even relocate should the opportunity arise. By the same token, partners of these people need not share their interests; it must merely be recognised that a wide circle of friends and range of interests are necessary to their well-being and, as a result, their ability to love.

Most important, the partners of people with Venus in the third house must never feel that they can be all people to their mates. It is important to recognise that while the placement of Venus in the airy third house requires that verbal communication and/or spiritual contact be the essence of a committed relationship, the detachment of this position can just as easily lend itself to short-term liaisons with no obligation. The dispassionate quality of a sensual planet (Venus) placed in a house that thrives on human connection (third house) is often found in individuals who do not place high value on monogamy, since they sometimes view sex as a means of communication and not necessarily as an expression of love or a testament to devotion.

Their short attention span, need for constant mental stimulation and never-ending appetite for travel usually impede long-term domestic planning. If Venus is conjunct the i.c. (the cusp of the fourth house), however, restlessness will be abated in favour of a proclivity towards the establishment of a home and family.

If positively aspected, these individuals bring an inspirational presence and originality into relationships, which will never suffer from boredom. While a well-aspected Venus indicates that these people have integrated, or attempted to integrate, their need for freedom with their desire for love, an afflicted Venus often creates an emotional detachment that desensitises them to the feelings of others. Individuals with Venus in the third house (to whom personal and professional freedom are imperative) must recognise that perpetual stimulation and mobility are not necessarily synonymous with independence or the fulfilment of artistic expression. With the realisation that freedom is, in actuality, a state of mind, the constant search for *new* horizons may be abandoned in favour of challenges closer to home, such as the rejuvenation of long-term relationships, jobs and/or creative projects that may have grown stale.

Because Venus is indicative of the desire to proliferate, its occupancy of the house representing communications and restlessness challenges the ability to maintain a committed relationship amid a variety of other activities (work, hobbies, friendships). Because the need for constant stimulation can present seemingly insurmountable obstacles, it is important to open the lines of communication with any romantic partners. Through rational and logical discussion, it may be discovered that it is indeed possible to nurture a family without surrendering personal freedom – the biggest fear confronting those with Venus in the third house. If Venus in the third house is conjunct the i.c., these people will be more inclined to balance their desire for outside stimulation with a need for a loving relationship. Furthermore, they may be writers, authors, musicians, artists, interior designers, real estate salespeople or involved in any profession in which they can earn a living by using their creative communication skills and affable personalities.

With Venus in Aquarius in the third house, Gloria Steinem's love of causes is filtered through the third house of writing, communications and short-term travel. Not only has Steinem been a successful editor, journalist and author (third house), but perhaps her greatest skill is her oratory ability and capacity for enthralling live audiences with her articulate, engaging and down-to-earth presentations. With Venus placed in Aquarius *and* the third house, it is understandable how she manages intense, meaningful love affairs yet has thus far avoided making a long-term commitment – attributable to the influence of both Aquarius *and* the third house. Because the sign and house recipient of her Venus are both categorised as the emotionally detached element of air, Steinem's most meaningful relationships have truly been her friendships with powerful, intelligent women (whom she calls her family), most of whom share her involvement with social and political activism. It is, in fact, this type of intense communication, love and respect that Plato attributed to the cerebral Aphrodite Urania and that I liken to the 'Libran' relationship-orientated Venus rather than to the 'Taurean' independent Venus. Unfortunately, the Greek philosopher erroneously assumed that: 1) this type of sharing could only occur between men and 2) this expression of love was more spiritual and, therefore, of a higher quality. Steinem's horoscope is a perfect example of the emphasis on relationships (Venus in air) expressed in a non-traditional way (Venus in Aquarius).

The ability to create (Venus) masterful dialogue (third house) is wonderfully epitomised by Noel Coward, George Bernard Shaw and Tennessee Williams – three of the twentieth century's leading playwrights and true masters of the English language. While Noel Coward was also known for his own commanding performances and charming personality, his ability to combine satirical wit and social commentary links him with Shaw. The emotional detachment of Venus in the third house is evident in the lives of Coward and Williams, whose homosexuality and colourful lifestyles are well documented. While Shaw was reputed to have had a long-time love affair with Mrs Patrick Campbell, who starred in many of his plays, he, too, never married.

Other notables with Venus in the third house include Paul Cezanne, Winston Churchill, Rudolph Valentino, Edward Kennedy, Jack Kemp, Robert Dole, Paul Tsongas, Stephen King and Frank Sinatra.

TAURUS AND LIBRA ON THE THIRD HOUSE CUSP

Those with Taurus on the third house cusp have slower minds and may be associative and/or visual thinkers who use intuition, images and colours the way others use logic and reasoning.

Those with Libra on the third house cusp will be eloquent speakers with a flair for journalism, poetry, acting and public speaking. They will have harmonious relationships with their siblings, who are usually talented and intelligent. They are likable, soft-spoken and diplomatic.

Venus in the Fourth House

Keywords: domestic, loving tranquillity, family-orientated, needing harmonious surroundings

The fourth house represents the emotional relationship we had with our parents which, in turn, affects how as adults we approach family, home and emotional commitment. Self-worth, therefore, is frequently measured in proportion to the strength of family ties. When Venus is placed in this sphere, it encourages a relationship or creative outlet that accommodates the intense desire for the steadfastness of home, family and community. Just as the fertility Goddesses prevented economic disaster by replenishing the earth, these fiercely protective individuals will stop at nothing to preserve and safeguard the stability of their immediate environment.

Because the fourth house represents the emotional nourishment received from the parents,* the placement of a well-aspected

---

*While traditional astrologers have always attributed the fourth house and the i.c. to the mother, some modern Jungian astrologers believe that they are representative of the father. For the purposes of this book, the fourth house will be viewed as emblematic of a person's emotional nourishment and family background – which, until recently, was almost exclusively the domain of the mother.

Venus may indicate a childhood replete with material comforts and parental affection. Empowered by a sound, supportive background, these people can, in turn, bestow boundless strength, creativity and unconditional love onto their *own* partners and children. Not only can they provide a strong emotional foundation on which not only families but companies, communities and organisations are built, but their sense of preservation extends to participating actively in the protection of the environment and the beautification of their communities.

If, however, Venus is afflicted in the fourth house, the search for emotional nourishment may lead to hastily formed and potentially destructive relationships. Parental models may have been indulgent, wasteful and/or irresponsible – behaviour patterns that these individuals do not wish to repeat – or they may have simply changed residences and schools several times during childhood. Lacking a harmonious family life or what they perceive represents a stable upbringing, these individuals may seek out partners whom they believe will provide what they have lacked; instead, their choices often eerily mirror their mothers and/or fathers, thus re-enacting turbulent parental relationships. Their instabilities and insecurities can result in possessive attitudes towards partners or unrealistic expectations of obtaining the devotion and attention withheld during their youth. It is vital that people with Venus in the fourth house go beyond childhood traumas so that these events are not re-enacted with their own partners or even children, to whom they may look for undying devotion.

While a positively aspected Venus enables these individuals to become loving partners who are hopelessly romantic and extremely loyal, the emotional or economic insecurity generated by an afflicted Venus in the fourth house may instead cause them to become jealous, possessive lovers and/or controlling, overprotective parents. Ironically, this stifling behaviour may further alienate their families and threaten the secure home base that they were attempting to build and maintain. Another manifestation is the desire to confine themselves and retreat into a cocoon-like existence devoid of social obligations. Retaining creative hobbies and engaging in activities outside the home will lessen the risk of living in their partner's shadow and decrease the likelihood that they will project unfulfilled ambitions onto their children – both courses ultimately detrimental.

In addition to representing the basis of the emotions and familial relationships, the fourth house symbolises the physical abode a person inhabits (as child and adult) which serves as an extension of the self. Hospitable and magnanimous, people with Venus in the fourth house take enormous pride in their homes, which are usually tastefully and comfortably decorated – reminiscent of or in reaction to the comforts and security of their own harmonious youth (or lack thereof). With creative, productive and loving Venus affecting one's domicile, these individuals truly enjoy activities that revolve around their homes, ranging from cooking and decorating to entertaining friends and family. They will also encourage their children to be equally hospitable hosts and hostesses.

The financial rewards of Venus in the fourth house emanate from occupations that involve either creative expression in the privacy of a home office (self-employed artists or writers, for example) or working in the areas of real estate, interior decorating, art collecting, gardening or cooking. Because Venus is a materialistic planet, idealistic and impractical pursuits are often sacrificed in favour of professions that provide financial stability and material comforts.

For those with Venus conjunct the i.c., the cusp of the fourth house and part of the parental axis, their parents will have displayed Venusian characteristics. If well aspected, one or both may have been loving, creative, prosperous and a source of strength. If afflicted, one or both may have been lazy, indulgent, manipulative or distant.

With Venus in Capricorn in the fourth house, Richard Burton's problems may have stemmed from an inability to shake off an impoverished youth. Instead of internalising his wonderful talents, Burton turned to powerful women for protection and to provide him with the self-worth that he lacked. Though opulence defined his years with Elizabeth Taylor, his alcoholism indicated that, despite having a beautiful wife and an illustrious career, he never overcame the insecurities of his impoverished background in Wales.

It may be speculated that Princess Diana's independence and popularity may have been difficult for Prince Charles to come to terms with, as his Venus in Libra in the fourth house demands that he have a wife who provides emotional security, nurturing and protection – impossible for a princess in the public eye. While they indeed had marital problems, it was ultimately the publicity surrounding the publication of Diana's biography that completely obliterated whatever privacy (fourth house) they may have had and precipitated the breakup of their marriage.

Notable personalities with Venus in the fourth house include Clara Schumann, Rock Hudson, Barbara Cartland, Ginger Rogers, Fred Astaire, Dianne Feinstein and Prince Charles.

TAURUS AND LIBRA ON THE FOURTH HOUSE CUSP

For those with Taurus on the fourth house cusp, their homes will be practical, comfortable and tastefully furnished. Their family background will have been financially secure and emotionally stable.

Those with Libra on the fourth house cusp seek partners who share their vision of a harmonious family life. It is also important that their homes are aesthetically pleasing and possibly decorated with works of art.

Venus in the Fifth House

Keywords: demonstrative, romantic, passionate, self-centred, creative

Corresponding to the fixed fire sign, Leo, the fifth house has traditionally been associated with love affairs, children, sports, entertainment, drama, gambling and creative/pleasurable pursuits – in other words, any activity or hobby that fulfils the need for self-expression. Contrary to the opposing eleventh house that is concerned with *group* activities, the operative word for the fifth house is 'self' and its gratification through the admiration and approval of others. To this end, those with Venus placed in the fifth house are able to inject passion, enthusiasm and a unique individuality into their relationships and the lives of their children. While these people may often be accused of being self-serving, egotistical, overdramatic and, at times, too overbearing, these are the very qualities that make them forceful, effective, tireless workers and advocates of causes for which they feel enormous conviction and passion.

If Venus is well aspected, these individuals are magnanimous, passionate, exuberant and compelling partners whose ability to co-operate goes hand in hand with a need for recognition. If, however, Venus is poorly aspected, these people may be insecure about their physical appearance, their capacity for love and/or their ability to share. This can lead to a search for these qualities within a relationship and while they may, indeed, be attracted to charismatic people who can provide what they themselves lack, they must discover their own sense of worth by learning to strike a balance between self-gratification and co-operation.

Represented by the fifth house, the enthusiasm that they bring into their love affairs does not necessarily result in marriage or long-term commitment. In fact, these people are so enamoured of themselves and the excitement of new conquests that they often have many flings prior to settling down. If they do settle down, it is important that they become involved with challenging and enjoyable activities outside the home, such as through the performing arts, exercise, sport or socialising; if they do not, there is a potential for all their excitable energy to manifest as demanding, childlike and domineering behaviour.

Although the second house represents the actual act of conception, the fifth house symbolises the result of procreative effort and the pride it evokes – whether it be a completed work of art, a blossoming romance or a child. While usually loving, attentive and encouraging parents, people with Venus in this house can also be overbearing, dominant and extremely resistant to change. Exceedingly individualistic and, at times, dictatorial, they will extend freedom of expression to others if it serves their self-interest. Frequently lacking true compassion and empathy, they can become so engrossed in the quest for self-glorification that friendships and relationships with partners and children ultimately suffer. It is vital for these individuals to utilise the power of Venus by cultivating a truly unselfish interest in their friends, colleagues, partners and children rather than simply using them as support networks.

In addition to affirming self-worth through creative and innovative accomplishments, people with this placement are often highly competitive and continually in pursuit of superiority and recognition for their talents. Because of an incessant, almost obsessive need to feel 'good', activities such as shopping, physical exercise, sex, sport and gambling can be extremely enticing and, if Venus is poorly aspected, these outlets become compulsive and potentially dangerous.

Because the fifth house is classified as fixed, the propensity for self-control of people with Venus in this placement is extraordinary, and though they may be somewhat hedonistic their indulgences will be short-lived – especially if these interfere with creative, romantic or financial goals. The tremendous need for sensual pleasure may find a positive outlet in dancing, dramatic arts, skiing or tennis – all of which produce feelings of exhilaration and a sense of physical well-being.

Although the fifth house has a reputation for endowing occupying and ruling planets with overbearing, self-centred traits, the desire for centre-stage and the quest for uniqueness transforms Venus into a symbol of innovative self-expression and boundless inspiration. At social gatherings (which they love hosting), individuals with Venus in the fifth house are easily recognised by their conspicuous, sometimes ostentatious clothing and/or flirtatious, gregarious manner. Fanatical about their own importance, individuals with this placement prefer self-employment or a job that offers creative control rather than to be a cog in the anonymous corporate wheel or to participate in group endeavours which could compromise their ideals.

Fostering self-expression, the fifth house exemplifies one's attitudes toward children – the arena in which we truly recreate and, therefore, perpetuate ourselves. While it is understandable how the fifth house symbolises the procreative act of child-bearing, it is just as comprehensible that, due to its self-involvement, the corresponding fifth sign of Leo, like all fire signs, is designated (by classical Hindu [Vedic] astrology) a barren, childless sign. This same system also states, however, that – as the Lesser Benefic – Venus brings emotional and financial rewards through offspring when it appears in the fifth house. When Venus or Jupiter transits or progresses through the fifth house or the planet ruling or occupying the fifth house, the time is ripe for childbirth (according to both Eastern and Western astrology). If Venus, Jupiter or the natal Moon, three beneficent planets (according to Hindu [Vedic] astrology) are situated in or rule the fifth house, the transit or progression of these planets will be even more effective.

Understandably, people with Venus in the fifth house often postpone or swear off having children due to their own self-involvement. When they learn to share, they make excellent parents because of the seriousness and commitment they bring to all their undertakings. Not surprisingly, when they and/or their friends become parents, their interest in children's issues soars and they may even change their profession to one concerning the education, health, entertainment and/or the welfare of youngsters – concerns unimaginable to them when they were young adults.

I clearly remember the horoscope of a female client who was a yoga instructor in her early thirties at the time I drew up her chart. The placement of Venus in her fifth house indicated to me that it would be beneficial if she were to become involved with children on a creative level, either as a parent or teacher. She insisted, however, that she had no affinity for this. By sheer coincidence we met several years later and I learned that after having had two children she had refocused her career and was teaching yoga to expectant mothers – linking her personal and professional life.

With Venus in Scorpio in the fifth house, Hillary Rodham Clinton (Figure 10.1, see page 261) exemplifies the control, power and influence (Scorpio) she has wielded in the area of children's rights and reform, for which she has won enormous recognition, respect and admiration (fifth house). While she did indeed 'follow her heart'* to Arkansas, Mrs Clinton was not content to be just

---

*This is her own description of her choice to marry Bill Clinton and move to Arkansas with him, thereby refusing lucrative job offers with several prominent law firms.[4]

a politician's wife. She was first a successful attorney and ultimately a partner in a prestigious Little Rock law firm; she presently heads a US national task force on health reform.

Mrs Clinton's self-esteem, which allows her to exercise multi-faceted roles (presidential advisor, First Lady, wife, mother) would not have been so strong had she not pursued her own interests, which garnered accolades from the legal community. Strongly individualistic, the First Lady announced that her official designation should include her maiden name.

Although she has only one child, her work with the Children's Defense Fund, a non-profit organisation dedicated to protecting the rights of minors, reiterates that the welfare of children (fifth house) has been a major focus in her life and has initiated many programmes ensuring the health and education of children throughout Arkansas and, hopefully, the rest of the U.S.

Celebrities with Venus in the fifth house include Marie Antoinette, Frederick Chopin, Percy Bysshe Shelley, William Wordsworth, Franklin D. Roosevelt, Indira Gandhi, Carl Sandburg, Mick Jagger, George Harrison and Princess Diana.

TAURUS AND LIBRA ON THE FIFTH HOUSE CUSP

If Taurus is on the fifth house cusp, there is sensuality, passion, jealousy and an attraction to people who spend money lavishly. While there is a definite affinity with having children, caution must be exercised not to regard them as possessions.

Those with Libra on the fifth house cusp adore flattery and admiration and demand respect. They are artistic, charming, sensual and passionate. There is a tendency towards creative collaborations, especially with a love interest.

Venus in the Sixth House

Keywords: health-conscious, amiable, possessing enormous creative discipline, desiring harmonious working conditions

With Venus in the sixth house (which corresponds to the mutable earth sign of Virgo) enormous value is placed on being of service and approaching work with a meticulous and analytical eye. Not particularly gifted with leadership abilities (the domain of the fifth sign/house), individuals with a well-aspected Venus in the sixth house bring to their personal and professional relationships a sense of loyalty, attention to detail and a flair for sustained productivity from which they garner self-validation. Due to the time and energy they expend working and/or volunteering their services, the classic description of Venus in the sixth house – 'falling in love (Venus) with a co-worker (sixth house)' – is likely to apply.

If the planet is afflicted, however, these sometimes shy or self-conscious individuals often question their own abilities. They may be attracted to people who are also extremely hard workers but who may not be able to offer the encouragement needed. Overly particular about and judgmental of colleagues, friends and lovers, they are, in actuality, most critical of themselves. For this reason they deny themselves the sensual pleasure that Venus so willingly offers; instead it is sublimated through their work and drive towards self-improvement.

To attain perfection, they may become fanatic about diet, exercise and health fads. While individuals with a well-situated Venus approach their bodies sensibly and with moderation, individuals with an ill-placed Venus may follow one of two extremes: 1) become obsessive about their exercise regiment or 2) become slovenly, careless and indulgent – leading, at its most extreme, to poor work habits, an inability to keep a job and poor health.

Advocates of excellence through hard work, good nutrition, physical exercise and service to others (sixth house), these prudent individuals often become committed social workers, counsellors, dietitians, health care practitioners, physical therapists or secretaries. Consummate professionals, their social skills, capacity for teamwork, noble dedication and efficiency enable them to bypass the frustrations of bureaucratic 'red tape' and become effective workers. They may also be attracted to craftswork, interior design, sculpture or architecture, which combine artistry with the meticulousness of the sixth house.

Dutiful workers concerned with the happiness and welfare of others – to the detriment of their own enjoyment – these individuals often feel guilty if they partake in frivolity and/or sensual pleasure. While it is, indeed, advisable that these tense workaholics learn to relax and 'let go', there is no doubt that even the slightest excess may adversely affect their sensitive constitutions and may even produce food allergies. The Venus-ruled throat, kidneys and skin may even present chronic problems that are likely to flair up during an allergic reaction or at times of emotional stress.

Moreover, an obsession with health and fitness often lends itself to vegetarianism (or some other special diet), yoga, meditation or regular physical exercise as part of a daily routine. Due to the practicality of the sixth house, people with Venus in this placement will make choices in their personal and professional lives that bring contentment, harmony and a comfortable income which will enable them to live healthy, fit and, thus, enjoyable lives.

Because Mercury, a symbol of intelligence and communications, is the natural ruler of the sixth house (corresponding to the Sixth sign of Virgo), romantic liaisons are based not merely on passion but on mutual respect and support. Since those with Venus in the sixth house have a propensity for working long hours working or volunteering their services, it is essential that they find partners whose professions and/or interests are equally fulfilling and who understand that gratifying work contributes greatly to their mental well-being.

If Venus is conjunct the Descendant, individuals are less reserved and the issues that concern them are what make them attractive to others. Their approach to work, service and health is intertwined with their choice of partner, who is either a colleague or deeply involved in the same lifestyle, causes or goals.

The sense of accomplishment and artistic perfection that they achieve through the methodical ' "fine-tuning" of their talents, skills and abilities'[2] is typical of Dustin Hoffman, one of the finest actors working today. His portrayal in the movie *Tootsie* of an obsessively meticulous, critical actor forced to find work disguised as a woman because no one would hire him as a man is said to have been an exaggerated portrait of his own methodical technique. While he may once have been reputedly difficult to work with, Hoffman has been in demand since his role in *The Graduate* (1968) catapulted him to fame. Like Marlon Brando and Robert Duvall (each of whom has Venus in the sixth house), Hoffman is a perfectionist who not only transforms himself but, if necessary, distorts his body to suit each character, thereby becoming unrecognisable with each new role.

Other personalities with Venus in the sixth house include Mary Cassatt, Sigmund Freud, Carl Jung, Marlene Dietrich, Joyce Carol Oates, Jonathan Winters, Bob Dylan, Natalie Cole, Richard Nixon, Betty Ford and Prince Andrew.

TAURUS AND LIBRA ON THE SIXTH HOUSE CUSP

For those with Taurus on the sixth house cusp, the sensitive areas of the body include the throat, neck, tonsils and eyes. Although generally in good health, there may be a tendency towards excess. They are slow but dependable workers.

Those with Libra on the sixth house cusp need harmony in their work environment and camaraderie among co-workers. Their work may involve sales, advertising, public relations or counselling. They may be prone to overindulgence or problems with the eyes, skin, kidneys and abdomen.

Venus in the Seventh House

Keywords: relationship-orientated, co-operative, diplomatic, objective, dependent

Traditionally signifying marriage, partnership, contracts and lawsuits,* the seventh house reveals the social self – namely, how we behave in a close personal or professional relationship. Because the descendant, which commences the seventh house, is directly opposed to the ascendant, the qualities inherent in this region of the chart – as defined by its occupying and/or ruling planet(s) – are not necessarily advantageous for developing an ability to function autonomously. Corresponding to the seventh sign of Libra, the seventh house represents any situation or circumstance – marriage being the exemplar – where diplomacy, sharing and co-operation must apply.

While the planet occupying or ruling the seventh house describes our behaviour towards a personal and/or professional partner, it also demonstrates how we relate one on one as opposed to within a group or the community at large. Towards this end, Venus in its natural seventh house, especially if conjunct the descendant, accentuates the necessity for teamwork, that is, the belief that it is only through another person – whether it be friendship, business or marriage – that best efforts can be made. Possessing objectivity, or the ability to view the self through another's eyes, those with Venus in the seventh house are keenly aware that individuals or situations will elicit their best qualities and/or supply them with the kind of lifestyle they lack and may not be able to achieve themselves. Given their Venusian charm, beauty, sensuality and ability to co-operate, listen and even manipulate others, they know how to win other people over and achieve the union they so desire.

The placement of Venus in the seventh house emphasises the planet's cerebral qualities and confers an approach to life

---

*In horoscope textbooks, this house also refers to 'open enemies' – that is, competitors, ex-spouses or anyone with whom a person is involved in a legal dispute – as opposed to the twelfth house, which represents 'secret or hidden enemies'. According to Hindu (Vedic) astrology, it is the sixth house that represents open enemies – especially at the workplace.

dominated by the need for harmony, romance and social acceptance. Because the self-esteem of those with this placement depends almost entirely upon the adulation of others, these individuals have carefully cultivated poised, charming personalities, agreeable dispositions and pleasing, stylish demeanours. Frequently espousing ideas that endear them to others, these beguiling and seductive individuals are loving, supportive and sexually desirable partners whose devotional strength and loyalty are the key factors in the success of any relationship.

In the professional sphere, those born with Venus in the seventh house have creative vision, diplomatic skills and keen marketing abilities – all qualities that make them desirable colleagues. Completely attuned to the needs of others, they are well-suited for careers in sales, public relations or advertising and have an affinity for supportive roles such as receptionist, secretary or administrative assistant. Intent listeners, they also possess the potential, like Librans, to become excellent mediators, therapists, counsellors and psychologists or, if their charts display a powerful Martian influence, attorneys with commanding presence and persuasive abilities. (Although people with seventh house emphases are fascinated with legal principles, it is a strongly placed Mars that makes them eminently suitable for the courtroom arena.) Rather than ambitiously pursue a career of their own, these individuals may simply choose to enable their spouse or partner to fulfil his or her professional obligations by providing a supporting but none the less vital role. For these individuals, the accolades and monetary rewards epitomise the success of their collaboration.

If Venus is well aspected, these people strive toward interdependence and know instinctively how to be supportive without compromising their own needs. Individuals with an afflicted Venus in the seventh house, however, may be motivated by their insecurity and craving for companionship to seek partners who are then given the impossible task of elevating their self-esteem. Such relationships are inevitably one-sided, dependent and unhealthy, based only on passion, sexual attraction or financial gain – activated during difficult transits and progressions through the seventh house. It is during these stressful times that these individuals must, as the quintessential Libran Venus, focus on healing and transforming the self in order to recapture the spirit of interdependence (rather than dependence) that makes for a healthy relationship.

Although the position of Venus in its natural house has traditionally been considered propitious in creating a loving, prosperous family life, it often produces a relentless obsession with wealth and glamour rather than with strength of character. While those with this placement may find that their relationships are not necessarily philosophically or intellectually motivated (as when the outer planets appear in the seventh house), these individuals crave a loving, creative and nurturing partnership and will stop at nothing to preserve their union. Because they are, at times, consumed with social standing and public image, Venus in the seventh house people strive to present a picture of marital bliss and contentment even during times of emotional and/or financial stress and obvious discord. If Venus is conjunct the descendant, sensuality, co-operation, sharing ideas and friendliness are especially evident in the way these people relate to others.

The positive application of this relationship-orientated Venus is perfectly exemplified by my creative and well-educated client, Mara, who has four planets (including Venus) situated in the seventh house. She confided to me that her greatest self-fulfilment was derived not from the attainment of professional goals but from her marriage to a loving, successful doctor. In fact, she could not even imagine actively pursuing a career without a partner to support her efforts and share her success. Not only did domestic happiness far outweigh professional aspirations, she was convinced that her financial goals would not have been met had she been left to her own devices. In her opinion, mutual co-operation is often mistakenly viewed by many goal-orientated people as dependency. She was not living her husband's dreams but fulfilling her own. Moreover, she defines a committed relationship as a source of strength – not a sign of weakness.

Notables with Venus in the seventh house include Robert Browning, Franz Schubert, Henri Matisse, Bertrand Russell, Annie Besant, Paul Verlaine, Michael Dukakis, Patty Hearst,

Charles Manson, Elizabeth Taylor, Princess Margaret and Paloma Picasso.

TAURUS AND LIBRA AS THE DESCENDANT (SEVENTH HOUSE CUSP)

If Taurus is the descendant there is a commitment to partnerships; yet these partnerships must guarantee economic security as well as passion and fidelity. In return for partners who are comforting and patient those with Taurus as the descendant will be generous and reliable though at times jealous and possessive.

Those with Libra as the descendant seek partners who will appreciate their beautiful, charming and sophisticated qualities. They have a keen awareness of how to attract a partner and quite often will be manipulative if they are insecure and unsure of themselves.

Venus in the Eighth House

Keywords: jealous, intense, charismatic, financially and sexually manipulative

While the seventh house describes the types of partnerships to which one gravitates as well as the ability to co-operate and share, the eighth house (second from the seventh) depicts the financial assets and liabilities acquired through marriage, business partnerships or family relationships, ranging from money, stocks and real estates to legacies, lawsuits and insurance benefits.* Corresponding to the fixed water sign of Scorpio, the eighth house also symbolises emotional, psychological, sexual and financial attitudes that colour personal and professional relationships – especially the use or misuse of power.

Just as Inanna and Dumuzi represented the convergence of sex, money and power, individuals with Venus in the eighth house seek the same type of adrenaline rush from their financial conquests,

---

*This is opposed to the possessive second house, which signifies the accumulation of assets by a single individual.

intimate and/or professional relationships. When the Goddess was sexually fulfilled, she was injected with a sense of potency that stimulated the prosperous growing season and, ultimately, empowered her people. Similarly, the self-worth of individuals with Venus in the eighth house is directly connected with sexual prowess, the ability to acquire money and/or the need to be in control.

Because the eighth house relates to emotional and sexual intensity, these individuals are aware that, in order to satisfy their complex needs and sustain their interests, relationships must have an element of challenge and excitement that quenches their sexual appetite and thirst for money and/or power. If Venus is well aspected these people are charismatic, attractive and filled with confidence, magnetism and a boundless sense of power and control over their lives which attracts equally magnetic, commanding and financially successful personal and business partnerships. Although these relationships may also be volatile and, in some instances, sexually motivated, there is the capacity for striking the balance between emotional compatibility and physical attraction.

If Venus is inharmoniously aspected, however (especially by Mars or Pluto), these people may seek someone who provides the kind of excitement they feel incapable of attaining through their own talents. The overriding passion and sexual power may become so overpowering that these emotions will be exceedingly difficult to control. While they may be physically attracted to and enticed by those who match their level of intensity, these unions are more often than not compulsive and ill-fated, often evoking jealousy, uncontrollable passion and destructive power games. Unless they learn to trust others and relinquish their inordinate need for control, their personal and professional relationships will always be threatened.

Rather than strive towards equality and/or develop the seventh house capacity for co-operation, these individuals thrive on the struggle for supremacy and often utilise their seductive charm and/or sexual prowess to achieve their goals by enticing others with promised rewards of sex, money and/or power. In fact, the difficulties incurred during relationships arise out of their egotism and the desire for constant self-gratification. With their self-esteem in question, they frequently seek adulating partners, friends and associates whom they can manipulate or dominate emotionally, psychologically and/or sexually.

While the placement of fertile, beneficent Venus in the amazingly creative but potentially destructive eighth house tests one's capacity to sustain a long-term relationship, the key lies in the ability to maintain a balance of power while constantly revitalising a partnership so it remains exciting and challenging. If their aggression, thrill-seeking and high level of energy are channelled through the performing arts (drama and dance), strenuous physical activities or competitive ventures that are creative and financially rewarding, individuals with Venus in the eighth house are less likely to express hostility towards their partners and might even learn to relax.

While their inexhaustible enthusiasm fuels successful and profitable business pursuits, it may also be their downfall should they succumb to negative emotions such as jealousy, combativeness, lust and greed. If Venus is poorly aspected, therefore, their ability for healthy competition may become as tenuous, ruthless and as potentially destructive as it could have been prosperous. Because there is an affinity for speculation, investment or using their powers of persuasion to market a product, idea or even themselves, these individuals will be attracted to the performing arts, politics or finance either as an avocation or, if Venus rules the second, sixth or tenth 'work' houses, as a vocation.

Fascination with the dark side of the psyche or underside of life also draws them to undercover/investigative work, occult research, psychology and astrology, often for the sheer excitement these areas evoke and not necessarily as a career. In fact, their love of intricate game-playing and risk-taking draws them into business dealings where speculation, investments and/or psychological challenges are at the forefront. Although they may profit wildly from these ventures, they are just as likely to incur devastating losses during difficult transits when their judgment is clouded by greed and the desire for instant gratification – one of Venus' most problematic characteristics.

Sean Connery's Venus in Libra in the eighth house is a prime example of the charm, mystique, infectious charisma and penetrating sexuality inherent in this placement. Even the role of James Bond, which catapulted him to fame, typifies the position's sense of adventure and intrigue. In fact, it is not uncommon for signatures in the horoscope to affect not only the individual's life but the content or motifs of their artistic endeavours.*

While we are not privy to the personal life of Sean Connery, we have, on the other hand, certainly been subjected to countless exposés about the love affairs of John F. Kennedy who, like his wife Jacqueline, had Venus situated in Gemini in the eighth house. Although his Venus in Gemini, the sign of the twins, allowed him to lead somewhat of a double life, its placement in the eighth house suggests that his self-image was linked to his sexual prowess. Not only did the eighth house placement of Venus endow him with an amazing charisma which endeared him to the American public despite near disastrous political crises, his clandestine liaisons were at the time well-concealed. It has since come to light that, although the press was aware of his tempestuous affairs, they guarded his secrets (which would be front page news in today's political climate). Jacqueline Kennedy Onassis' Venus in the eighth house is indicative of her powerful husbands from whom she inherited enormous wealth.

Warren Beatty's Venus in Taurus in the eighth house fostered his reputation as one of the most available, sexually active ladies' men in Hollywood until he eventually settled down with self-assured Annette Bening. Moreover, Beatty has always been as committed to producing films as he is to acting and directing, highlighting his need to maintain both financial and creative control.

Other notables with Venus in the eighth house include Johann Kepler, Dwight D. Eisenhower, Angela Davis, Sophia Loren, Henry Fonda, John Raitt and Burt Reynolds.

---

*We have already seen how the position of Venus affected the subject matter of the writers Joyce Carol Oates and Agatha Christie.

TAURUS AND LIBRA ON THE EIGHTH HOUSE CUSP

If Taurus is on the eighth house cusp there is a definite affinity for business, banking and gambling as well as long- and short-term investing. Those with this sign in the cusp of this house may be obsessive by nature with an inordinate need for control and a tendency towards compulsive sexuality, passion and jealousy.

Those with Libra on the eighth house cusp have an amazing allure that enables them to attract partnerships. There is a bit too much laziness, poor foresight and extravagance, however, which may interfere with their need for making investments and taking risks.

Venus in the Ninth House

Keywords: interested in publishing, creative thinking, living abroad, marriage to someone exotic

Corresponding to the mutable fire sign of Sagittarius, the ninth house has traditionally been associated with foreign travel, higher education, philosophy, religion, publishing and the law. Most significantly, each of these concerns reflects a preoccupation with the exploration of profound social, philosophical and religious values that reach beyond the attainment of financial rewards and romantic/sensual gratification. Whereas the diametrically opposed third house concerns learning – the accumulation of ideas – the ninth house represents teaching – the assemblage of those concepts into a system that can be transmitted to others.* While the third house individual may, for instance, perform or write as a means of communicating ideas, the ninth house personality aspires to direct or publish in order to oversee, instruct, cultivate and guide the development of others' skills and talents in keeping with his/her own overall vision.

Individuals with Venus in the ninth house rely on the knowledge obtained from independent research, academic studies

---

*In the patriarchal society of India, the ninth house, not the tenth, represents the father and the values he imparts.

or an in-depth understanding of philosophical, religious and legal principles to gain admiration and deference, resulting in their attainment of self-respect (fire house). To elevate their self-esteem even further, they tend to inundate themselves (often to the point of fanaticism) with as much worldly experience (for example foreign travel, attending conferences, participating in cultural events) as possible in order to impress others. Since relationships are not usually fulfilling for them unless there is constant growth and something they are continually learning, many people with this placement marry either their students or teachers. It is important to remember that, as with Venus in Sagittarius, a relationship in which the roles of student and teacher are being enacted will often end once the student catches up with the teacher. If the relationship is to endure, it is necessary to transform it into one of equals.

Because the ninth house symbolises the search for freedom of expression, it is not unusual for this position to promote people with highly individual, creative and even flamboyant behaviour that is reflected in their wardrobe, hairstyles, cultural interests and friends. By the same token, personal and professional relationships require independence, the exploration of broader horizons and a need for constant intellectual stimulation. It is not uncommon for these people to marry foreigners and relocate to their spouse's homeland either temporarily or permanently, since this breeds a situation in which the two are continually teaching each other about their respective cultures.

Although Venus enjoys luxury and economic prosperity, its position in the ninth house is one of the planet's least materialistic locations. In their search for love and creative self-expression, those with Venus in this house are not motivated by personal gain but seek an outlet for their knowledge and fervent convictions. Extremely passionate, arrogant and, at times, fanatical in their need to instruct others and share their points of view, these people often feel compelled to convert others to their religious, political or philosophical beliefs. Their magnetism and judiciousness make them excellent spokespeople, advocates and lobbyists – positions that demand the patience, determination and diplomacy of Venus as well as the brutal honesty, directness and idealism for which the ninth house and its corresponding sign, Sagittarius, are best known.

Blessed with an incredible lust for life and authentic love of people, these restless individuals enjoy travelling, socialising and attending cultural and media events. An almost obsessive need to explore new avenues of thought, however, makes it extremely difficult for them to forego their independent and stimulating lifestyles. To maintain their arrogance, sense of authority and need to be right, Venus in the ninth house produces an attraction to partners who either share their 'wanderlust' or encourage the pursuit of new ideas, studies and projects. Not unlike individuals with Venus in the third house, those with Venus in the ninth house will avoid intimacy unless they are convinced that intellectual stimulation, excitement and freedom can still be maintained.

Emblematic of their quest for knowledge and spiritual truth through higher education, foreign travel and intellectual exchanges, the ninth house is affiliated with researchers, academicians, teachers, attorneys, writers (especially journalists), politicians, publishers or translators. If Venus is conjunct the midheaven, it is even more important for these people to be recognised for their knowledge, which they feel compelled to share through one of the aforementioned professions. This often results in the formation of creative collaborations (actor/director, writer/editor) or professional partnerships (law firm, joint research) through which their strong convictions or philosophy of life may be expressed. If these particular fields of interest are not further developed or utilised, they may simply search for a partner who either practises one of the aforementioned professions or who is passionate and opinionated about the very subjects these individuals wish to learn more of.

While individuals with Venus placed in this area of the horoscope may indeed be passionate about ninth house issues such as philosophy, religion, law and politics, they refuse to teach or practise professionally unless they can inject creativity into areas that may otherwise be dry and dull. While the ninth house is long on theory and devoid of practicality, Venus provides these people with diplomacy, a sense of ethics, the powers of persuasion and the facility for expressing their strong opinions and points of view both passionately and convincingly.

If Venus is positively aspected, these people derive their validation from opinions, travel and worldly knowledge – this is part of what makes them attractive to others. If Venus is poorly situated, however, the need to be right prevents compromise and being able to see another person's point of view – both of which are vital for any successful relationship.

The writer F. Scott Fitzgerald chronicled the decadent, 'careless' lifestyles of the rich, whom he both envied and disdained. Ruling the ninth house and positioned in Libra on the eighth-ninth house cusp, Fitzgerald's Venus fits the ninth house profile as much as it does the eighth.* Having acquired fame and fortune in his early twenties with his first novel *This Side of Paradise*, Fitzgerald aspired to and ultimately pursued the free and exciting lifestyle (ninth house) that he perceived was synonymous with money and recognition (Venus). Not only did Fitzgerald and his wife Zelda embark on an adventurous, fun-filled, undisciplined way of life marked by midnight swims in public fountains and champagne savoured out of evening shoes, but Fitzgerald idealised and characterised Zelda (Venus) – as ninth house Venuses are apt to do – in his stories as the 'Flapper Girl' – a term he coined. They even followed the ninth house road to the Riviera, a paradise for expatriate artists and writers who managed to produce some of this century's most provocative literature and works of art (Venus) despite drinking and pontificating until the early morning hours (ninth house).

Unfortunately, Fitzgerald is a prime example of the negative manifestation of this placement – the inability to balance romantic idealism with the practicalities of everyday life. Zelda, in pursuit of her own unrealistic ambition of becoming a ballerina, suffered a breakdown and was confined to a mental institution, where she died when the facility burned down. Fitzgerald eventually moved to Hollywood (the land of illusion) where, at a young age, he died of a heart attack probably exacerbated by years of alcohol abuse.

Due to the overwhelming Venusian influence in his horoscope

---

* For all the charts in this book I have used the Koch house system.

(Sun, Mercury, Venus in Libra, Moon in Taurus), Fitzgerald was desirous of uplifting himself to become larger than life. The love and devotion of his wife and readers (Venus in Libra) coupled with his accomplishments as an author (Venus in the ninth house) gave him the euphoric feeling that he could conquer the world. Unfortunately, he was unable to internalise his self-worth, and his indulgent, abusive lifestyle continued to fuel his insecurities, destroy his marriage and prevent him from utilising his talents to their fullest potential.*

Celebrities with Venus in the ninth house include King Louis XIV of France (known as the Sun King), Harry S. Truman, Doris Day, Billie Jean King, Marilyn Monroe, Robert Kennedy, Princess Anne, Lorna Luft, Coretta Scott King, Sean Penn and Bonnie Raitt.

TAURUS AND LIBRA ON THE NINTH HOUSE CUSP

Those with Taurus on the ninth house cusp have a practical philosophy of life. They are determined to reach their goals when it comes to higher education and may earn their money through foreign business or with something related to foreign goods.

Those with Libra on the ninth house cusp may marry foreigners or highly educated people, or may even live abroad. Due to their eloquence and ability to express themselves lucidly, they make good lawyers and teachers.

Venus in the Tenth House

Keywords: creative goals, projecting beauty, glamour and illusion, harmonious or creative father figure

Commencing the tenth house, the midheaven is the horoscope's most elevated point and aptly describes the highest professional

---

* The jealousy and competition fuelled by the Fitzgeralds' union is obviously indicative of his Venus in the eighth house.

achievements for which we consciously strive. While the ascendant, which defines our immediate impression upon our environment, is, like breathing, automatic and unconscious, the midheaven and, ultimately, the tenth house describes how we wish to be perceived and whether that image has been successfully achieved. Because the tenth house has always represented the conscious choices we make and the position in life to which we aspire, it is defined as the sphere of professional achievements, recognition, public service and fame.

Just as the fourth house has traditionally been the house of the mother or the provider of emotional nourishment, the tenth house represents the father or the goal-setter and authority figure. Due to the interchangeability of parental role models, the two houses can be viewed as the parental axis, the fourth house signifying the more nurturing parent and the tenth house typifying the professional role model and the attributes he or she inspires. With Venus in the tenth house, the most admired parent has instilled – by example or instruction – the importance of diplomacy, salesmanship and popularity in attaining one's goals. On the negative side, people with Venus in this house have learned to associate success with a beautiful, friendly and good-tempered personality at such an early age that their public image often becomes confused with their private feelings. With so many children presently raised in single-parent households, it is not necessarily the father who is the career-orientated parent and, as a result, the tenth house also represents how we are viewed publicly while the fourth house denotes what we are really like in the sanctity of our own home. If the tenth house, its ruler and/or occupying planet are harmonious, this image is, for the most part, successfully conveyed. If they are afflicted, there will indeed be a conflict between the private and public image. There may also be too much dependence on the approval of others, or ambitions may be lived out through a successful partner – which ultimately leads to a sense of frustration.

In light of this, individuals with Venus in the tenth house wish to be recognised for their boundless creativity, compassion, patience, determination and, most obviously, their beauty. While this placement commonly appears in the charts of actors, models and other luminaries whose charismatic charm, beauty and/or artistry have been carefully nurtured and thrust upon the public, the idolatry that they generate also satisfies their need for acknowledgement. While it is certainly not easy to second-guess the public or methodically to cultivate an attractive and infectious image, it is this unique ability to connect with the masses that makes these individuals excellent actors and politicians.* While their 'people skills', social concern and facility to mediate tense situations make them well suited for careers in public office, it is their ability to project a likable image that attracts voters and gets them elected. Other professions which employ the aesthetics, diplomacy and prosperity of Venus include singing, architecture, interior design, banking and law.

Not merely satisfied with excelling artistically, those with this placement demand that the fruits of their labour be respected, acknowledged professionally and rewarded financially. Due to their practicality, sobriety and vast ambition (tenth house), people with Venus in the tenth house take their relationships quite seriously and are unlikely to indulge in a frivolous sexual union or even to contemplate a relationship unless there are indications of permanence. Fiercely loyal and devoted mates, they are usually attracted to accomplished, prosperous partners who may not strike a passionate chord but who can be counted on to support their quest for artistic and/or financial success. If their approach to life includes the desire to have children this will usually be impeded until economic stability is assured and, if they do opt to steer their lives in that direction, parenthood is undertaken with the same commitment and seriousness as any other project or relationship.

A prime example of a conscious effort to change one's image is Janet, a client of mine with four planets (including a well-aspected Venus) in Leo in the tenth house. She rejected her role as the wife of a prominent businessman to become a painter. Unable to integrate the new image into her former lifestyle, Janet upped stakes to Greece where she presently earns her living

---

* Due to its benevolence and hunger for power, Jupiter is also prominent in the charts of actors, politicians and, of course, astrologers.

selling portraits to tourists. Although Venus in the fixed sign of Leo gave her the determination to seek a lifestyle that allowed her to be highly creative, the tenth house placement (intensified by the stellium) deemed it important that her friends and family accept her new identity. Knowing they could never comply, Janet relocated, revamped her image and re-emerged as a successful but reclusive artist. Although Janet's tenth house describes how she appears to her Grecian friends, traces of the flamboyant Southern belle she once was still linger beneath the surface.

During the 1992 Democratic primary race former Governor of California Jerry Brown was accused of reinventing his image during each political campaign. This is a perfect description of those with Venus in the tenth house. There is always room for suspicion as to whether their compassion emanates from the heart or is strictly for the sake of appearance. While Brown has never been known for his subtlety (Sun in Aries), he would like to be recognised for his work with Mother Theresa in Calcutta and as a liberal defender of the poor.

As the manifestation of forbidden love and unbridled sexuality, Venus in the tenth house describes the career of Henry Miller, whose reputation (tenth house) was established after the publication of *Tropic of Cancer* and *Tropic of Capricorn* – novels that contained such uncensored eroticism that they were initially banned in his native United States. Anais Nin's diaries portray Miller as a man who both understood and loved women – though his actual behaviour often negated the image he tried to convey.

Well-known personalities with Venus in the tenth house include Vincent Van Gogh, Salvadore Dali, J. P. Getty, Oliver North, Jimmy Carter, Sarah Ferguson, Gwen Verdon and Maxwell Perkins.

TAURUS AND LIBRA ON THE MIDHEAVEN
(TENTH HOUSE CUSP)

Those with Taurus on the midheaven will choose money-making professions that will support their extravagances. They may be attracted to financial careers – such as banking, entrepreneurial activities and the stock market – or to artistic careers, especially in the realm of sculpture and music. Most important, they wish to be known for their stability and capacity for holding things together.

Those with Libra on the midheaven are attracted to politics, show business or some other glamorous field where they can project their diplomatic, charming images. They wish to be known as co-operative people who are an asset to every venture in which they participate. They also make fine attorneys, salespeople, consultants or therapists.

Venus in the Eleventh House

Keywords: enjoying group activities and friendships, having high ideals and hopes

Just as the placement of Venus in the third and seventh air houses focuses on the ease with which individuals form interpersonal relationships, its position in the airy eleventh house encourages group activities that accommodate creative ideas, love and the need to be associated with a unit. Because the eleventh sign/house represents an attempt to align with a force greater than the self, that is, the 'limiting' sphere of home and family, those with Venus in this house only value themselves if they can identify with a particular group – whether it be their circle of friends, the community, the nation or their belief system – political, philosophical or religious.[3] In fact, the placement of Venus in this area of the chart almost guarantees that part of the reason one attracts or is attracted to a particular partner lies in shared political, social, cultural and/or artistic ideals.

Passionate, diplomatic, charming and well-spoken, those with Venus in the eleventh house are often called upon to mediate or be spokespeople for an organisation, idea or product. Dedicated to the improvement of their social, political and cultural milieu, they often devote more time to community activism than to their own families, whom they are often accused of neglecting. For this reason it is vital for them to select socially concerned partners who either share or, at least, respect their ideological points of view. Most important, their partners must provide the friendship, intellectual stimulation and freedom of expression that go beyond the sensual enjoyment and monetary security so important to other placements of Venus. (The need for a spouse or partner who is valued as a friend is particularly acute if Venus is the ruler of the descendant, that is, Taurus or Libra, on the seventh house cusp.)

While Aquarius (the eleventh sign) and the eleventh house are often promulgated as representing social, political and religious values, the placement of Venus describes the precise relationship formed within the group, community or organisation espousing those ideals. Because Venus is directed towards harmony, artistry and beautification, individuals with this planet in the eleventh house are attracted to creative arts organisations or troupes whose vision may also extend to the social and political arenas. Their functions within the group structure may range from being observers to being a vital part of the group's artistic or public relations staff – each role utilises their powers of persuasion.

While traditional astrological texts infer that one's friendships (eleventh house) are primarily with women (Venus), it is more appropriate to describe Venus in the eleventh house as the ability to maintain long-lasting friendships (eleventh house) with individuals (regardless of sex) who are creative, passionate and loyal (Venus). This position also suggests that the ideal situation is one in which the spouse or love interest is also a friend and/or colleague – because people with Venus in this house tend to spend a fair amount of time away from home.

Since the eleventh house is categorised as one of air, the placement of Venus there epitomises the ethereal, cerebral Goddess who assigns more importance to platonic love than physical love. Since the eleventh house signifies one's hopes and dreams, those with Venus in this house have extremely high and often unrealistic expectations for their partners, whom they expect to live up to the ethical standards of the organisations to which they belong – an almost impossible task. It is very important that these individuals separate everyday reality from their exaggerated idealism without relinquishing their dedication and activism. On the other hand, an afflicted Venus may cause such devotion to causes or even to friends that elements of insecurity and jealousy may enter their relationships, thus jeopardising otherwise meaningful associations in both the personal and professional sphere.

The impracticality of those with Venus in this house may also result in a misuse or neglect of their finances, which can simply be overlooked in favour of indulging (Venus) their social activism (eleventh house). On the other hand, they may just be donating their earnings to their favourite charitable causes. It may be advisable for these individuals to choose efficient, level-headed partners to handle their practical affairs and balance out their idealism.

As the second house (finances) from the tenth house (profession), the eleventh house represents, according to Hindu (Vedic) astrology, that which we have earned. With Venus placed in the eleventh house, there is not only the ability to profit from the fruits of one's labour, but a tendency to squander it just as easily. Because the eleventh house is impractical, these people will probably not amass possessions but will contribute to charitable causes or support worthwhile organisations.

Because self-affirmation is often measured by the group with whom we identify or 'belong', individuals with this placement of Venus are often hesitant to take on family responsibilities for fear these will complicate or interfere with their social, political and/or religious obligations. While there may be an innate conflict and even trepidation about settling down into domesticity, the eleventh house has, according to ancient tradition, long been regarded (along with the fifth house) as an indicator of fertility and the timing of childbirth. To this end, if a well-aspected Venus or Jupiter is situated in the eleventh house, circumstances revolving around the birth of a child should be beneficial. By the same token, if the aforementioned planets transit the eleventh house, the time is ripe for planning a pregnancy.

Lord Lawrence Olivier was a perfect example of the effects of Venus when placed in pioneering, self-centred Aries in the eleventh house of inspirational groups. In Olivier's horoscope, the self-absorbed Venus in Aries worked wonders by transforming his conceit and need for constant admiration into the unabashed passion and confidence which enabled him to portray any character he wished. Acclaimed as an excellent physical actor, Olivier had the unique ability through makeup and mental and physical control to alter his entire body to accommodate the mannerisms and physical characteristics necessary to play a part. Although his intensity and versatility (Sun, Ascendant in Gemini) brought him recognition the world over, his true creative visions were fulfilled as founder and director of the National Theatre – a breeding ground for Britain's finest actors, directors and, especially, budding playwrights.

Not only did the formation of this theatre allow Olivier to choose his own creative vehicles, the company was the culmination of an aesthetic, cultural and social vision shared by a cohesive group of artists. As a result, the National Theatre became a showcase where relevant, contemporary and experimental works could be presented alongside the classics, providing accessible, affordable theatre to the masses as well as the intellectual elite. While each of his three wives was an actress in her own right, Joan Plowright (his wife at the time) was an equally strong force in the formation of the National Theatre.

Luminaries with Venus in the eleventh house include Queen Victoria, Karl Marx, Auguste Rodin, Arthur Conan Doyle, Ernest Hemingway, Zelda Fitzgerald, Martin Luther King, Aristotle Onassis, George Bush, Glenda Jackson, Queen Juliana of the Netherlands, Henry Kissinger, Harold Wilson, Princess Caroline of Monaco, Tony Curtis, Jane Fonda and Carlo Ponti.

TAURUS AND LIBRA ON THE ELEVENTH HOUSE CUSP

For those with Taurus on the eleventh house cusp, friendships are loyal, steadfast and often last a lifetime. Their beliefs and ideals are usually practical and fit in with their everyday lives.

Those with Libra on the eleventh house cusp usually belong to artistic groups or patronise the performing arts. They are attracted to artistic, compassionate circles of friends and especially gravitate towards friendships with woman.

Venus in the Twelfth House

Keywords: compassionate, secretive, indulgent, reclusive

Like Venus in the twelfth sign of Pisces, its exalted position, the planet's appearance in the twelfth house endows its recipients with a gentle, loving and sympathetic nature – recalling the more tender aspects of the Love and Fertility Goddesses. Because individuals with this placement possess an abundance of warmth, soft-heartedness and compassion, they often feel compelled to sacrifice their own desires and give of themselves in order to feel validated and worthy of love. The need to give and receive love is, at times, so overpowering that their affection is bestowed upon undeserving recipients. Deriving their self-worth from helping those in emotional and/or financial need, these tireless workers and selfless volunteers must learn to preserve their own mental health by leaving work at the office.

While their willingness to help others is certainly a virtue, the insecurity and fragility associated with the twelfth house often produce in them a compulsion to befriend and even romance unstable or addictive personalities in order to reaffirm their own self-worth. While there is a genuine wish to see partners improve or recover, they often become 'enablers' who unintentionally maintain, rather than curb, their partners' illnesses. Should their companions improve and their role as helpmate no longer be required, the optimism and overwhelming creative instincts supplied by Venus in the twelfth house must be utilised to redirect the course of the relationship.

Extremely compassionate and highly imaginative, these individuals are attracted to the emotionally demanding professions of social work, nursing and medicine, as well as to the creative fields of the visual and performing arts (such as film, dance and drama). In order to succeed, however, they must put aside their personal dilemmas and channel their emotions into their work. (This is more likely to occur if the chart also displays either a preponderance of earth and fire signs or a strongly aspected Sun, Mars and/or Saturn.)

A lack of confidence and fear of criticism inherent in people with Venus in the twelfth house frequently prevent their imaginative ideas from finding a productive, creative outlet; instead these ideas are dissipated by escapist behaviour. They have also been known to conceal or repress their emotions, which can result in clandestine, ill-fated love affairs or, at its most extreme, a reclusive lifestyle.

These people may have been awkward, bashful or lonely as children and their adult behaviour patterns often stem from these deep-seated insecurities. Due to the sense of alienation that lies at the very core of people with this placement, they do not understand the meaning of sharing – regarding it as something that is being taken away from them. While they often look to a relationship to bring them out of their shell, it is important for their partners to recognise that their need for privacy and solitude must nevertheless be respected.

If Venus is well aspected, the hidden aspect of personality may involve meditation, creativity or helping others who are either lonely, hospitalised, institutionalised or imprisoned. If Venus is poorly aspected, there is an accompanying inability to open up to others and, at its worst extreme, a failure to form close relationships at all. Ironically, however, it is this alienation that aids in the quest to help others in favour of confronting the complexities of interpersonal relationships.

While the twelfth house is the domain of physical or emotional confinement, this area of the chart, according to Hindu (Vedic) astrology, also governs expenditures and spending habits. The placement of Venus in this house accentuates the planet's affinity with opulence, resulting in the purchase of beautiful, costly and often frivolous items. If Venus is poorly aspected, however, these individuals will measure their self-esteem by their earning power and will try to impress others with their expensive possessions, resulting in extravagant, wasteful spending, borrowing and, if taken to the utmost degree, perpetual debt.

Barbra Streisand is an example of someone with both Venus in Pisces, the twelfth sign and place of exaltation, and in the twelfth house. As the ruler of the second house of finances, Venus (indicative of her singing ability) is placed in the twelfth house, which signifies that, due to her compassionate nature, Streisand has contributed a portion of her earnings (second house) to worthy and humanitarian causes (twelfth house) – most notably to AIDS research and women's rights. Her fundraising efforts in support of the Democratic Party and its support of human rights was established firmly during the 1988 Presidential race when, in support of Democratic candidate Michael Dukakis, Streisand gave a rare concert at her home and donated all the proceeds to the campaign. Due to the planet's position in the twelfth house (fears), she has readily admitted in interviews to being terrified of performing live despite her extraordinary singing voice and the enticement of huge financial rewards. Although it is difficult to believe that someone so talented would be afraid of an audience, one explanation lies in the fact that with a stellium of planets in the fixed sign of Taurus, Streisand is a creature of habit; she has publically admitted that she is unable to forget the stage fright and nausea she experienced nightly while starring on Broadway in the musical *Funny Girl* – over 25 years ago.

The humanitarian but ultimately lonely Venus in the twelfth house is depicted in the chart of Mia Farrow, whose Venus in Aries in the twelfth house endows her with the need to be admired (Venus in a fire sign) for her compassion and humanitarianism (twelfth house) in adopting numerous children – many of them developmentally, emotionally or physically disabled. In fact, the need to adopt her last child was cited by the press as having been one bone of contention between her and Woody Allen, precipitating their infamous breakup. We can only speculate that with Venus (sharing) in wilful Aries in the twelfth house of isolation, Farrow was more devoted to an idealistic cause than to Allen, who – with Venus in Libra in the second house – needs adulation from (Libra) and control over (second house) a partner – needs Farrow was only able to fulfil when playing actress to his director.

Notables with Venus in the twelfth house include Claude Debussy, D. H. Lawrence, Françoise Sagan, Lyndon Johnson, Jeremy Thorpe, Janis Joplin, Jimi Hendrix, Lenny Bruce, Kim Novak, Ted Turner, Meryl Streep, Chris Evert, Liza Minnelli and Cher.

TAURUS AND LIBRA ON THE TWELFTH HOUSE CUSP

Those with Taurus on the twelfth house Cusp may be quite economical. They may spend much of their time alone due to their devotion and disciplined artistry. They feel imprisoned by money, which they either hoard or spend foolishly.

Those with Libra on the twelfth house cusp are often quite possessive of their lovers, with whom they wish to spend time away from the rest of the world. They are lavish spenders who like to impress people with what they have.

9

VENUS IN ASPECT

Just as the sign reveals *how* and the house relates *where* (in which area of life) a planet is expressed, it is the aspects – the harmonious and inharmonious relationships between two planets based on certain longitudinal distances – that penetrate the core of the horoscope by divulging *why* the planets and, therefore, we react as we do. Revealing both the overt and subtle facets of an individual's character, aspects display precisely what occurs when a planetary symbol such as Venus interacts with another.

Although the following delineations are based on the observation of major and minor aspects formed by the 360-degree circle's division by multiples of two and three, they may be applied to any positive or negative planetary contact.

Among the major aspects I have utilised, the sextile (60°) and trine (90°) are considered favourable, while the square (90°) and opposition (180°) are unfavourable. Amid the minor aspects, the semi-sextile (30°) is regarded as auspicious, while the semi-square (45°), sesquiquadrate (135°) and inconjunct (150°) are inauspicious. Labelled neutral, the conjunction (0°) becomes harmonious if its two planets are well aspected, and inharmonious if poorly aspected.

The following delineations illustrate how our capacity for love, proliferation and creativity is affected by other planetary energies. Beneficial aspects increase our level of self-confidence – which, in turn, radiates outwardly allowing us to form meaningful relationships and to become abundant and prosperous in everything we do. Adverse aspects, on the other hand, almost always generate a degree of low self-esteem, which we may try to compensate for with excessive indulgences.

To grasp the positive aspects fully, it may be helpful to envision the Sumerian Inanna whose passion rejuvenated the earth, strengthened economic prosperity and won her the love and respect of her nation. To examine the inauspicious aspects, it may be equally beneficial to visualise the Babylonian Ishtar – the temptress who led men to their deaths – or Aphrodite, whose obsessive vanity resulted in a string of narcissistic love affairs and destructive sexual liaisons. According to astrologer Richard Lamm, aspects are analogous to sub-personalities, which are described by Roberto Assagioli, founder of Psychosynthesis and author of a book of the same name, as the various roles, often contradictory, that each of us plays.

> Each one of us has different selves – according to the relationships we have with other people, surroundings, groups, etc., and it is well for us not to identify ourselves with any of these 'selves,' and to recognise that these are all roles that we play. And that although it seems paradoxical it is yet true that the less we are identified with a particular role the better we play it. It is good to emphasise this 'playing of roles.' The goal is the freed self, the I-consciousness, who can play *consciously* various roles.[1]

While each aspect represents a significant sub-personality, or character trait, it is vital to 'synthesise these sub-personalities into a larger organic whole'[2] to understand the aspect's full impact within the context of an entire horoscope.

Venus–Sun

Positive Keywords and Phrases

- affectionate, sociable, nurturing, pleasure-seeking, creative, harmonious

Negative Keywords and Phrases

- indulgent, lazy, loving luxury, not true to the self

Since the Sun and Venus never lie more than 48 degrees apart, the only aspects that can be formed between them are the neutral conjunction (0°), the auspicious semi-sextile (30°) and the difficult semi-square (45°). Possessing only half the strength of the sextile (60°) and square (90°), the semi-sextile and semi-square, two minor aspects, nevertheless provide insight into an individual's character.

Reflecting the familial affiliation between the Mesopotamian Sun God Utu/Shamash and his sister, the Venusian Goddess Inanna/Ishtar, Venus–Sun aspects impart the ability to maintain meaningful relationships (Venus) without relinquishing one's identity and/or professional goals (Sun). With the individualistic Sun 'fallen', or weakened, in Venus-ruled Libra – the sign representing partnerships, social obligations and diplomacy – Venus–Sun people place more value on exuding love, beauty and co-operation than asserting their will. As opposed to ancient astrologers' view that relying on a partner was a sign of weakness, the strength of these people lies in their recognition that the only way to fulfil their aspirations is in conjunction with a partner. Additionally, these individuals measure success (Sun) in terms of peer acceptance and prosperity (Venus).

Acutely aware that the key to personal and professional achievement lies in the ability to co-operate with and, if need be, appease business and/or marriage partners, Venus–Sun people often deflect their convictions and compromise their ideals by cultivating non-argumentative, amiable personalities to avoid conflict with colleagues, friends and lovers. Although they are regarded as loyal friends, these individuals cannot react to crises for fear of making the wrong decision or subjecting themselves to unpleasantness.

These charming, diplomatic and thoroughly convincing individuals are perfectly suited to careers in cosmetology, modelling, entertainment, law and politics – all of which necessitate the projection of good will, illusion and/or glamour. Cognizant of their ability to mesmerise, they have an uncanny way of seducing the public into adhering to their points of view and enticing partners with rewards of optimism, loyalty and love.

Endowed with the Taurean attributes of infinite patience, perseverance and single-minded determination, Venus–Sun individuals have the ability to sustain long-term relationships, bring creative projects to fruition and attain economic well-being. Their unequivocal sense of impartiality, honesty and responsibility also enables them to become excellent business managers, accountants and mediators. While generally fair-minded and benevolent, they will not hesitate to dismiss a disloyal co-worker, friend or lover at a moment's notice if they suspect betrayal.

The ability to nurture long-lasting relationships naturally extends to the maintenance of a stable home environment. While positive aspects signify that they are warm and attentive to the needs of their families, the negative aspects indicate that they are often unable to say 'no' to loved ones and, as parents, are unable to discipline for fear they will be resented or considered insensitive. It is essential that they develop confidence in their decision-making abilities and realise that they will not be judged by their actions but loved for who they are.

The position of the astrological Sun and how it is aspected describes the father as well as the parent* after whom the individual has most modelled his or her values, personality and goals. While favourable Venus–Sun aspects indicate that the desire to gain recognition for one's achievements was instilled by that parent, the unfavourable aspects may reveal a weak parent whose desire to please others and conform to society overshadowed his or her own ambitions.

Note: This description may also be applied to the Sun in Taurus and the second house, the Sun in Libra and the seventh house and Venus in Leo and the fifth house.

Venus–Moon

Positive Keywords and Phrases

- affectionate, good-natured, charming, nurturing, fertile, friendly, able to express love

*Although the Sun and Moon have traditionally represented the father and mother respectively, the Sun may be categorised as the parent who has influenced a person's worldly values, and the Moon as the parent from whom a person has received emotional nourishment.

Negative Keywords and Phrases

- vain, self-obsessed, lazy, self-indulgent, addictive by nature, extravagant, oversexed, protective

The interpretation of Venus–Moon aspects is perfectly embodied by the Roman Goddess of Love (Venus) whose maternal and devotional strength (Moon) guided her heroic son Aeneas safely to Rome. Despite the obstacles the lad encountered from rival deities who brought on bad weather, the Goddess remained loyal and steadfast until Aeneas reached his destination.

Combining motherly love (Moon) with physical affection (Venus), the amalgamation of the Moon and Venus, two fruitful planets, marks one of the most compassionate and nurturing aspects in the zodiac. Dutiful and sensitive to the needs of family, friends and community, individuals whose charts boast favourable Venus–Moon aspects frequently overprotect and place the needs of their partners and children above their own. While not necessarily diehard social activists, these soft-spoken, gentle and loving individuals tend to direct their energies towards improving the environment both ecologically and educationally.

Although favourably aspected individuals are quite content to be 'homebodies', unfavourable Venus–Moon aspects impart a conflict between needs (Moon) and desires (Venus) that may manifest as a battle pitting belonging to a family unit (Moon) against exercising romantic and sexual freedom (Venus).

Whereas the placement of the Sun traditionally characterises paternal lineage (father and grandfather), the sign, house and aspects of the astrological Moon describe the mother and grandmother (Moon). While harmonious aspects suggest that the emotional climate in the home was loving, artistic and protective, inharmonious aspects may have provided the individual with a maternal figure who was moody, domineering and, at times, neurotic. Replete with insecurities and emotional instability, the mother may have demanded constant reassurance and attention from the father and, if not forthcoming, from the children.

Lacking healthy emotional nourishment, these individuals consequently associate relationships with suffocation and frequently opt not to marry or not to have children. Rather than seek comfort within a loving but 'restrictive' environment, they often find solace in the instant gratification offered by food, alcohol, drugs or sex. Because the Moon and Venus both influence the reproductive cycle, however, it is not unusual for parenthood to be thrust upon them unexpectedly. Often 'fated' to face parental responsibilities, they must learn to associate love with stability and trust instead of insecurity and disappointment to prevent the destructive cycle from recurring in the next generation.

In addition to representing fecundity, Venus–Moon aspects repeatedly appear in the charts of sensitive, artistic individuals who are vulnerable to the rigours and stresses of modern life. Craving serenity, their appreciation of beauty and the arts leads to the creation of an aesthetically balanced home and work environment – which are ideally one and the same and located away from the city's hustle and bustle. On the other hand, the obsessive need for tranquillity can result in the emergence of a passive, unmotivated personality who, by avoiding life's challenges, eludes its greatest joys.

Note: This description may also be applied to the Moon in Taurus and the second house, the Moon in Libra and the seventh house and Venus in Cancer and the fourth house.

Venus–Mercury

Positive Keywords and Phrases

- cheerful, friendly, creative in speech and writing, musical, achieves a balance between speaking and listening, has a good sense of humour

Negative Keywords and Phrases

- self-involved, speaks but does not listen

Because Mercury and Venus are never more than 76 degrees apart, the only aspects linking these two planets are the conjunction

(0°), the harmonious sextile (60°), the helpful semi-sextile (30°) and difficult semi-square (45°). Characterised by the lack of major inharmonious aspects, Venus–Mercury contacts do not present the difficulties inherent in other inauspicious Venus combinations.

Mythologically speaking, Aphrodite/Venus and Hermes/Mercury (the fleet-footed messenger of the Olympians) were half brother and sister – related through their father, Zeus/Jupiter, King of the Gods. Except for a brief interlude with Aphrodite/Venus that produced Hermaphrodite and Eros/Cupid, Mercury is never mythologised in an amorous context and, as a result, is the only planet classified as 'neutral'.

The astrological union of these two planets signifies a non-sexual amalgamation whereby Mercury's desire for honest communication and intellectual compatibility neutralises the passion and physical pleasures of Venus. Individuals endowed with favourable aspects define an ideal partnership as one in which friendship and respect are placed on an equal footing with romance and sexual expression. They firmly believe that open discussion with their partners can prevent minor annoyances from escalating into resentment and open hostility.

Blessed with affable personalities, crystal-clear speaking voices and gentle manners, Venus–Mercury people are exceptionally kind, sincere and loyal to their friends and siblings. Possessing unusual communication skills and mediating abilities, they can be captivating speakers as well as intent listeners – vital qualities for public relations, sales and advertising. In addition, their powers of persuasion and amiability and eloquence render them equally effective as educators, attorneys, speechwriters or literary agents.

Praised for having outgoing personalities and even temperaments, Venus–Mercury individuals, potentially more ignitable than their agreeable dispositions indicate, tend to dissociate themselves from any offensive or unpleasant thoughts and emotions that may be inimical to their 'genial' image. If their stifled feelings of anger and hostility do arise, however, they can erupt with uncontrollable rancour. While a facility for cultivating and maintaining long-lasting friendships and professional contacts is, in part, dependent on their agreeable dispositions, these individuals should realise that it is quite normal, even healthy, to verbalise unfavourable opinions or feelings from time to time. Although suppressing opinions and/or emotions may be more prevalent among those possessing the difficult Venus–Mercury aspects, this tendency also exists in favourably aspected people – but to a lesser degree.

Note: This description may also, in part, be applied to Mercury in Taurus and the second house, Mercury in Libra and the seventh house and Venus in Gemini, Virgo, the third and sixth houses.

Venus–Mars

Positive Keywords and Phrases

- physically demonstrative, passionate, sexually active, enthusiastic, having physical endurance, enjoying freedom of expression

Negative Keywords and Phrases

- self-indulgent, promiscuous, belligerent, impatient, provocative

The astrological aspects between Venus and Mars that reveal the individual's attitudes towards the enigma of love (Venus) and sex (Mars) is best epitomised by the adulterous relationship of their namesake deities – Aphrodite/Venus and Ares/Mars. Although this tragic, immoral liaison resulted in great sorrow, the union did spawn a daughter, Harmonia (Harmony), whose name denotes the serenity that can be achieved when love (Venus) tempers aggression (Mars).

To this end, favourable Venus–Mars aspects enable individuals to replace meaningless outbursts of rage (Mars) with the application of diplomacy, understanding and boundless procreative strength (Venus). Endowed with an outgoing personality and inordinate magnetism, Venus–Mars people may be equally blessed with an exceedingly healthy and well-balanced attitude towards relationships and sex that allows them to distinguish spiritual love from physical expression and, as a result, successfully combine the two.

Due to their projection of sexuality, many Venus–Mars individuals were seduced and 'deflowered' while still rather young, thereby discovering sex to be a reliable method of releasing tension, satisfying strong physical urges or simply escaping adolescent problems and/or restrictive parents. To prevent sexuality from becoming a panacea, however, these people are advised to discover other outlets (such as dancing, athletics, etc.) to accommodate their intense need for physicality. More skilled in expressing physical love than in the art of verbal communication, they often gauge their well-being and the strength of relationships by the level of their sexual fulfilment. Proficient in the art of seduction and their facility to attract, they are confident that, should a marriage or love affair dissipate, initiating a new one will be a simple task.

Whereas harmonious aspects foster long-term committed partnerships (personal and professional), inharmonious aspects frequently produce one-sided, unstable and/or volatile entanglements fraught with hostility, anger and, very possibly, violence. Sometimes the victims of physically or sexually abusive parents, these negatively aspected individuals may have at an early age learned to associate love with brutality. As a result, they are empowered (Venus) by brandishing sexual prowess and brute force (Mars) leading to promiscuity or extramarital affairs and, in extreme cases, sadomasochism and/or rape. On the other hand, childhood traumas may have been so demoralising that they deem themselves deserving of punishment and, as a result, become casualties of the aforementioned scenarios.

Because this aspect combination reflects the type of fervent passion that spurred the clandestine and ultimately tragic affair between Aphrodite/Venus and Ares/Mars, it is of paramount importance that Venus–Mars people learn to regard sex as an expression of love – otherwise they may be destined, as were both deities, to be alone. Individuals with difficult Venus–Mars aspects are advised to embark on a course of serious self-examination (which may or may not include counselling or psychotherapy) to work out their fears, anger and hostility (Mars) towards intimacy (Venus). As with all difficult Venus aspects, these individuals must first recognise their own worthiness before they can extend unselfish love to another.

Regarding family matters, auspicious Venus–Mars aspects nourish relationships that combine friendship (Venus) and physical passion (Mars) resulting in a desire to procreate. Whether planning an enterprising venture, a vegetable garden or a family (Venus), each undertaking, approached with impassioned enthusiasm (Mars), will inevitably be seen to its logical conclusion. On the other hand, beneficent interpersonal relationships and creative projects begun by individuals with inharmonious aspects are often abandoned due to their own impatience and rage. To transform this destructive pattern into a constructive one, such people are advised to confront head-on their tendency to injure or destroy (Mars) what they have nurtured (Venus) before they can replace anger with love and serenity.

Note: This description may also be applied to Mars in Taurus and the second house, Mars in Libra and the seventh house and Venus in Aries and the first house.

Venus–Jupiter

Positive Keywords and Phrases

- able to recognise opportunities, generous, optimistic, expansive, honest

Negative Keywords and Phrases

- slovenly, excessive, indulgent, wasteful of resources

Jupiter and Venus are traditionally referred to as (respectively) the 'Greater' and 'Lesser' Benefic. Together they form one of the zodiac's most potentially auspicious planetary combinations. Just as the King of the Gods (Enki, Zeus) could always be depended upon to rescue and/or support the fertility Goddess (Inanna, Aphrodite), Jupiter, an expansive and magnanimous planet, elevates Venus by presenting endless opportunities (Jupiter) for upward mobility and financial growth (Venus) as well as fortuitous circumstances (Jupiter) regarding creative endeavours, marriage and children (Venus). When linked by inauspicious aspects, however, the altruism and longing for instant gratification inherent in both these planets become overexaggerated, resulting in self-indulgent, excessive and, ultimately, self-destructive behaviour.

Although the difficulties intrinsic to unfavourable Venus–Jupiter contacts have always been minimised as being 'just a bit' extravagant or wasteful, they are, in actuality, exceedingly hazardous aspects and are prominently displayed in the horoscopes of people addicted to drugs, alcohol, food and even sex. Even seemingly harmless excesses like promiscuity, gambling and compulsive shopping, which may initially raise self-esteem by inducing a false sense of well-being, are potentially as self-destructive as the more obvious food, drug and alcohol dependencies.

Extremely optimistic, flamboyant and convinced of their own immortality, Venus–Jupiter individuals believe that they are immune to the perils of addiction and are quite confident that, should the need arise, friends and family will succumb to their unbounding charm and come to their aid. Although both positive and negative aspects do, in fact, bestow a certain degree of good fortune – that is, being in the right place at the right time – these individuals cannot, unlike their namesake deities, extricate themselves from every life-threatening situation and will ultimately suffer the consequences of their excesses. (Because the pleasure principle applies to both these planets, even the harmonious aspects cannot always alleviate compulsive behaviour patterns. If Venus is positively aspected to Saturn, Mars and Pluto, however, the hedonistic tendencies of Venus–Jupiter may be somewhat offset.)

To understand the essence of this aspect (and the general nature of Venus), it is extremely important to remember that in each of her manifestations – from the Sumerian Inanna to the Roman Venus – the Love Goddess was affiliated with the regeneration of the earth; in fact, the second sign (Taurus) and second house are both associated with material security and procreative strength. Beset with the influence of expansive Jupiter, however, these individuals, dependent on an inordinate amount of emotional nourishment and sexual gratification, tend to luxuriate in an excess of sensual pleasure (eating, drinking and making love), resulting in the slowing down of their body's metabolism. Although they are proud of their appearance, these individuals display a need for physical satiation and, therefore, tend towards obesity – a lifelong bane that they must struggle to overcome. On the other hand, excessive vanity extends to the desire to be admired, touched, perfumed, made up and dressed in luxurious fabrics – reminiscent of Homer's 'Hymn to Aphrodite' in which he elaborates on the scents and fabrics of the room where she and the shepherd Anchises consummated their love.

Venus–Jupiter people's yearning for the limelight precipitates their attending parties and/or social gatherings where they can be seen hobnobbing with influential people who may further their careers. Although Venus–Jupiter aspects do indeed present an inordinate number of opportunities, these 'lucky breaks' are, in actuality, the result of careful networking and the successful marketing of their talents. While harmonious aspects bestow an uncanny ability to recognise and seize the moment, inharmonious aspects appear in the charts of people who lack the self-confidence to avail themselves of the very same advantages. Moreover, individuals with favourable aspects invest their money wisely while those with unfavourable aspects spend lavishly to create the illusion of success.

Just as Aphrodite/Venus, the world's most desirable woman, and Zeus/Jupiter, King of the Olympians, were adored by their sycophantic subjects, individuals with this planetary aspect rely on the admiration of others for their self-worth. Because success and recognition are of the utmost importance to them, these charming, seemingly self-assured individuals effectively project an alluring and powerful image that, unfortunately, is sometimes more impressive than the actual quality or depth of their work.

Maintaining a veil of optimism to conceal their excesses is often an inheritance from parents whose boasting masked their own imperfections and hid family problems. To ensure their children's social acceptance, the parents of Venus-Jupiter individuals will have reinforced the importance of popularity by overemphasising good looks and participation in athletic activities. For fear of disappointing their parents, Venus-Jupiter children often will have camouflaged their scholastic failures and social rejection with outward gaiety or by resorting to a variety of potentially dangerous habits (such as overeating, alcohol, drugs) that suppressed the pain and provided temporary relief. While positive Venus-Jupiter aspects supply the resiliency to recover from major impasses, individuals with negative aspects can benefit by developing the inner strength to accept rejection without reproach and move on to the next experience with ease.

The coupling of expansive Jupiter with abundant Venus defines one of the most fertile placements in the entire zodiac. Never loners, their desire to proliferate extends not only to their families but to the acquisition of friends and possessions. In fact, any form of expansion from the purchase of a new home to the conception of a child frequently occurs during Jupiter's transits either to natal Venus or to the ruler of the second house. Because these are the two most excessive planets, the entire horoscope should be analysed before immediately thinking that this combination will bring nothing but luck – an erroneous assumption that is often made.

Note: This description may also be applied to Jupiter in Taurus and the second house, Jupiter in Libra and the seventh house and Venus in Sagittarius and the ninth house.

Venus-Saturn

Positive Keywords and Phrases

- faithful, dutiful, sober, economical, affectionately undemonstrative, practical in relationships

Negative Keywords and Phrases

- fearful of relationships, lonely, late to marry, cold

Just as the difficulties inherent in Venus–Jupiter aspects have traditionally been underrated, the problems triggered by Venus–Saturn contacts tended to be overexaggerated – until the publication of Liz Greene's insightful, classic text, *Saturn: A New Look at an Old Devil* (1976). The sorrowful destinies that used to be cited for Venus–Saturn ranged from spinsterhood/childlessness to the premature death of a spouse.

Traditionally labelled the 'Greater Malefic', Saturn represents, according to Dr Greene, the attainment of knowledge through the recognition of fears and limitations. When coupled with this long-suffering planet, self-indulgent Venus has the potential to steer her procreative power in the direction of relationships (Venus) which are structured, long lasting and amazingly productive (Saturn).

Saturn's effect on self-image and the capacity for love (Venus) is symbolised by the story of Chronos (Saturn), who castrated his tyrannical father Ouranos (Uranus) resulting in the latter's maimed appearance and sexual incapacitation. While positively aspected individuals may simply display a modest approach to the body (such as, wearing conservative clothes or preferring to make love in the dark), negatively aspected people harbour deep-rooted feelings of inadequacy which radiate outwardly and influence how they (and others) perceive their physical self. Maintaining a modest or even unkempt appearance may also validate their mistaken belief that they, like Ouranus, deserve to be disfigured – often the backlash of emotional scars left by a parent (usually the father) who was critical, stern, unaffectionate, cruel or absent due to career demands, estrangement or death.

On the other hand, just as the magnificent, powerful and fruitful Aphrodite ultimately emerged from Ouranos' deformity, these individuals may go to the other extreme and attempt to elevate their self-esteem (Venus) by altering their looks to suit society's standards (Saturn). In the case of women, physical 'improvements' may include dying their hair, applying lots of makeup, wearing glamorous clothes and/or undergoing cosmetic surgery. In the case of men, these 'enhancements' make take the form of expensive clothes, moustaches and/or beards and toupees. The success of these embellishments, however, ultimately depends on whether the individual's self-confidence and inner beauty have truly been bolstered by the external metamorphosis. While it may be difficult to believe that some successful actors, models or other public figures have at times battled shyness, awkwardness or low self-esteem, their accomplishments force us to realise that their fierce determination to succeed was instrumental in achieving their goals and ultimately reversing a poor self-image.

> the typical Venus–Saturn woman carries deep feelings of inferiority and unattractiveness – regardless of how physically appealing she may be. It is common also to find Venus–Saturn women in the performing arts, as models, and even as the modern equivalent of the hetaira, with perhaps less glamour. For these women it is terribly important to be loved, admired, and thought beautiful . . .*[3]

Although Venus–Saturn individuals profess to crave emotional fulfilment, a fear of intimacy frequently leads them to form ill-fated relationships with abusive, unfeeling and/or self-destructive partners. These relationships only reinforce their self-doubt and further compound the injuries to an already fragile self-image. While positive aspects provide enough resiliency to bounce back from disappointing love affairs, individuals with negative aspects do not recover as easily – withdrawing for long periods in an effort to rebuild their confidence. Due to the restrictive influence of Saturn, however, those with both harmonious *and* inharmonious aspects usually experience a certain degree of aloneness which, if utilised constructively and meditatively, can lead to extraordinary self-knowledge. Once Venus–Saturn individuals conquer their fears and insecurities, they are capable of attaining enough confidence to form meaningful committed relationships.

Whereas Mars provides a dynamic, physical outlet for one's sexual appetite, Saturn supplies Venus with the maturity, responsibility and fidelity necessary to maintain a long-lasting marriage replete with the joys of parenthood – if so desired. While positive Venus–Saturn contacts signify steadfast, co-operative

---

*Although Dr Greene attributes this description specifically to women, I feel that it also applies to men with Venus/Saturn contacts.

partnerships, its negative aspects denote difficulties arising from: 1) marriage to someone much older or younger, 2) 'late' marriage or 3) no marriage at all.

Burdened with responsibilities at an early age (either caring for other family members or earning a living), Venus-Saturn individuals are instinctively drawn to mature friends and, ofttimes, to older, more worldly partners who can provide the companionship, devotion and financial security (Saturn) they lacked as children. Conversely, fear of emotional vulnerability may drive these individuals into the arms of younger men or women who admire *their* worldliness and to whom they can be caretaker and instructor. It is quite common for Venus-Saturn females to gravitate to older men until they are about the age of 35, when they attract younger men enamoured of experienced women. Conversely, Venus-Saturn males typically remain bachelors or have relationships with experienced, older women until they reach mid-life, by which time they are ready to start a family – usually with someone younger. Because older women/younger men relationships have become socially acceptable, they presently fall under the domain of both harmonious and inharmonious Venus-Saturn aspects. While favourable Venus-Saturn contacts precipitate extremely successful 'May-December' romances, individuals with unfavourable combinations perceive these relationships as problematic because they lack the judgment to select suitable mates. The partner, frequently a parental substitute, reinforces the truth that they have settled for a secure relationship devoid of passion and vitality – a painful reminder of their own weakness and fear of risk-taking.

No longer socially stigmatised for waiting until they are emotionally mature and financially stable (Saturn) before committing to marriage and family (Venus), these goal-orientated individuals are none the less beset by the ever-present task of balancing their relationships (Venus) and careers (Saturn). Because professional success (Saturn), vital to their self-esteem, is more accessible than expressing affection, these individuals may opt to avoid conflict and immerse themselves in work.

In much the same way that intimacy is feared and often delayed, parenthood, too, is viewed with trepidation due, in part, to their own absent, uncommunicative or strict parents who may have found that reaching an equilibrium between family (Venus) and profession (Saturn) was frustratingly difficult. Terrified that they, too, will be unsuccessful at juggling love (Venus) and career (Saturn), these people, with their overwhelming sense of duty, responsibility and desire for perfection, may simply choose to remain childless. By recognising their parents' vulnerabilities and forgiving their failures, however, they may discover that child-rearing need not be limiting and difficult but a rewarding experience.

Note: This description may also be applied to Saturn in Taurus and the second house, Saturn in Libra and the seventh house and Venus in Capricorn and the tenth house.

Venus-Uranus

Positive Keywords and Phrases

- having unusual, rebellious or independent relationships or modes of artistic expression

Negative Keywords and Phrases

- provocative, having unstable relationships

To interpret the astrological relationship between Venus and Uranus, it is worth while to review Hesiod's account of Aphrodite's emergence from the castoff genitals of Ouranos, the Sky God, who could, in fact, be considered her biological father. While this unique, motherless birth endowed Aphrodite (Venus) with independence, it also transformed her into a social outcast whose individuality, rebelliousness and singular beauty became the target of Olympian wrath. Although Homeric legends depict *Zeus* as her father, he was not a warm, paternalistic figure but an authoritarian whose edict forbidding his daughter to bed mortals led to her defiant affair with Anchises and the birth of her son Aeneas – the progenitor of the Roman race.

The aforementioned descriptions of the Goddess epitomise the nature of Venus–Uranus contacts, which instil the compulsion to rebel against authority and assert independence through innovative, creative expression and/or unconventional relationships. While individuals with positive aspects utilise their uniqueness and magnetism to: 1) achieve creative and professional success, 2) champion social and political causes and/or 3) constantly revitalise personal relationships, those burdened by difficult aspects are often 'rebels without a cause' who become involved in unorthodox, self-destructive love affairs.

Just as the Goddess ascending from the sea was a magnificent vision to behold, Venus–Uranus individuals, though not always 'classically' beautiful, nevertheless generate an inordinate amount of charisma, magnetism and 'electricity'.* Acutely aware of their effect on others, they must learn to use this 'power' wisely and not, as is too often the case, confuse sexual desirability with love and respect. Not unlike Aphrodite, whose procreative strength was, at times, veiled by carnality, these provocative people are frequently identified with flamboyance and a lack of inhibition rather than individualism, ingenuity and social activism – traits for which they would prefer to be known.

While individuals with positive aspects are indeed admired (Venus) for their brilliance and originality (Uranus), those with the harder aspects are frequently admonished for their defiance and provoking ways (Uranus). Even when expressing a heartfelt though unconventional point of view, they are still considered intentionally defiant due to their abrasive manner. Repelling the very people they wish to attract, negatively aspected individuals are frequently plagued with the lifelong dilemma of seeking acceptance (Venus) while maintaining their ideals (Uranus).

Goal-orientated individuals with positive Venus–Uranus aspects seek supportive marriage partners who share and/or respect their need for creative self-expression and independence. On the other hand, individuals with unfavourable aspects lack the Venusian ability to synthesise relationships with ambition and, as

---

*In fact, 'electricity' has always come under the traditional domain of Uranus. Consequently, transits to and from Uranus have always been blamed for blackouts, electrical fires and other electricity-related occurrences.

a result, avoid meaningful romantic involvements which could interfere with their work. Often the product of an unhappy childhood or unstable home life, these aloof males *and* females have the ability to maintain an active, enjoyable sex life *sans* emotional involvement.

A prime example involved a female client with an exact Venus–Uranus square who had three successive relationships with musicians whom she accompanied on concert tours, thereby fulfilling her desire for a thrilling, creative lifestyle. Desirous of excitement and freedom, these emotionally distant and unstable men (Uranus) provided constant stimulation but were incapable of extending the love and attention (Venus) she so desperately needed. My client finally realised that she unconsciously chose ill-fated relationships because she was terrified of a commitment (to work or to a relationship) and the permanence it would entail. Furthermore, she recognised that she lacked the courage to explore her own creative avenues and, instead, lived hoping that she would absorb some creativity vicariously through her lovers. Venus–Uranus people may ultimately require intense self-examination and, quite frequently, counselling or psychotherapy to learn that freedom need not be compromised in a meaningful relationship or creative endeavour.

The arrogance, self-assurance and compulsive professionalism that drive Venus–Uranus individuals is, at times, attributable to a dynamic parent (or parents) whose progressive philosophy and/or occupational achievements dominated the child's life. Because the parents were perceived as successful, strong-willed and, possibly, unapproachable, these individuals often sought attention, respect and love from other role models such as teachers and, later in life, a boss or partner. Unless they learn to balance marriage and family (Venus) with the desire for independence (Uranus), these people will remain obsessed with the need for esteem and admiration gained through professional success to replace the warmth and support denied them in their youth.

Just as Venus–Uranus individuals can be cynical about long-lasting relationships, the prospect of parenthood is alternately welcomed and feared due, in part, to witnessing their parents' unconventional approach to professional and familial life. Not easily deterred by challenging situations, positively aspected individuals ultimately accept the responsibilities of combining home and family, whereas negatively aspected people frequently choose to remain childless. When Venus–Uranus contacts do become parents, an unorthodox yet loving approach to child-rearing is, more often than not, inimical to mainstream ideas about raising children and, therefore, open to criticism.

At its most extreme, the ambivalence of inharmonious Venus–Uranus individuals towards parenthood can manifest in unplanned pregnancies, terminations or an inability to conceive, especially if either of these planets rules or occupies the fifth house. Uranus transits and progressions to Venus, if it rules or occupies the second, fifth, seventh or eleventh houses, may precipitate unexpected pregnancies as well as the sudden formation of a relationship, business or creative project.

Note: This description may also be applied to Uranus in Taurus and the second house,* Uranus in Libra and the seventh house and Venus in Aquarius and the eleventh house.

Venus–Neptune

Positive Keywords and Phrases

- compassionate, romantic, devotional, optimistic

Negative Keywords and Phrases

- deceptive, masochistic, unsympathetic, dishonest

Although there are no recorded legends coupling Aphrodite/Venus with Poseidon/Neptune, Lord of the Waters, the sea was vital to the worship of both Aphrodite and Astarte, who, as 'Mistresses of the Sea' provided sailors with sexual favours and inexperienced maidens with initiation rites. Aphrodite's best-

---

*Because Uranus in Taurus and Libra lasts for a period of approximately seven years, it is considered to be a generational aspect and, therefore, does not really pertain to the individual *per se*.

known affiliation with Neptune, however, is her emergence from the Mediterranean Sea's foam intermingled with the sperm of Ouranos' castrated genitals. This motif was innumerably replicated by generations of diverse visual artists including the Greek Apelles (fourth century BC), the Italian Botticelli (fifteenth century), the Flemish Rubens (late sixteenth–early seventeenth century), the French Ingres (late eighteenth–mid nineteenth century) and the contemporary American lithographer Nancy Spero. While Rubens' rendering of the 'Birth of Venus' portrays a full-bodied Goddess emerging from the water, Spero's collage 'Fertility Figure/Birth' (1987) depicts the sea as amniotic fluid in which the foetus languishes awaiting birth. An inspiration to countless artists, the legend of Aphrodite's birth provides a clearer understanding of Venus–Neptune aspects.

Just as the fruitful, powerful and beautiful Aphrodite represented the power of women, Venus–Neptune contacts also represent compassion which can transcend senseless violence. And just as Aphrodite's origins were shrouded in mystery, Venus–Neptune individuals, unwilling or unable to distinguish fantasy from reality, may adopt an illusory, glamorous and often deceptive (Neptune) persona. Because those with positive Venus–Neptune aspects successfully interchange their public image with their private identity, they actively pursue and often achieve their visions of a romantic lifestyle. When Venus is positively aspected, Neptune adds the elements of spirituality, idealism, imagination and compassion to one's image of the self. Positively aspected Venus–Neptune people view themselves, therefore, as harbingers of spirituality, idealism, imagination and compassion. Projecting placidity, sensitivity and love, other people simply want to be around them and they have the unique power and illusion of being able to absorb others' problems. (This is, of course, why this aspect is found in the horoscopes of politicians, film stars, religious leaders and medical practitioners. It may also be found in the charts of evangelists, con artists and salespeople.)

On the other hand, inharmonious Venus–Neptune aspects frequently appear in the charts of people who, as children, escaped unpleasant or emotionally abusive family situations by inventing imaginary playmates or weaving fanciful, fantastic stories about their backgrounds. Lacking coping skills and the ability to concentrate, they were often labelled 'dreamers' by parents and teachers who did not understand their 'escape mechanisms' as signals for help. As a result, these individuals were not given the practical tools that would allow them to organise their thoughts and channel their imaginations. Prone to depression and inertia due to an inability to distinguish between fantasy and reality, there is a tendency to escape societal pressures via alcohol, drugs or even 'love addictions', all of which provide them with a temporary sense of well-being. The desire to elude the stresses of everyday life may lead to relocation to another state or country where they can escape the judgment of friends and family and begin anew. Although an altered personality and appearance may indeed attract a new set of companions, unacknowledged fears and anxieties will eventually re-emerge during a domestic or professional crisis.

Appropriately nicknamed 'the universal solvent', the planet Neptune is, in fact, noted for the ability to dissolve any project or relationship with which it is aligned. It is not unusual during Neptune transits and progressions for a business, career or marriage to literally drown in a sea of troubles without the possibility of resuscitation. While Saturn limits endeavours and Pluto demands reorganisation, Neptune simply disintegrates and the only recourse is to begin anew.

Possessing the unique ability to project glamour (Venus) and illusion (Neptune), Venus-Neptune aspects often appear, as mentioned above, in the horoscopes of actors, models, politicians and religious leaders. Each of these professions commands public support and mass approval. Like those with difficult Venus-Neptune contacts, these people may also have had family backgrounds which they would prefer to conceal. Positive aspects of Venus-Neptune provide the social skills, charm and ability to adopt a successful persona in order to rise above an abusive, addictive or unstable upbringing and successfully fulfil their aspirations – often with the aid of a partner.

Exuding a potentially deceptive (Neptune) allure (Venus), these people have an uncanny ability to convince the public that what they have to offer will undoubtedly improve the quality of life.

While individuals with positive Venus–Neptune contacts are more likely to strike a balance between their charismatic image and their private lives, those with the inharmonious combination often become so enamoured of pleasing others that their own personal points of view gradually fade into oblivion as they fulfil the roles defined by others. Because the key to believable acting lies in the ability to tap into and, thus, project honest emotions, the further these appealing individuals stray from their basic beliefs, the more unconvincing their portrayals become. (This is especially noteworthy in the case of dishonest politicians or bad actors whose superficiality will inevitably surface.)

Just as priestesses of the Goddess provided sexual gratification (Venus) to sailors (Neptune), the capacity to bestow pleasure colours positive and negative Venus–Neptune contacts which, in addition to the aforementioned professions, are also prominent in the horoscopes of makeup artists, hostesses, call girls and dutiful spouses. While individuals with harmonious aspects possess confidence in their appearance and talent, individuals with inharmonious aspects often look to relationships for creative stimulation and self-affirmation. Because their approach to partnership (Venus) is frequently cloaked in self-deception (Neptune), these sympathetic, devoted and hopelessly romantic individuals tend to idealise their mates; this can lead to submissiveness and, at its most extreme, masochism and abuse.

Similar to the effects of Venus in Pisces, Venus, the symbol of personalised, individual love, aspected to Neptune, the emblem of spiritual, universal love,* forms one of the most compassionate placements in the entire zodiac. Inundated with an enormous sense of guilt about life's injustices, these individuals have an overwhelming desire to be of service either professionally or through volunteer work. In extreme cases, an obsessive need to champion the downtrodden can extend to the selection of 'needy' partners whom they hope to reform. Though compassion is indeed an enviable quality, the compulsion to be the recipient of another's gratitude is not a substitute for genuine love and respect.

---

*Because it represents universal love, a 'higher' form of individual love, esotericists refer to Neptune as the 'higher octave' of Venus.

(If these people have strong aspects from down-to-earth Saturn, the illusory effects of Neptune can be counteracted and kept in tow.)

Attitudes towards partnership may have been modelled after a 'co-dependent' parent whose role was that of caretaker for an addictive, sick or problematic spouse or child. Because their parents did not always provide positive reinforcement, it is advisable for these individuals to develop a sense of self-worth so that they do not project unfulfilled hopes and dreams onto their own offspring. Romanticising the rewards of parenthood and, at the same time, minimising its responsibilities may cause Venus–Neptune people to become depressed after the birth of a child. It is imperative that they understand the dynamics of their relationships with their own parents in addition to learning good coping and parenting skills before nurturing families of their own. (If Venus is also aspected by Jupiter [co-ruler of the illusory sign of Pisces], this tendency will be even more emphatic and detrimental. On the other hand, the harsh realities created by aspects from Mars, Saturn and/or Pluto may offset the idealism of Venus–Neptune.)

Note: This description may also be applied to Neptune in Taurus* and in the second house, Neptune in Libra and in the seventh house and Venus in Pisces and the twelfth house.

Venus–Pluto

Positive Keywords and Phrases

- powerful, charismatic, compassionate, creative

Negative Keywords and Phrases

- jealous, possessive, demanding of self and others, needing love and admiration

The interpretation of Venus–Pluto aspects is perfectly illustrated by the universal Mourning Myth – constant throughout world

---

*Because Neptune in Taurus and Libra lasts for a period of approximately 14 years, it is considered a generational aspect and, therefore, does not really pertain to the individual *per se*.

mythologies – wherein the Fertility Goddess (Venus) grieves for her loved one who has been abducted to the Underworld (Pluto). Because Inanna was the earliest embodiment of the planet Venus, it is the Sumerian Mourning Myth which best epitomises the complexity of Venus–Pluto contacts.

Provoked by a desire to confront her lustful, vengeful sister, Ereshkigal, Inanna journeys to the Netherworld and is condemned to die. Persuaded by Enki, King of the Gods, Ereshkigal ultimately releases Inanna with the stipulation that Dumuzi, the Vegetable Lord, spends half the year in the Underworld and the other half sharing Inanna's throne.

The psychological battle for supremacy between Inanna, the 'good' Goddess of Procreation (Venus), and Ereshkigal, the 'bad' Goddess of Death (Pluto), characterises the conflict faced by most individuals with Venus–Pluto aspects. While they yearn for Inanna and Dumuzi's procreative passion (Venus), these people also demand a challenging, multi-levelled relationship which includes the mutual discovery of innermost fears, hopes and dreams (Pluto). In fact, more than any other planetary combination, Venus–Pluto aspects have the capacity to provide a powerful, in-depth and fulfilling union combining intellectual, spiritual and physical love.

Committing to a loving relationship comes naturally to harmoniously aspected individuals whose openly affectionate, supportive parents created a trusting and secure environment in which they learned that true intimacy involves an ability to give and take. Although Venus–Pluto individuals have the potential themselves to be understanding, nurturing parents, they are usually compelled to fulfil their intense creative urges before committing to a long-term relationship or even to begin to contemplate having a family of their own.

Functioning at its optimum level, this planetary combination endows an unfailing magnetism, charismatic charm and potency that can be utilised to attract partnerships, business ventures and creative projects. Due to the abundance of love (Venus) and explosiveness (Pluto) contained in the positive and negative manifestations of this aspect, the full capacity of their creative power does not usually emerge until they reach their mid-thirties or a comparable level of maturity.

While individuals with positive Venus-Pluto aspects do not fear the range of emotions (love, sadness, anger, fear) which may surface in the course of a relationship or marriage, those with negative aspects are usually hindered in their attempts at intimacy by guilt, fear, shame and/or anger, which are often related to traumatic or painful childhood experiences. Despite efforts to ignore disturbing memories, if not addressed and properly understood these memories often resurface and will be re-enacted in the course of their own relationships.

Whereas positively aspected individuals may have had parents who were almost inspirational, the negative combination indicates parents who were perceived as devourers or strict disciplinarians and whose love was contingent upon the child's ability to achieve their unfulfilled goals. Entering into adulthood with overwhelming insecurity, fear, and self-deprecation, the compulsive need to satisfy the parent may be transferred to the partner, who serves as guide, protector and surrogate mother or father. Because of the volatility of Venus-Pluto aspects, unresolved hostility or anger towards the parents may be expressed in the form of obsessive jealousy, temper tantrums and/or coldness which may drive the partner away or, at its most extreme, provoke verbal, emotional or even physical abuse.

Confronting one's past for the sake of a healthy partnership is illustrated in 'Inanna's Descent'. Ereshkigal's intense jealousy has festered for so long that the mere sight of her sister arouses not only sibling rivalry but an outpouring of vengeance and evil. Just as Inanna (Venus) exposes herself to Ereshkigal's lust, envy and retaliation in order to address her own repressed feelings, individuals with negative Venus-Pluto contacts must face their own potentially volatile emotions. With the help of a counsellor, therapist or mediator, one can emerge from the emotional prison (Underworld) ready to embark on a procreative relationship (Venus) which incorporates the recognition of painful past experiences (Pluto).

Like Campbell's 'The Hero With 1,000 Faces' whose triumphant rite de passage prepared him for the responsibilities of adulthood, individuals with Venus-Pluto contacts usually experience one, or perhaps several, failed relationships before changing recurrent self-destructive behaviour patterns. Addressing unresolved feelings and discovering self-worth often coincide with Pluto's transit of the natal Venus, which demands (Pluto) re-evaluating one's life and reassessing the approach to relationships (Venus). It is, in fact, advisable that these intensely demanding individuals pursue independent interests and/or spend time away from their partners – not unlike Inanna and Dumuzi, whose separation regenerated their marriage and, ultimately, the earth.

Utilising the inordinate magnetism and power inherent in both favourable and unfavourable aspects, these individuals are distinctly aware of their ability to attract romantic and professional opportunities. In addition to possessing perseverance, magnanimity and boundless creativity, Venus–Pluto people have difficulty relinquishing control and often use sex to dominate or manipulate others. Unlike Venus–Mars aspects, which merely confuse love and sex, Pluto's influence (similar to the position of Venus in Scorpio or the eighth house) is psychologically motivated and potentially more damaging. Utilising sexual prowess to win love and further one's self-esteem is epitomised by Ishtar who, in the *Epic of Gilgamesh*, first entices men with promises of ecstasy (Venus) and then eliminates them (Pluto).

Unable to handle the intensity of their allure or overwhelming sexuality, these troubled individuals may anaesthetise their feelings by saturating themselves with food and sex – addictions which, in the short term, provide a sense of comfort but, in the long term, further undermine self-esteem and the ability to control life.

The power of this planetary combination is perfectly illustrated in the chart of Allison, a therapist whose Venus–Pluto conjunction in Leo in the eighth house* supplied the confidence and magnetism necessary for professional success. Overcompensating for youthful mediocrity, this attractive, corpulent woman commanded attention with her booming voice, anecdotal wit and conspicuous attire, which usually consisted of outlandish, gaudy

---

*Because the eighth house correlates to Scorpio, the eighth sign of the zodiac, the effect of the conjunction between Venus and Pluto, the ruler of Scorpio, is further intensified.

outfits, ornate jewellery and wide-brimmed hats. Her home was decorated with lush carpets, opulent furniture and expensive works of art – all signs of monetary success. But it was Allison's proficiency as a counsellor and her compelling flair for making clients feel important which attracted a steady clientele of prominent businesspeople and celebrities who solidified her reputation and financial security. While her powerful persona initially bolstered her self-confidence, it was Allison's successful practice – an acknowledgement of her counselling skills – which strengthened and ultimately sustained her self-worth.

Note: This description may also be applied to Pluto in Taurus and the second house, Pluto in Libra and the seventh house and Venus in Scorpio and the eighth house.*

Unaspected Venus

When Venus is not aspected to any other planet, the desire to attain prosperity, form relationships and radiate love is hampered. As a result, a person with an unaspected Venus in his or her chart may become introverted. Since the ability to connect with other people is often misguided, this person may find it difficult to express warmth and affection. When Venus is unaspected, however, it is most important to view the house it rules and the house it occupies, since it is this/these area(s) that often remain unfulfilled in the individual's life. Whereas harmonious aspects are assets at the person's disposal and inharmonious aspects present conflicts which demand resolution, unaspected planets symbolise areas in the person's life that are difficult to synthesise. With an unintegrated Venus, the individual must employ the positive resources of the rulers of the second and/or seventh house for the self-confidence, relationship skills and procreative strength ordinarily provided by Venus.

---

* Because Pluto's transit through a sign can last from 12 to 20 years, it is considered a generational aspect and, therefore, does not really pertain to the individual *per se.*

10

VENUS IN PREDICTION

TRANSITS AND PROGRESSIONS

Whereas progressions are *symbolic* planetary movements charted from the day of birth, transits are the *actual* present positions of the planets affecting the horoscope. While progressions set the stage for patterns, the transits trigger events which, like progressions, are defined by the combination of planetary energies. Once we have determined the role Venus plays in a horoscope, it is then possible to surmise how the planet will manifest when it aspects or is aspected by another planet by transit or progression.

Transits to Natal Venus

Because Venus represents love, beauty, prosperity and abundance, it is these areas that are affected when a transiting planet aspects natal Venus. While a harmonious transit fosters ease, happiness and increased productivity, a challenging transit to natal Venus ignites a period when one's self-esteem and values are tested.

Although felt for a relatively brief period of time, the effects of transiting Sun, Moon, Mercury, Venus and Mars on natal Venus (lasting from two hours [as with the Moon] to three days [as with Mars]) generate similar circumstances as the corresponding planetary aspect (see Chapter 9). More noteworthy, however, are aspects formed by the transiting slower-moving planets (Jupiter, Saturn, Uranus, Neptune and Pluto) to natal Venus – which can last from two days to two years depending on the planet involved – since their impact is more intense and far-reaching.*

---

*While each of the major aspects formed by a transiting or progressed planet affects natal Venus, it is the conjunction and the square that create the tension that forces confrontation, action and change.

TRANSITING JUPITER ASPECTING NATAL VENUS

When natal Venus is aspected by transiting Jupiter, social and financial opportunities usually present themselves. One must be cautioned, however, that the combination of these two traditional benefics fosters indulgence, ease and sloth as much as it promotes contentment and satisfaction. People experiencing this transit should not merely depend on fortuitous circumstances and opportunities that may present themselves, but must act on them before the transit is over. Due to the expansion (Jupiter) of one's relationships (Venus), this transit may precipitate a marriage, the birth of a child, creative and financial success or even an inheritance. A perfect example of this expansion is Bill Clinton, whose Venus, Mars *and* ascendant were transited by Jupiter when he was elected President of the United States.

TRANSITING SATURN ASPECTING NATAL VENUS

When transiting Saturn contacts natal Venus, one must come to terms with external and internal limitations on oneself and, therefore, on one's relationships, creativity and attitude towards finances. Consequently, the individual is usually forced to view personal and professional relationships with brutal honesty, often resulting in the recognition and acceptance of one's own limitations and those of any union or partnership. If these obstacles cannot be overcome, the transit might signal the relationship's demise, though that is not necessarily the only outcome. If the individual is not currently involved in a relationship, the transit may signal the beginning of a serious and committed relationship with a partner who is either older or who has a sobering influence on the individual. Because Saturn represents work, persistence and dedication, business partnerships and financial speculations formed under this transit will yield slow but steady results.

TRANSITING URANUS ASPECTING NATAL VENUS

As the planet of sudden and dramatic change, Uranus not only alters one's self-image and values but frequently does so without warning. While we try to prepare for Saturn transits by accepting our limitations, nothing can ever prepare us for the complete unpredictability, eccentricity and abruptness of Uranus contacting a planet or angle. Because Venus craves love, harmony, sensuality and comfort this transit is especially disruptive, often resulting in the unexpected end of a relationship, the release of pent-up feelings or the revelation of a partner's secrets (extramarital affairs, debts, addictions, etc.).

On the other hand, it is during this transit that an individual (regardless of marital status) might have a whirlwind romance with someone who is independent, sexual, charming yet emotionally detached (Uranus). It is advisable, however, to wait until after the transit subsides (which can last up to a year and a half) before assessing one's true feelings and deciding whether this relationship has the potential to evolve into a long-term commitment.

TRANSITING NEPTUNE ASPECTING NATAL VENUS

When transiting Neptune aspects natal Venus, the idealism, romanticism and fantasy inherent in all Neptune contacts are injected into the individual's image of him- or herself, thereby affecting any relationships and projects he or she has been nurturing. On the positive side, liaisons formed at this time usually answer the need for a more childlike, fanciful and spiritual approach to life. More people are swept off their feet by the 'love of their life' during Venus/Neptune transits than at any other time, astrologically speaking. While this is indeed exciting and romantic, it is important to come down to earth since imminent danger always lurks under the Neptunian mystery and fantasy that pervades this transit.

Because a wish to be enveloped in the throes of passion

accompanies this transit, it is not uncommon for an individual to fall in love with an idea or image of someone rather than with the actual person at this time. As with the transits of Uranus, it is advisable to wait until the transit passes before making any long-term commitment.

TRANSITING PLUTO ASPECTING NATAL VENUS

When transiting Pluto aspects natal Venus, the individual often questions his or her self-worth, resulting in a re-evaluation of his or her ability to love and to nurture. Under this transit the individual often experiences the same emotional roller-coaster ride that Inanna (Venus) took when she journeyed to the Underworld (Pluto) and back again. Experiencing this transit, the individual often undergoes a series of transformations consisting of: 1) an initial disappointment or rejection (usually in love) that wounds the self-esteem, 2) pain, suffering and, at times, despair and 3) the realisation that one's life must change drastically. This final awareness is often accompanied by the dissolution of an important relationship or, at the other extreme, the onset of a romantic liaison that is highly passionate and sexual albeit potentially destructive due to the range of emotions it arouses.

Because Pluto strips the individual of everything he or she values (including self-worth), there arises, through the pain and suffering, a feeling of liberation and the freedom to start anew. Unfortunately, the emotional turmoil and dejection cannot be ignored and counselling or therapy may be the only key to emerging from the web of insecurities that surface during this transit. If the Pluto-Venus contact is positive, however, the individual's ego attachments can be left behind. One's values are then transformed, resulting in the ability to approach relationships with a true enjoyment of one's sexuality (Pluto) and a better understanding of sharing (Venus).

TRANSITS AND HOUSE RULERSHIP

When determining the effects of transits on natal Venus, it is also necessary to view Venus as the ruler of a particular house. Transits to natal Venus will, in general, bestow love, abundance, creativity and prosperity on the following areas of life when Venus is the house ruler of:

- *The ascendant and first house* – one's personality, general constitution and overall approach to life
- *The second house* – attitudes towards finances, possessions, skills and talents
- *The third house* – siblings, mobility, oral and written communications
- *The i.c. and fourth house* – childhood roots, family, home, land, emotions
- *The fifth house* – children, love affairs, creativity, dramatic expression
- *The sixth house* – health, work environment, colleagues and employees, pets
- *The descendant and seventh house* – marriage, partnerships, co-operation, contracts, lawsuits
- *The eighth house* – investments, business interests, sexuality, inheritances
- *The ninth house* – pursuit of knowledge, higher education, philosophical and religious beliefs, foreign travel
- *The midheaven and tenth house* – father, career, status in society, reputation
- *The eleventh house* – friendships, ideals, aspirations, community work
- *The twelfth house* – solitude, research, sadness, hidden secrets, enemies

TRANSITING VENUS

Though its effects are not as dramatic as the transits of the outer planets, transiting Venus is none the less noteworthy. Because its journey through each house is relatively swift (depending on the length of the particular house), Venus' entrance into a new house marks a transition from one sphere of influence to another. Since Venus represents that which we love and value, its transits through each house bring opportunity and harmony to the area that particular house represents. Due to the empowerment Venus provides, fortuitous circumstances, offers and liaisons may materialise in connection with the house through which the planet is travelling. By the same token, Venus may bring laziness, extreme sensuality and indulgent behaviour patterns. The following are brief descriptions of what might occur when Venus transits each house.

First House

Whereas the preceding month or two (depending on the length of the twelfth house) may have been a time of introversion, the transit of Venus over the ascendant and into the first house usually brings a marked change in personality and the desire to socialise. There is a renewed confidence in the way one is able to express oneself and radiate one's energy to the outer world.

Second House

When Venus transits the natal second house there is a concentration on productivity and prosperity – a direct result of the renewed confidence of the first house. This may also be a time when one begins a new project, whether it be planning a marriage or a child, expanding one's business or even, as in the case of one of my client's, adding an extension to one's home.

Third House

When Venus transits the third house there may be opportunities for media work, writing, travel and pleasant meetings, along with the desire to increase one's circle of friends and neighbours. Renewed relationships with siblings should also be encouraged. There may be an urge to beautify one's immediate environment.

Fourth House

When Venus crosses the i.c. and passes through the fourth house there is a desire to bask in the comforts of home and to enjoy the closeness of family ties. It may be a good time to beautify the home, making it more comfortable for entertaining or even working in. Most important, however, during this transit relationships with loved ones will be strengthened and valued.

Fifth House

After feeling homebound during Venus' transit of the fourth house, the fifth house brings a sudden burst of energy and the desire to have some fun. When Venus transits the fifth house, love affairs are likely to begin or to take centre-stage. There may be a wish for creative ventures, and children may play a special role. On the other hand, beware of the indulgences and impetuous romantic liaisons that may be on offer at this time.

Sixth House

When Venus transits the sixth house there should be increased harmony among co-workers, with the possibility of a promotion or pay rise. In fact, this might be an ideal time to ask for a wage increase, due to the negotiating skills that can be mastered during this transit. On the other hand, there may be a tendency towards laziness – to just sit back on one's haunches.

Seventh House

When Venus crosses the descendant and travels through the seventh house, the time is ripe for resolving any tensions which may exist in personal and professional relationships. It may also be indicative of a period when new ventures, contracts and projects which call for co-operation, diplomacy and/or dealing with the public may be initiated.

Eighth House

During this transit, investment opportunities and/or the fruits of prior speculation may actually materialise. Due to the desire for excitement and an elevated level of charm, charisma and sexuality, many different types of people will enter one's life and there may be temptation to be excessive and indulgent. As a result, there must be careful discrimination as to who can and cannot be trusted.

Ninth House

When Venus transits the ninth house, the traditional meaning of falling in love or being attracted to either a foreigner or someone whose lifestyle is different may certainly hold true. It is a time when strong convictions may finally find their outlet and there may be opportunities in the areas of education, law and/or publishing. If there is an offer for travel at this time, it is important to grab it.

Tenth House

The transit of Venus through the tenth house may bring the confidence needed to finally pursue that elusive job opportunity. It may also be indicative of the ability to change one's appearance, personality and/or image to suit professional demands. There may be increased respect and admiration from important and well-connected people, but it is important to distinguish between public, personal and private self.

Eleventh House

When Venus transits the eleventh house, there may be an overwhelming desire for new social contacts and friendships as well as participation in creative ventures. Due to a renewed sense of optimism and self-esteem, political and social concerns will define the nature of new acquaintances and group activities. A special relationship may also take shape with someone who shares your ideals.

Twelfth House

During Venus's transit through the twelfth house, there may be disappointment in terms of one's relationships, resulting in lower self-esteem and a period where one retreats and goes inward. This can be an extremely positive time, since values and self-image may be reassessed in preparation for the transit of Venus over the ascendant, when socialising will once again predominate.

TRANSITING RETROGRADE VENUS

While the 1-2 day transits of Venus to natal planets and angles often go completely unnoticed, the transits of retrograde Venus are significant especially when conjoining a planet or angle in the chart. About 21 days before inferior conjunction with the Sun (which occurs every 580-584 days midway through the retrograde cycle), Venus retrogrades for 41-42 days and influences the populace at large by reversing the planet's usually harmonious, loving and nurturing influence and causing indulgence, argumentation and, oft-times, chaos. When retrograde Venus contacts a planet or angle in the natal chart, however, the framework of a normally 1-2 day transit extends to become a transit of 2-3 months' duration, encompassing the time that Venus stations, that is, goes 1) direct, 2) retrograde and 3) direct again. If transiting retrograde Venus contacts an individual's planets and/or angles the effects of this planet, which may encompass love, harmony, creativity and prosperity, will be reversed and the individual may experience wasteful behaviour, dissension and an inability to give or receive pleasure.

Let's look at how Venus retrograde affected Bill Clinton in 1993. In February 1993, Venus began slowing up until it reached its first retrograde station on 11 March 1993 at 20° Aries. After retrograding through Aries, it reached its direct station on 22 April 1993 at 3° Aries.

On 9 February 1993, transiting Venus initially conjoined Bill Clinton's descendant at 5° Aries. On 13 April 1993, Venus retrograded over his descendant until it went direct and transited his descendant for the final time on 3 May 1993. Whereas many people felt a certain frustration with relationships, projects and finances between March and April 1993, Clinton (and others whose planets or angles were conjoined by transiting Venus) experienced enormous difficulties between 9 February (when Venus transited his descendant for the first time) and 3 May (when it transited for the last time). Because the transit of Venus over his descendant also opposed his ascendant, Mars and Neptune, the effects were especially marked. The transit ignited a three-month period during which Clinton's usual Venusian talent for pleasing, convincing and even manipulating the public completely backfired, causing his popularity to decline in the early months of his presidency. In fact, at the time of this writing,* his overall popularity rating with the American public is under 50 per cent – less than that of any other American president in recent history.

Because Venus conjoined his descendant, the popularity of Hillary Rodham Clinton, on the other hand, suddenly rose and, contrary to what was the case during the months preceding the election, she won over the American public with her charm, enthusiasm and intelligence. It is this author's hope that Clinton will once again regain his ability to please people while remaining true to his beliefs.

Progressions

Although there are a variety of progressions employed to interpret the birth chart, the most commonly utilised are secondary and solar arc progressions. Like the transits, progressions are defined by the particular combination of planetary energies and are most

*November 1993.

noteworthy when natal Venus is conjoined or squared by a progressed planet or when progressed Venus conjoins or squares a natal planet or angle. While a transit of Venus takes a day or two, progressions encompass a one- to three-year period lasting from the moment the aspect applies until it separates.

If one is born with natal Venus retrograde, the year in which Venus goes direct by secondary progression affects the person's life by reversing the patterns previously set up by natal Venus. If, for instance, there was low self-esteem due to a natal retrograde Venus, the individual will probably enter a period of elevated self-confidence and desire to form relationships once Venus goes direct by progression.

By the same token, if Venus retrogrades by secondary progression during one's lifetime, there will be a definite transformation of one's attitude towards oneself, one's relationships and the area represented by the house Venus rules. There may even be setbacks and obstacles not previously encountered, or a period in which the individual decides to re-examine goals and self-definition.

Although progressed Venus conjoining any natal planet or angle sets the stage for the unfolding and flowering of one's esteem and creativity, the most singular progression involves the Sun and Venus – which, according to Mesopotamian mythology, were brother and sister. This belief was founded largely on the fact of their brilliance, which caused these heavenly bodies to appear as if they accompanied each other as they rose and set.

Because the Sun and Venus are, at their maximum, 48 degrees apart, many people experience the progressed Sun–Venus conjunction by solar arc (which advances each planet approximately one degree per year based on the approximate daily motion of the Sun) within their lifetime – though never after they have reached the age of 50–51.

Secondary progressions, based as they are upon the concept that each day beyond the birthday represents one year, are not as straightforward. Because the Sun's daily motion is faster than that of Venus, it will take a shorter period of time for the progressed Sun to conjoin natal Venus as Evening Star than for progressed Venus as Morning Star to conjoin the natal Sun. When natal Venus appears as the Evening Star, the progressed Sun conjoining natal Venus occurs at the same time by secondary and solar arc progression. When Venus is the Morning Star, however, progressed Venus conjoins the natal Sun at a completely different time than the solar arc progression. The secondary progressed conjunction of Venus (as Morning Star) to the Sun may occur up to the age of 70, especially if the individual was born during the time or immediately before Venus goes retrograde (which slows up the planet's daily motion and, ultimately, the time it advances during a progression). If the progressed conjunction occurs late in life it does not mean the individual will not marry or attain prosperity; it simply means he or she will not come under planetary influence and what it represents.

Because the Sun is the truest expression of the self and Venus is the value we place upon that self, individuals with a positive natal Sun-Venus relationship (see Chapter 9) easily radiate an inner beauty to the outside world. Because they feel worthy of giving and receiving love, they usually have no problems forming relationships. To the same end, the progressed conjunction represents a time of fulfilment when the individual truly values and loves the self, resulting in marriage, the conception and birth of a child, the fulfilment of one's creativity or simply success in a project one has nurtured for several years. The progression may also induce financial productivity, material acquisitions or moving into a new home.

It is significant to point out that if the Sun-Venus progression occurs early in life, it may simply be indicative of the formation of a special friendship, popularity at school, creative achievement or any fulfilling activity likely to occur at a young age. The progression may even be suggestive of the birth of a sibling. Although most people experience the progressed Sun-Venus conjunction in their lifetime, the progressed conjunction between Venus and any other planet or angle will likewise activate the pleasure and self-worth that this planet, like the Goddess, is capable of bestowing.

Supporting the representation of Venus as the planet of fertility, I have found that in a substantial number of charts the conception or birth of a child often occurs when progressed Venus contacts a natal planet or angle, or when a progressed planet or angle contacts natal Venus.* Because procreation is the truest expression of bringing forth one's creative energy into the world, this is not difficult to understand.

Hillary Rodham Clinton experienced an exact conjunction between her secondary progressed Mercury and natal Venus at 11.24 p.m. on 27 February, 1980 – the day that her daughter Chelsea was born.[1] Bill Clinton was elected President of the United States – the culmination of a childhood dream – when his progressed Sun conjoined his natal Venus.

It is also important to consider which houses Venus rules, since this will better define the means by which an individual is fulfilled. When my own Venus (ruler of my third and tenth houses) conjoined my natal Sun by solar arc progression, I was asked to write my first book, *Indian Astrology*. At the time *Venus* was being readied for publication, progressed Venus conjoined my Taurus midheaven by solar progression – which, to emphasise the point, is ruled by Venus.

Solar Returns

Understanding the orbit of Venus is not only important for transits and progressions but is significant for the solar return – an annual chart drawn for the moment the Sun returns to its natal position. Venus will only be found at its natal position in the solar return every eight years. Therefore, the Sun and Venus repeat their identical natal positions every eight years, at which time one must confront any issues that arise from the natal relationship formed between these two heavenly bodies.

Although Bill Clinton's Sun will appear at 26° Leo in every solar return, his Venus will be found at 11° Libra in his natal chart and his solar returns for the years 1954 (when he was eight years old),

---

* Although I have not yet conducted a statistically controlled study, I have found that in a large percentage of charts (men and women), conception and/or the birth of a child occurred during a conjunction (one degree orb) involving either natal or progressed Venus.

Venus in Prediction 261

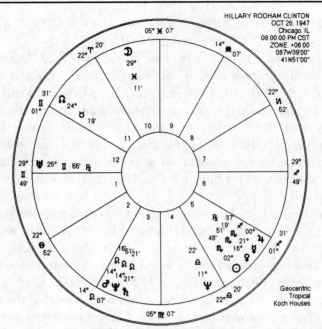

Figure 10.1: Hillary Rodham Clinton's horoscope.

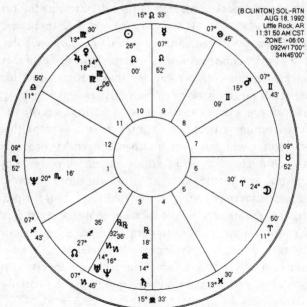

Figure 10.2: Bill Clinton's solar return.

1962 (16), 1970 (24), 1978 (32), 1986 (40), 1994 (48), 2002 (56), 2010 (64), 2018 (72), 2026 (80) and 2034 (88).

The position of Venus, therefore, also appears at 22° Leo in the solar returns for Bill Clinton's 1st, 9th, 17th, 25th, 33rd, 41st, 49th, 57th, 65th, 73rd, 81st, 89th (etc.) year. The position of Venus will also be identical in the solar returns for the 2nd, 10th, 18th, 26th, 34th, 42nd, 50th, 58th, 66th, 74th, 82nd, 90th (etc.) year. These eight-year intervals are significant due to the fact that the particular concerns represented by the position of Venus and its relationship with the Sun, if any, will be repeated in every eighth solar return.

Looking at Bill Clinton's solar return (not precession corrected) for 1992 (Figure 10.2), the year he was elected President, we may be prepared for the potential repetition of the same patterns or circumstances symbolised by Venus in the solar returns for 1984, 1976, 1968, 1960 and 1952. In November, 1976, Clinton was elected to his first public office as Attorney General of the State of Arkansas. In November 1984 he successfully ran for Governor after losing the previous election. This ability to make a political comeback also marked his successful 1992 Presidential campaign – eight years later. In his solar return for 1992 there are in fact many striking positions: Saturn conjunct the i.c. and solar return Mercury at the same position as his natal Mercury. As far as Venus is concerned, however, we can see that it is conjunct Jupiter in the eleventh house, which can be interpreted as 'great fortune in the area of one's hopes and dreams'. If we look up the definition of Venus-Jupiter aspects in Chapter 9, it is evident that while Venus-Jupiter will bring fortuitous occurrences, prosperity and social contacts, it will also present overly optimistic circumstances and therefore bring on the need to be cautious about squandering one's opportunities. This aspect also emphasises the importance of social acceptance (to the extent of caring more about public opinion than adhering to one's true voice and acting accordingly). Because the Venus-Jupiter conjunction falls in Virgo, Clinton must be co-operative, prudent and cautious and must refrain from riding the coattails of his popularity.

Appendix

BIRTH DATA

Bill Clinton, 19 August, 1947, 8:51 CST, Lat. 33N40, Long. 93W36. *Source:* Bill Clinton's mother.

Hillary Rodham Clinton, 26 October, 1947, 20:00 CST, Lat. 41N52, Long. 87W39. *Source:* Hillary Rodham Clinton to a reporter.

Gloria Steinem, 25 March, 1934, 22:00 EST, Lat. 41N39, Long. 83W33. *Source:* Birth certificate as cited in Mackey-Saunders Data Collection, Astrolabe, Orleans, MA, 1989.

Jacqueline Kennedy Onassis, 28 July, 1929, 14:30 EDT, Lat. 40N54, Long. 72W23.

John Fitzgerald Kennedy, 29 May, 1917, 15:00 EST, Lat. 42N20, Long. 71W07. *Source:* Rose Kennedy as cited in Blackwell Data Collection, Astrolabe, Orleans, MA, 1989.

(Note: on 27 November, 1957, Caroline Kennedy's birth, Jackie's progressed Venus by solar arc conjoined her natal Pluto and JFK's secondary progressed Mars conjoined natal Venus.)

Princess Diana, 1 July, 1961, 19:45 British Summer Time, Lat. 52N50, Long. 0E30. *Source:* Charles Harvey quoting Diana's mother as cited in *The Only Way to Learn About Relationships*, Marion March and Joan McEvers, ACS Publications, San Diego, CA, 1992.

Prince Charles, 14 November, 1948, 21:14 GMT, Lat. 51N30, Long. 0W08. *Source:* Official records as cited in Blackwell Data Collection.

Lord Laurence Olivier, 22 May, 1907, 5:00 GMT, Lat. 51N14, Long. 0W20. *Source: The Oliviers* by F. Barker as cited in *Astrological Quarterly*, Summer 1956.

Barbra Streisand, 24 April, 1942, 5:08 EWT, Lat. 40N38, Long. 73W56. *Source:* Edwin Steinbrecher quotes a mutual friend as cited in *The Only Way to Learn About Relationships*, Marion March and Joan McEvers, ACS Publications, San Diego, CA, 1992.

Woody Allen, 1 December, 1935, 22:55 EST, Lat. 40N50, Long. 73W52. *Source:* Birth certificate as cited in Mackey-Saunders Data Collection, Astrolabe, Orleans, MA, 1989.

Mia Farrow, 9 February, 1945, 11:27 PWT, Lat. 34N04, Long. 118W15.

Source: Birth certificate as cited in Mackey-Saunders Data Collection, Astrolabe, Orleans, MA, 1989.

F. Scott Fitzgerald, 24 September, 1896, 15:30 LMT, Lat. 44N57, Long. 93W05. *Source: The Far Side of Paradise* by Arthur Mizener.

The charts in this book were supplied by the New York Astrology Center, 545 Eighth Avenue, New York, NY 10018 (212) 947-3609. Mail orders can also be obtained from there.

REFERENCES

Chapter 1
1. Carl Jung, *Man and His Symbols* (New York: Bantam Doubleday Dell, 1968) p.98
2. Monica Sjoo, *The Great Cosmic Mother* (New York: Harper & Row, 1987), p.46
3. Marija Gimbutas, *Language of the Goddess* (San Francisco: Harper SanFrancisco, 1989), p.15
4. Elinor Gadon, *The Once and Future Goddess* (San Francisco: Harper SanFrancisco, 1989), p.12
5. Ibid.
6. Marija Gimbutas, *The Goddesses and Gods of Old Europe* (Berkeley and Los Angeles: University of California Press, 1982), p.17
7. Ibid., p.11
8. Ibid., p.176
9. Ibid., p.152
10. Merlin Stone, *When God Was a Woman* (San Diego, CA: Harcourt, Brace Jovanovich, 1976), p.17
11. Gimbutas, *The Gods and Goddesses of Old Europe*, p.80
12. Ibid., p.146
13. Stone, *When God Was a Woman*, pp.200-1
14. Ibid., p.202

Chapter 2
1. William Hallo and J. J. A. Van Dijk, *The Exaltation of Inanna* (New Haven, CT: Yale University Press, 1968), pp.15, 32-3
2. Jack Lindsay, *Origins of Astrology* (London: Muller, 1971), p.71
3. Diane Wolkstein and Samuel Noah Kramer, *Inanna: Queen of Heaven and Earth* (New York: Harper & Row, 1983), p.122
4. Ibid., p.155
5. Ibid., p.xiii
6. Ibid., p.38
7. Joseph Campbell, *Hero of 1,000 Faces* (Princeton, NJ: Princeton University Press, 1985), p.105
8. Joseph Campbell and Bill Moyers, *The Power of Myth* (Garden City, NY: Anchor Books, 1991), p.152

9. Ibid., p.157
10. Sylvia Brinton Perera, *Descent to the Goddess* (Toronto: Inner City Books, 1981), p.61
11. Campbell and Moyers, *The Power of Myth*, p.212
12. Joseph Campbell, *The Masks of God: Occidental Mythology* (New York: Viking Penguin, 1962), p.83
13. Merlin Stone, *Ancient Mirrors of Womanhood* (Boston: Beacon Press, 1984), p.106
14. Stone, *When God Was a Woman*, pp.94–5
15. Paul Friedrich, *Meaning of Aphrodite* (Chicago: University of Chicago Press, 1978), p.17
16. H. W. Saggs, *The Might That Was Assyria* (New York: St Martin's Press, 1988), p.275
17. Ibid., p.275
18. Franz Cumont, *Astrology and Religion Among the Greeks and Romans* (New York: Dover Publications, 1960), p.15
19. Ibid., pp.7–8
20. Erica Reiner, *The Venus Tablet of Amisaduqa* (Santa Monica, CA: Undena Books, 1980), p.29
21. Ibid., p.13
22. Ibid., p.29
23. T. S. Pattie, *Astrology* (London: British Library Publications, 1980), p.13
24. Ibid., p.12
25. Lindsay, *Origins of Astrology*, pp.50–1

Chapter 3

1. Willis Barnstone (trans.), *Sappho* (Garden City, NY: Anchor Books, 1965), p.27
2. Umberto Cassuto, trans. Israel Abrahams, *The Goddess Anath* (Jerusalem: Magnes Press, 1971), p.58
3. Samuel Noah Kramer, *Mythologies of the Ancient World* (New York: Anchor Books, 1961), p.197
4. Stone, *When God was a Woman*, p.164
5. Gadon, *The Once and Future Goddess*, p.177
6. Dr J. M. Hemelrijk, *Venus te Lijf* [*Venus Alive*] (Amsterdam: Allard Pierson Museum Publications, 1985), p.22
7. Sir James Frazier, *The Golden Bough* (New York: Macmillan, 1951), p.328
8. Ibid., pp.346–47
9. Ibid., p.330
10. Robert Graves, *The Greek Myths*, Part I (London: Penguin Books, 1955), p.194
11. Ibid., pp.341–2
12. Sarah Pomeroy, *Goddesses, Whores, Wives and Slaves* (New York: Schocken Books, 1975), p.32

13. Jean Shinoda Bolen, *Goddesses in Everywoman* (New York: Harper & Row, 1984), p.18
14. Hesiod, trans. M. L. West, *Theogony* and *Works and Days* (New York: Oxford University Press, 1988), p.39
15. Homer, *Iliad* (trans. E. V. Rieu; London: Penguin Books, 1950), p.100
16. Ibid., p.101
17. Ibid., p.103
18. Karl Kerenyi, *The Gods of the Greeks* (London: Thames and Hudson, 1951), p.72
19. Geoffrey Grigson, *The Goddess of Love* (New York: Stein & Day, 1977), p.59
20. Stone, *When God Was a Woman*, p.160
21. Carol Christ, *Laughter of Aphrodite* (New York: Harper & Row, 1987), p.164
22. Barnstone, *Sappho*, p.35
23. Plato, trans. Alexander Nehamas and Paul Woodruff, *Symposium* (Indianapolis: Hackett Publishing Co., 1989), p.14
24. Walter Burkert, *Greek Religion, Archaic and Classical* (Cambridge, MA: Harvard University Press, 1960), p.152
25. Friedrich, *Meaning of Aphrodite*, p.218
26. Hemelrijk, *Venus te Lijf*, p.24
27. Burkert, *Greek Religion, Archaic and Classical*, p.152
28. Pomeroy, *Goddesses, Whores, Wives and Slaves*, p.145
29. Cumont, *Astrology and Religion Among the Greeks and Romans*, p.27
30. Lindsay, *Origins of Astrology*, p.73
31. Christopher McIntosh, *The Astrologers and Their Creed* (London: Century Hutchinson, 1969), p.17
32. Pattie, *Astrology*, p.7
33. Lindsay, *Origins of Astrology*, p.124
34. Ptolemy, trans. J. M. Ashmand, *Tetrabiblos* (North Hollywood: Symbols and Signs, 1976), p.60
35. Ibid., p.112
36. Ibid., p.31
37. Ibid., p.101
38. McIntosh, *Astrologers and Their Creed*, p.23
39. Ptolemy, *Tetrabiblos*, p.45
40. John Ferguson, *The Religions of the Roman Empire* (Ithaca, NY: Cornell University Press, 1970), p.71
41. Grigson, *The Goddess of Love*, p.219
42. Ibid.
43. Lawrence Durdin-Robertson, *The Year of the Goddess: A Perpetual Calendar of Festivals* (London: The Aquarian Press, 1990), p.94
44. Edith Hamilton, *Mythology* (New York: New American Library, 1969), pp.92–103
45. Hamilton, *Mythology*, p.230

46. Michael Grant, *Roman Myths* (New York: Scribner's, 1970), p.60
47. G. Karl Galensky, *Aeneas, Sicily, and Rome* (Princeton, NJ: Princeton University Press, 1969), p.213
48. David Ulansey, *The Origins of the Mithraic Mysteries* (New York: Oxford University Press, 1989), p.41
49. Geoffrey Ashe, *The Virgin* (London: Penguin Books, 1988), p.195
50. Cumont, *Astrology and Religion Among the Greeks and Romans*, p.108
51. Lindsay, *Origins of Astrology*, p.349
52. Tester, *A History of Western Astrology*, p.49

Chapter 4
1. Erich Neumann, *The Great Mother* (Princeton, NJ: Princeton University Press, 1955), p.145
2. H. W. Janson, *History of Art* (New York: Harry Abrams, 1962), p.367
3. Kenneth Clark, *The Nude* (Princeton, NJ: Princeton University Press, 1956), p.78
4. Mirella Levi D'Ancona, *Botticelli's Primavera* (Florence: Leo S. Olschki Editore, 1982), p.105
5. Frederick Hartt, *History of Italian Renaissance Art* (NY: Harry N. Abrams, Inc., 1987), p.335
6. Thomas Moore, *The Planets Within* (Great Barrington, Massachusetts: Lindisfarne Press, 1990), p.137
7. Janson, *History of Art*, p.345
8. H. Diane Russell, *Eva/Ave: Women in Renaissance and Baroque Prints* (Washington, DC and New York: National Gallery of Art and The Feminist Press, 1990), p.131
9. Ibid.
10. Clark, *The Nude*, p.171

Chapter 5
1. Bolen, *Goddesses in Everywoman*, p.238
2. Ibid., pp.240-1

Chapter 6
1. Alice Howell, *Jungian Synchronicity in Astrological Signs and Ages* (Wheaton, Illinois: Quest Books, 1990), pp.131-2
2. Dr E. C. Krupp, *Beyond the Blue Horizon* (New York: HarperCollins*Publishers*, 1991), p.204

Chapter 7
1. Dr Susan Forward and Joan Torres, *Men Who Hate Women and the Women Who Love Them* (NY: Bantam Doubleday Dell, 1987), p.87

Chapter 8
1. Alan Oken, *Alan Oken's Complete Astrology* (New York: Bantam Doubleday Dell, 1980) p.313
2. Howard Sasportas, *The Twelve Houses* (Wellingborough: The Aquarian Press, 1985), p.204
3. Ibid., p.92

Chapter 9
1. Robert Assagioli, *Psychosynthesis* (London: Penguin Books, 1976), pp.74-5
2. Ibid., p.75
3. Liz Greene, *Saturn: A New Look at an Old Devil* (York Beach, Maine: Samuel Weiser Publications, 1976), p.171

Chapter 10
1. Rex Nelson with Phillip Martin, *The Hillary Factor* (NY: Richard Gallen & Co., Inc., 1993), p.213

BIBLIOGRAPHY

Ashe, Geoffrey, *The Virgin* (London: Routledge & Kegan Paul, 1988).
Assagioli, Robert, *Psychosynthesis* (London: Penguin Books, 1976).
Aveni, Anthony, *Conversing with the Planets* (New York: Random House, 1992).
Baigent, Michael, Campion, Nicholas and Harvey, Charles, *Mundane Astrology* (Wellingborough: The Aquarian Press, 1984).
Barnstone, Willis (trans.), *Sappho* (Garden City, NY: Anchor Books, 1965).
Bolen, Jean Shinoda, *Goddesses in Everywoman* (New York: Harper & Row, 1984).
Burkert, Walter, *Greek Religion, Archaic and Classical* (Cambridge, MA: Harvard University Press, 1960).
Campbell, Joseph, *The Hero With A Thousand Faces* (Princeton, NJ: Princeton University Press, 1949).
–, *The Masks of God: Occidental Mythology* (New York: Penguin Books, 1964).
–, *Transformations of Myth through Time* (New York: Harper & Row, 1990).
– and Moyers, Bill, *The Power of Myth* (Garden City, NY: Anchor Books, 1991).
Campion, Nicholas, *An Introduction to the History of Astrology* (London: Institute for the Study of Cycles, 1982).
Cassuto, Umberto, trans. Israel Abrahams, *The Goddess Anath* (Jerusalem: The Magnes Press, The Hebrew University, 1971).
Christ, Carol, *Laughter of Aphrodite* (New York: Harper & Row, 1987).
Clark, Kenneth, *The Nude* (Princeton, NJ: Princeton University Press, 1956).
Cumont, Franz, *Astrology and Religion among the Greeks and Romans* (New York: Dover Publications, 1960; first published by G. P. Putnam's Sons, 1912).
D'Ancona, Mirella Levi, *Botticelli's Primavera* (Florence: Leo S. Olschki Editore, 1982).
Dalley, Stephanie, *Myths from Mesopotamia* (New York: Oxford University Press, 1991).
Durdin-Robertson, Lawrence, *The Year of the Goddess: A Perpetual Calendar of Festivals* (Wellingborough: The Aquarian Press, 1990).
Eisler, Riane, *The Chalice and the Blade* (New York: Harper & Row, 1987).
Ferguson, John, *The Religions of the Roman Empire* (Ithaca, NY: Cornell University Press, 1970).
Forward, Dr Susan and Torres, Joan, *Men Who Hate Women and the Women Who Love Them* (NY: Bantam Doubleday Dell, 1987).
Frazier, Sir James, *The Golden Bough* (New York: Macmillan, 1951).
Friedrich, Paul, *Meaning of Aphrodite* (Chicago: University of Chicago Press, 1978).

Gadon, Elinor, *The Once and Future Goddess* (San Francisco: HarperSanFrancisco, 1989).
Galensky, G. Karl, *Aeneas, Sicily, and Rome* (Princeton, NJ: Princeton University Press, 1969).
Garin, Eugenio, *Astrology in the Renaissance* (London: Routledge & Kegan Paul, 1983).
George, Demetra, *Asteroid Goddesses* (San Diego: ACS Publications, 1986).
Gettings, Fred, *The Secret Zodiac* (London: Routledge & Kegan Paul, 1987).
Gimbutas, Marija, *Goddesses and Gods of Old Europe* (Berkeley and Los Angeles: University of California Press, 1982).
—, *Civilization of the Goddess* (San Francisco: HarperSanFrancisco, 1991).
—, *Language of the Goddess* (San Francisco: HarperSanFrancisco, 1989).
Grant, Michael, *Roman Myths* (New York: Scribner's, 1970).
Graves, Robert, *The Greek Myths*, Part I (London: Penguin Books, 1955).
—, *The White Goddess* (London: Faber & Faber, 1961).
— and Patai, Raphael, *Hebrew Myths: The Book of Genesis* (New York: McGraw-Hill Book Company, 1983).
Greene, Liz, *Saturn: A New Look at an Old Devil* (York Beach, Maine: Samuel Weiser Publications, 1976) (London: Arkana, 1992).
Grigson, Geoffrey, *The Goddess of Love* (New York: Stein & Day, 1977).
Hall, Nor, *The Moon and the Virgin* (New York: Harper & Row, 1980).
Hallo, William and Van Dijk, J. J. A., *The Exaltation of Inanna* (New Haven, CT: Yale University Press, 1968).
Hamilton, Edith, *Mythology* (New York: New American Library, 1969).
Harding, M. Esther, *Women's Mysteries: Ancient and Modern* (New York: Harper & Row, 1976).
Hartt, Frederick, *History of Italian Renaissance Art* (New York: Harry N. Abrams Inc., 1987).
Hemelrijk, Dr J. M., *Venus te Lijf* [*Venus Alive*] (Amsterdam: Publication in connection with exhibit at Allard Pierson Museum, University of Amsterdam, 1985).
Hesiod, trans. M. L. West, *Theogony and Works and Days* (New York: Oxford University Press, 1988).
Homer, trans. E. V. Rieu, *Odyssey* (London: Penguin Books, 1946).
—, *Iliad* (London: Penguin Books, 1950).
Howell, Alice, *Jungian Synchronicity in Astrological Signs and Ages* (Wheaton, Illinois: Quest Books, 1990).
Janson, H. W., *History of Art* (New York: Harry Abrams, 1962).
— *The Western Experience* (New York: Knopf, 1974).
Jung, Carl, *Man and His Symbols* (New York: Bantam Doubleday Dell, 1968).
Kerenyi, Karl, *The Gods of the Greeks* (London: Thames and Hudson, 1951).
Kitson, Annabella (ed.), *History and Astrology* (London: Unwin Paperbacks, 1989).
Kovacs, Maureen Gallery (trans.), *The Epic of Gilgamesh* (Stanford, CA: Stanford University Press, 1985).

Kramer, Samuel Noah, *Mythologies of the Ancient World* (New York: Anchor Books, 1961).
–, *The Sacred Marriage Rite* (Bloomington, IN: Indiana University Press, 1969).
–, *In the World of Sumer* (Detroit: Wayne State University Press, 1986).
Krupp, Dr E. C., *Beyond the Blue Horizon* (New York: HarperCollins*Publishers*, 1991).
Lacks, Roslyn, *Women and Judaism: Myth, History and Struggle* (New York: Doubleday & Company, 1980).
Lehman, J. Lee, PhD, *Essential Dignities* (West Chester, PA: Whitford Press, 1989).
Lerner, Mark, *Mysteries of Venus* (Eugene: Great Bear Press, 1986).
Lindsay, Jack, *Origins of Astrology* (London: Muller, 1971).
Lubsen-Admiraal, Stella and Crouwel, Joost, *Cyprus and Aphrodite* ('s-Gravenhage, Netherlands: SDU Uitgeverij, 1989).
McIntosh, Christopher, *The Astrologers and their Creed* (London: Century Hutchinson, 1969).
Meyer, Michael, *Handbook for the Humanistic Astrologer* (New York: Anchor Books, 1974).
Moore, Thomas, *The Planets Within* (Great Barrington, MA: Lindisfarne Press, 1990).
Neumann, Erich, *The Great Mother* (Princeton, NJ: Princeton University Press, 1955).
Oken, Alan, *Alan Oken's Complete Astrology* (New York: Bantam Doubleday Dell, 1980).
Olyan, Saul M., *Asherah and the Cult of Yahweh in Israel* (Atlanta, GA: Scholars Press, 1968).
Orenstein, Gloria, *Reflowering of the Goddess* (Elmsford, NY: Pergamon Press, 1990).
Ovid, trans. Mary Innes, *Metamorphoses* (London, Penguin Books, 1955).
Pattie, T. S., *Astrology* (London: British Library Publications, 1980).
Perera, Sylvia Brinton, *Descent to the Goddess* (Toronto: Inner City Books, 1981).
Pingree, David, *Babylonian Planetary Omens* (Malibu: Undena Publications, 1976).
Plato, trans. Alexander Nehamas and Paul Woodruff, *Symposium* (Indianapolis: Hackett Publishing Co., 1969).
Pomeroy, Sarah, *Goddesses, Whores, Wives and Slaves* (New York: Schocken Books, 1975).
Ptolemy, trans. J. M. Ashmand, *Tetrabiblos* (North Hollywood: Symbols and Signs, 1976).
Qualls-Corbett, Nancy, *The Sacred Prostitute* (Toronto: Inner City Books, 1988).
Reiner, Erica, *The Venus Tablet of Amisaduqa* (Santa Monica, CA: Undena Books, 1980).
Rudhyar, Dane, *An Astrological Study of Psychological Complexes* (Boulder, CO: Shambhala Publications, 1976).

Rufus, Anneli S. and Lawson, Kristan, *Goddess Sites: Europe* (San Francisco: HarperSanFrancisco, 1991).
Russell, H. Diane, *Eva/Ave: Women in Renaissance and Baroque Prints* (Washington, DC and New York: National Gallery of Art and The Feminist Press, 1990).
Saggs, H. W., *The Might That Was Assyria* (New York: St Martin's Press, 1988).
Sandars, N. K. (trans.), *Poems of Heaven and Hell from Ancient Mesopotamia* (London: Penguin Books, 1971).
Sasportas, Howard, *The Twelve Houses* (Wellingborough: The Aquarian Press, 1985).
Schilling, Robert, *La Religion Romaine de Venus* (Paris: E. de Boccard, 1982).
Sjöö, Monica and Moor, Barbara, *The Great Cosmic Mother* (New York: Harper & Row, 1987).
Spretnak, Charlene, *Lost Goddesses of Early Greece* (Boston: Beacon Press, 1984).
Steinem, Gloria, *Revolution from Within* (Boston, MA: Little, Brown, 1992).
Stone, Merlin, *When God Was a Woman* (San Diego, CA: Harcourt, Brace Jovanovich, 1976).
—, *Ancient Mirrors of Womanhood* (Boston: Beacon Press, 1984).
Sullivan, Erin, *Retrograde Planets* (London: Arkana, 1992).
Teubal, Savina J., *Sarah the Priestess, The First Matriarch of Genesis* (Athens, OH: Swallow Press/Ohio University Press, 1984).
Tester, S. J., *A History of Western Astrology* (Woodbridge, UK: The Boydell Press, 1987).
Ulansey, David, *The Origins of the Mithraic Mysteries* (New York: Oxford University Press, 1989).
Virgil, trans. Allen Mandelbaum, *Aeneid* (Berkeley: University of California Press, 1981).
Walker, C. B. F., *Cuneiform* (London: British Museum Publications, 1987).
Warmington, Eric H. and Rouse, Philip G. (eds.), trans. W. H. D. Rouse, *Great Dialogues of Plato* (New York: New American Library, 1956).
Wolkstein, Diane and Kramer, Samuel Noah, *Inanna: Queen of Heaven and Earth* (New York: Harper & Row, 1983).
Woolley, Sir Charles Leonard, *The Sumerians* (New York: AMS Press, 1970).

INDEX

'A Prayer to Aphrodite' 60, 81
Abraham 62
Adam and Eve 63
Adonai 62, 66
Adonia 79
Adonis 65, 66, 78-81, 96, 99, 100, 102, 106, 115
Aeneas 48, 74, 76, 101-3, 134, 224, 236
Aeneid, The, 75, 101, 102
Age of Aries 41, 58, 128
Albumasar 107
Alexander the Great 86
Alighieri, Dante 108, 151
Allen, Woody 158, 164, 181, 182, 218, 263
Almagest 90
Anath 61, 62
Anatolia 20-5, 41, 64, 103
Anchises 74-6, 101, 102, 231, 236
Apelles 84, 85
Aphaca 64, 65
Aphrodisias 103
Aphrodite 11-13, 21, 23, 24, 27, 35, 43, 58, 60, 65-88, 90, 91, 92, 93, 95-103, 106, 113, 115, 119-21, 123, 125, 133, 134, 139, 141, 144, 166, 169, 176, 177, 185, 221, 226-8, 230, 231, 233, 236, 237, 239, 240
Aphrodite-Euploia 83

Aphrodite-Hathor 65, 86, 91, 92
Aphrodite-Hetaira 70, 83, 85, 98
Aphrodite of Knidos 84, 113
Aphrodite-Ourania 72, 73, 82, 83, 87; *see also* Urania
Aphrodite-Porne 70, 83, 85, 98
Aphroditos 83
Apollo 73
Aquarius 125, 128, 157, 167-70, 181, 184, 185, 213, 239
Ariadne 68, 69
Aries 41, 58, 89, 91, 118, 124, 128, 139, 141-5, 151, 163, 166, 173, 211, 214, 218, 229, 253
Artemis 72, 75, 96, 104, 121
Asherah 62-3
Ashteroth 61
Ashurbanipal, King 53
Asia Minor 71, 74, 75, 79, 81, 84, 86, 89, 94, 99, 103, 105
Assyrians 48, 49
Assyro-Babylonian Empire 43, 45
Astarte 60, 61, 64-70, 72, 75, 97, 103, 121, 239
Astarte Plaques 64
Atargatis 61
Athens 67, 70, 72, 75, 83
Attar 61
Attis 106
Atunis 96
Autumn Equinox 33, 45, 93, 133

Index

Baal 61-2, 64-6, 68, 106
Babylon 44, 45, 50, 57, 86, 87
Babylonia 37, 44, 45, 47, 49, 57, 58, 65, 66, 83, 86, 89, 91, 106, 111, 119, 129
Babylonian Astrology 50-6, 87
Baru Priests 50, 51, 52
Beatty, Warren 203
Bergen, Candice 148
Berosus 89
'Birth of Venus' 11, 112, 240
Boccaccio 108
Bolen, Jean Shinoda 121
Botticelli, Sandro 11, 111-16, 133, 158, 240
Bronze Age 24, 25, 28, 29, 95, 128, 133
Brown, Jerry 211
Bull, as symbol 19-21, 23, 26, 36, 46, 48, 58, 68, 91-3, 104, 131, 156
Bull of Heaven 48
Burton, Richard 166, 188
Byblos 65

Caesar, Julius 99, 102
Caesar, Octavius 102
Callas, Maria 166
Campbell, Joseph 40, 185, 245
Canaan 37, 61, 62, 111
Cancer 124, 149-51, 153, 174, 211, 225
Capricorn 125, 164-7, 174, 188, 211, 236
Carthage 65, 70, 96, 101
Catal Huyuk 22, 23
Ceres 104, 105
Chalcolithic Era 19, 24
Chariot 46, 49, 60
Charles, Prince 146, 158, 189, 263
Christianity 104, 105

Christie, Agatha 160
Chronos 71, 72, 106, 121, 233
Clinton, Bill 122, 136, 157, 158, 161, 177, 178, 192, 193, 249, 253, 254, 257, 258, 263
Connery, Sean 158, 203
Constantine 105
Copernicus 90
Corinth 65, 70, 72, 76, 79, 83
Coward, Noel 167, 185
Cranach, Lucas 116
Crete 21, 24-8, 40, 65, 68, 69, 128
Cuneiform tablets 52, 57, 61
Cuneiform writing 29
Cupid 77, 100, 101, 112, 115
Cybele 104
Cyclades 24, 94
'Cycle of Inanna' 34, 35, 39
Cyprus 24, 25, 65-7, 69, 71, 72, 76, 81, 83, 86, 94, 98, 103
Cythera 65, 71-2, 113

Dark Ages 66, 95, 107
Decameron 108
Delphi 83
Delphic Oracle 83
Demeter 73, 74, 76, 80, 104, 105, 121, 123, 125
De Niro, Robert 156
Diana, Princess 146, 189, 193, 263
Dido 101
Dionysus 69, 73, 77
Divine Comedy 108
Double axe 22
Dove 84, 113
Dual rulership 124, 125
Dumuzi 12, 34-40, 46, 47, 61, 80, 85, 92, 106, 120, 123, 131, 144, 157, 200, 244, 246
Duncan, Isadora 143

Egypt 25, 37, 40, 65, 67, 83, 86, 87, 96, 99, 106, 128
El 61
Enheduanna 28, 42, 43
Enki 31, 35, 36, 38, 47, 229, 244, 245

Enuma Anu Enlil 52, 53
Enuma Elish 44
'Epic of Gilgamesh' 46-8, 246
Ereshkigal 37-9, 46, 47, 244, 245
Eros 72, 77, 100
Etruscans 95-6
Euphrates River 23, 28, 29, 35, 42, 44
Europa 68, 69, 92
Evans, Sir Arthur 25, 161
Eve 36, 63, 73, 116
Evening Star, Venus as 27, 31, 32, 35, 39, 40, 44, 45, 51, 53, 55, 57, 58, 61, 62, 64, 75, 86-8, 90, 91, 93, 95, 106, 119, 124, 129, 255, 256
'Exaltation of Inanna' 28, 42

Ficino, Marsilio 110-12
Fitzgerald, F. Scott 148, 158, 203, 207, 215, 263
Florence 11, 109, 110, 112, 113
Fonda, Jane 144, 161, 163, 164, 203, 215
Fonteyn, Dame Margot 151

Gaia 71
Galatea 99, 155
Garbo, Greta 153
Garden of Eden 35, 36, 62, 116
Gardens of Adonis 79
Gemini 124, 139, 146-8, 150, 157, 203, 214, 227
Gilgamesh 36, 46-8, 58, 63, 246

Gimbutas, Dr Marija 18, 21, 22
Giorgione 114, 115
Graces 72, 77, 100, 112, 113
Grace, Princess 158
Greece 22, 27, 37, 41, 58, 65, 67, 69-71, 78, 82-4, 87, 88, 93, 96, 98, 99, 106, 119, 129, 210
Greek Astrology 86-95
Greene, Dr Liz 233

Hades 73
Halaf 23, 49
Hammurabi 44, 45
Harmony of the Spheres 87
Helen of Troy 75
Heliacal rising and setting 54
Heliopolis 64
Helios 76, 106
Hellenistic Egypt 83, 96
Hephaistos 73, 77, 100, 102, 125
Herodotus 45, 50, 65, 66
Hesiod 69-74, 78, 82, 100, 121, 236
Hestia 73, 121
Hindu (Vedic) Astrology 119, 179
Hipparchus 89, 91
Hoffman, Dustin 151, 196
Homer 70, 71, 72-6, 78, 82, 100, 101, 231, 236
Homeric Hymns 74
Humanism 109, 113, 116

Iliad, The 74, 75, 101
Inanna 12, 23, 27, 28, 31-40, 42, 43, 45, 46, 49, 55, 58, 61, 63, 72, 75, 80, 85, 87, 92, 103, 106, 113, 119, 120-2, 129, 139, 141, 144, 157, 178, 200, 222, 229, 230, 244-6, 250
'Inanna's Descent' 35, 37, 39, 40, 46, 245

India 29, 41, 86, 95, 107
IndoEuropean 24, 27, 41, 43, 45, 49, 58, 71, 72, 104
Ingres 116, 240
Iraq 20, 23, 28, 41
Iron Age 49, 76
Ishtar 40, 42-52, 55, 57, 58, 61, 73, 75, 80, 87, 88, 91, 119, 129, 141, 221, 222, 246
'Ishtar's Descent' 46, 47
Israel 41, 61

Jackson, Michael 155
Jordan 41, 61
Jung, Carl G. 17, 128, 151, 196
Juno 96, 101, 102

King, Dr Martin Luther 171, 215
Kition 65
Knossos 25, 27, 69
Kos 89
Kramer, Samuel J. 34, 35

Layard., Sir Henry 53
Lebanon 41, 61, 64, 65
Leo 124, 151-3, 156, 163, 168, 181, 189, 210, 223, 246, 257
Lerner and Loewe 100
Lesbos 80, 81
Levant, The 41, 61, 64, 65, 79
Libra 11, 92, 93, 95, 100, 107, 111, 115, 116, 118, 124-6, 132-4, 138, 140, 156-8, 160, 174, 177, 178, 179, 181, 182, 186, 189, 193, 196, 197, 200, 203, 204, 207, 208, 212, 215, 218, 219, 222, 223, 225, 227, 229, 232, 236, 239, 257
Lilith 36, 63
Linear A and B Tablets 25, 70
Loren, Sophia 156, 203
'Ludovisi Throne' 84

Malle, Louis 148
Malta 24
Manilius 106, 126
Marduk 44, 45, 49, 51, 88, 89
Mars 51, 53, 86, 91, 92, 96, 98, 100, 106, 115, 124-7, 133, 141, 182, 201, 216, 227-30, 234, 243, 246, 248, 249, 253
Maternus, Firmicus 107
Mediterranean Islands 25, 65
Mellaart, Sir James 23
Mercury 51, 53, 86, 106, 125, 125, 146-8, 154, 195, 207, 225, 226, 227, 248, 257, 258
Mesopotamia 20, 27, 29, 41, 44, 49-51
Middle Ages 95, 108, 119
Minerva 96
Minoan Empire 24-7, 66
Minos, King 25, 68
Minotaur 68, 69
Mithras 58, 104, 105
Monroe, Marilyn 143, 208
Moon 19, 31, 42, 44, 45, 51-3, 57, 86, 87, 89, 90, 106, 111, 120, 122-4, 127, 149, 192, 207, 223-5, 248
Moon God 31, 42, 44
Morning and Evening Star 27, 31, 32, 35, 39, 40, 44, 45, 51, 53, 55, 57, 58, 61, 62, 64, 75, 86-8, 90, 91, 93, 95, 106, 119, 129
Morning Star, Venus as 32, 55, 65, 87, 124, 256
Mot 61, 62
Mourning Myth 37, 80, 243, 244
Mt. Olympus 71, 72, 74
Muses 73
My Fair Lady 100
Myrrha 78, 99

Nanna 31, 42
Neptune 121, 122, 124, 125, 171, 239-43, 249, 250, 254
Neumann, Erich 17, 108
Newman, Paul 166, 167, 178
Nineveh 49, 53
Ninib 51, 88
Nixon, Richard 171, 172, 196

Oates, Joyce Carol 151, 196
Odyssey, The 74, 77
Oken, Alan 175
Old Europe 21-4, 64
Old Testament 62, 63, 69
Olivier, Lord Laurence 144, 215, 263
Ouranos 71-3, 82, 87, 122, 233, 236, 240
Ovid 99, 100, 106, 109, 115, 171

Paleolithic Era 12, 23
Palestine 41, 50, 62, 63
Pandemos 82, 93, 110, 112, 115, 144, 156, 174
Pandora 73
Paphos 65-7, 72, 77, 99, 103, 112, 113
Pasiphae 68
Perrera, Sylvia Brinton 40
Persephone 78-80, 121, 125
Persia 41, 67, 83, 86, 94, 106, 129
Phaethon 46, 106
Phoenicia 22, 63, 65-70, 83, 97
Phryne 85
Pingree, Dr David 53
Pinter, Harold 160
Pisces 94, 118, 125, 128, 170-2, 215, 217, 242, 243
Plato 82, 87, 88, 93, 108, 110, 115, 116, 134, 144, 147, 156, 185

Pluto 124, 125, 159, 182, 201, 230, 241, 243-8, 250
Poseidon 73, 77, 97, 122, 239
Praxiteles 84, 85, 113, 116, 158, 240
Presley, Elvis 166
'Primavera' 112, 113
Prostitution 44, 45, 48, 67, 70, 79, 83, 98
Psyche 17, 39, 100, 128, 202
Ptolemy (Claudius Ptolemaius) 86, 89-92, 94-5, 107, 111, 120
Pygmalion 100, 155, 166, 171
Pythagoras 87, 88

Raging Bull 156
Reiner, Dr Erica 53
Remus 102
Renaissance 11, 43, 75, 95, 107-9, 111, 113-16, 119, 120, 133
Renoir, Auguste 116, 131
Rice, Anne 160
Rivera, Geraldo 153
Rock of Aphrodite 67
Roman Astrology 106-7
Roman Empire 95, 101, 102, 105
Rome 67, 95-102, 104, 105, 111, 112, 119, 129, 224
Romulus 102
Roosevelt, Eleanor 155
Rubens, Peter Paul 116, 131, 240
Rudhyar, Dane 111, 144

'Sacred and Profane Love' 115
Sacred Marriage Rites 34, 38, 42, 44, 45, 47, 62, 64, 79, 92, 93
Sappho 60, 80-2
Sargon 42

Index

Saturn 51, 53, 86, 106, 121, 125, 132, 164, 169, 216, 230, 232, 233-6, 241, 243, 249, 258
Saturn: A New Look at an Old Devil 233
Scorpio 118, 124, 125, 151, 159-61, 162, 181, 192, 200, 246, 247
Selene 106
Seleucid Era 58, 89
Serpent 22, 26, 36, 46, 63
Serpent Goddess 26
Shad Bala 124
Shamash 44, 50, 51, 222
Shaw, George Bernard 100, 154, 185
Shiva 46
Sicily 24, 65, 70, 95, 97, 98, 101
Sin 44, 50, 51
Sinatra, Frank 166, 186
Sparta 65, 75, 76, 83
Spero, Nancy 240
Spring Equinox 33, 45
Steinem, Gloria 169, 185, 263
Stellium 124, 210, 218
Stoicism 88, 106
Streisand, Barbra 172, 217, 218, 263
Sumer 25, 28-43, 128
Sumer-Akkad 41-3
Sumerians 23, 29-34, 38, 41, 43, 51, 52, 144, 178
Sun 11, 31, 32, 44, 45, 51, 53-5, 57, 58, 73, 75, 76, 87, 89, 90, 92, 93, 104, 106, 122-4, 128, 133, 153, 154, 156, 157, 207, 208, 211, 214, 216, 221-2, 248, 253-8
Sun God 31, 44, 76, 104, 122, 222
Sun Goddess 31
Symposium 82, 110

Syria 20, 41, 50, 61, 64, 65

Tammuz 106
Taurean Epoch 26, 127, 128
Taurus 11-13, 25, 28, 29, 39-41, 58, 68, 91-5, 98, 100, 107, 111, 112, 115, 116, 118, 123-30, 133, 134, 137, 139, 140, 144-6, 156, 159, 173, 174, 178, 180, 181, 182, 186, 189, 193, 196, 200, 203, 204, 207, 208, 211, 212, 215, 218, 223, 225, 227, 229, 231, 232, 236, 257
Taylor, Elizabeth 143, 166, 188, 200
Tetrabiblos 90, 95, 107, 120
Theogony 71
Theseus 69
Tiamat 45
Tigris River 23, 28
Timaios 88
Titian (Tiziano Vecellio) 11, 111, 113-16, 131, 144
Trojan War 74, 75
Tropic of Cancer 211
Tropic of Capricorn 211
Tropical Zodiac 89, 91
Troy 74-6, 101
Turan 96
Turkey 20, 22, 66, 83, 103
Turner, Ted 161, 164, 218
Tyre 68

Uffizi Gallery 11
Unaspected Venus 247
Underworld 35, 37-40, 46-8, 55, 62, 73, 78, 79, 101, 244, 245, 250
Ur 30, 62
Urania 83, 93, 110, 112, 116, 134, 147, 156, 169, 174, 185; see also Aphrodite-Ourania)

Uranus 121, 122, 124, 125, 169, 233, 236-9, 249
Utu 31, 222

Vegetable God 12, 35, 61, 66, 78, 79
Veneralia 92, 98
Venice 110, 113, 114
Venus and Adonis 115
'Venus and the Lute Player' 114
Venus, aspects of:
　Venus-Jupiter 229-32, 233, 258
　Venus-Mars 227-9, 246
　Venus-Mercury 225-7
　Venus-Moon 223-5
　Venus-Neptune 171, 239-43, 250
　Venus-Pluto 243-7
　Venus-Saturn 232-6
　Venus-Uranus 236-9
Venus Erycina 98, 101
Venus Genetrix 99, 105
Venus in Aquarius 167-70, 184, 185, 239
Venus in Aries 141-5, 151, 163, 166, 214, 218
Venus in Cancer 149-51, 225
Venus in Capricorn 164-7, 188, 236
Venus in Gemini 146-8, 150, 203, 227
Venus in Leo 151-3, 224
Venus in Libra 156-8, 160, 181, 189, 203, 207, 218
Venus in Pisces 170-2, 217, 242, 243
Venus in Sagittarius 161-4, 205, 232
Venus in Scorpio 159-61, 192, 246, 247
Venus in Taurus 144-6, 156, 203
Venus in Virgo 154-6
Venus in the first house 175-8
Venus in the second house 178-82
Venus in the third house 175, 182-6, 206
Venus in the fourth house 186-7
Venus in the fifth house 189-94
Venus in the sixth house 194-6
Venus in the seventh house 174, 197-200
Venus in the eighth house 200-4
Venus in the ninth house 204-8
Venus in the tenth house 208-12
Venus in the eleventh house 212-15
Venus in the twelfth house 216-19
'Venus of Laussel' 19
'Venus of Lespugue' 18
Venus Obsequens 97
Venus Phosphorus 87
'Venus of Urbino' 11, 114
'Venus of Willendorf' 18, 19
Venus, Roman Goddess of Love 95-107, 134, 141, 230
Venus Tablet of Amisaduqa 50, 53-7
'Venus with the Mirror' 114
Vesper 106
Vesta 98
Vinalia 92, 98
Virgil 75, 100-2, 109
Virgin Mary 103-6, 109, 111-13, 115, 116, 144, 151, 196
Virgo 94, 118, 124, 125, 154-6, 194, 195, 227, 258
Vulcan 11, 75, 99, 101, 106, 126

Wolkstein, Diane 35, 39
Woodward, Joanne 167, 182
Works and Days 71, 73

Yahweh 36, 62

Zeus 27, 60, 68, 71, 73, 74, 76-80, 82, 88, 92, 96, 97, 101, 102, 106, 110, 226, 229, 231, 236

Ziggurats 30

By the same author . . .

Indian Astrology

A Western approach to the ancient Hindu art

Indian Astrology is a comprehensive summary of the ancient Eastern astrological tradition and a practical guide to the way in which Hindu interpretive and predictive techniques may be applied to Western horoscope analysis.

Skilfully weaving together a concise history of the earliest roots of astrology – from the great Babylonian Empire's astrological notations on cuneiform tablets – Ronnie Gale Dreyer describes the Indian contribution to the field of astrology, including the usage of the sidereal zodiac techniques determining planetary strength and weakness. Navamsa and other degree divisional charts – including the model for Harmonic charts and the Vimshoddhari Dasa System – a method of forecasting planetary cycles unique to Indian astrology. The role of the Hindu astrologer as general seer, confidante and communicator of sacred knowledge is also discussed. *Indian Astrology* is thus an invaluable source of ancient wisdom which complements contemporary astrological interpretation.

Ronnie Gale Dreyer studied Hindu astrology both privately and at Sanskrit University in Benares, India. She lived in Amsterdam for 10 years where she maintained an astrological practice and conducted classes and workshops throughout the Netherlands. She lives in New York City.

ISBN 0 85030 738 4